DIRECT OBJECTS AND LANGUA

Direct object omission is a general occurrence, observed in varying degrees across the world's languages. The expression of verbal transitivity in small children begins with regular uses of verbs without their object, even where object omissions are illicit in the ambient language. Grounded in generative grammar and learnability theory, this book presents a comprehensive view of experimental approaches to object acquisition, and is the first to examine how children rely on lexical, structural and pragmatic components to unravel the system. The results presented lead to the hypothesis that missing objects in child language should not be seen as a deficit but as a continuous process of knowledge integration. The book argues for a new model of how this aspect of grammar is innately represented from birth. Ideal reading for advanced students and researchers in language acquisition and syntactic theory, the book's opening and closing chapters are also suitable for nonspecialist readers.

ANA T. PÉREZ-LEROUX is Professor of Spanish and Linguistics, and Director of the Cognitive Science Program at the University of Toronto. Her research seeks to understand how children learn the syntax and semantics of the smallest and silent components of sentence grammar, including determiners, prepositions, number, tense, mood and aspect, null objects and subjects, and how grammatical complexity develops from these components.

MIHAELA PIRVULESCU is Associate Professor of French and Linguistics in the Department of Language Studies, University of Toronto Mississauga. Her research looks at the morphosyntactic expression and acquisition of verbal argument structure, and how bilingualism and multilingualism impacts the course of language acquisition.

YVES ROBERGE is Principal of New College and Professor of Linguistics in the French Department at the University of Toronto. His research focuses on the syntax and semantics of French and other Romance languages, especially Canadian French, as well as dialectal variation, first language acquisition, and the syntax-morphology interface.

CAMBRIDGE STUDIES IN LINGUISTICS

General Editors:

P. AUSTIN, J. BRESNAN, B. COMRIE,

S. CRAIN, W. DRESSLER, C. J. EWEN, R. LASS,

D. LIGHTFOOT, K. RICE, I. ROBERTS, S. ROMAINE,

N. V. SMITH

In this series

Earlier issues not listed are also available.

DIRECT OBJECTS AND LANGUAGE ACQUISITION

ANA T. PÉREZ-LEROUX
University of Toronto

MIHAELA PIRVULESCU
University of Toronto Mississauga

YVES ROBERGE
University of Toronto

CAMBRIDGE
UNIVERSITY PRESS

CAMBRIDGE
UNIVERSITY PRESS

University Printing House, Cambridge CB2 8BS, United Kingdom

One Liberty Plaza, 20th Floor, New York, NY 10006, USA

477 Williamstown Road, Port Melbourne, VIC 3207, Australia

314-321, 3rd Floor, Plot 3, Splendor Forum, Jasola District Centre, New Delhi - 110025, India

79 Anson Road, #06-04/06, Singapore 079906

Cambridge University Press is part of the University of Cambridge.

It furthers the University's mission by disseminating knowledge in the pursuit of education, learning and research at the highest international levels of excellence.

www.cambridge.org
Information on this title: www.cambridge.org/9781108941013
DOI: 10.1017/9781139086264

First published 2017
First paperback edition 2020

A catalogue record for this publication is available from the British Library

ISBN 978-1-107-01800-6 Hardback
ISBN 978-1-108-94101-3 Paperback

Contents

Figures

Tables

Foreword

This is an absolutely marvelous book full of delightful insights into what may be the favorite topic of linguistics, interpreting invisible constituents, in this case, missing objects. Its greatest value, though, lies in its demonstration of how to reason simultaneously across all the domains of linguistics: theory, acquisition, experimentation, syntax, semantics, pragmatics, learning theory and cognition. This is not simple virtuosity, but an important method which will characterize – or fail to characterize – future work in linguistics. In particular, the authors show that a variety of syntactic options for null objects co-vary with subtle pragmatic options, which, in turn interact with a child's growing lexicon. In contrast, the tradition in acquisition work has been to treat linguistic theory – syntax for instance – as fixed, then look at its acquisition consequences rather than attempting to allow a variety of insecure theoretical claims to co-exist with a variety of insecure acquisition claims, and then reason about the details of each with an eye on the other. It is important that we all feel empowered to reason across different domains, notations, methodologies, even though we cannot command equal expertise in them all. This should lead everyone to more sophisticated collaborations.

Where do languages divide on null objects? One division is the hot/cool distinction articulated by Huang (1982). He observed that "hot" languages (for instance, many Asian languages) allowed more direct reference to context, which can sometimes cross over into L2. Once a visitor from Japan came and offered me a gift and said, *"Let me give you!"* and handed the gift to me. In English, it is simply impossible not to express the contextually superfluous "this" (*let me give you this*). A child must make a parametric decision between hot and cool languages. This book is aimed at the subtler null object that differentiates a language like Portuguese from English, where a null *pro* (a DP) allows reference to context. In English, a null object is possible, in general, with nonreferential objects only, as in *I like to cook*. The core of the authors' analysis is that there is a universal Transitivity Requirement (TR) carried by all verbs, even seemingly intransitive ones. A transitivity requirement means, essentially, that a grammatical object (a Theme) is automatically projected.

Since it does not follow from syntax narrowly conceived of as Merge, the TR seems to refer to a so-called Third Factor effect: the cognitive complexity of transitive verbs, which involve Agents, intentions and responsibility (*John hit Bill*).

I think that this approach may be couched in a stronger UG claim, what I call "Strict Interfaces" (Roeper 2014). This is essentially a version of what Rizzi (2016)[1] has recently called "broad UG" keeping the critical notion of cross-modular innateness in grammar. Chomsky (pc) likewise agrees that the interfaces are themselves subject to strong innate constraints. The concept of Strict Interfaces seeks to represent how various factors are expressed – or distorted – at the point of an innate interface. Biology is full of strict interfaces: hand-eye coordination is clearly innate and involves a notion of three-dimensionality in vision that is mapped onto an implicit three-dimensional map carried by the organization of muscles, so that we can effortlessly reach for what we see. In the same vein, the authors argue that verbs are "intrinsically combinative" toward delivering a transitive reading. That is another way to say that there is an innate strict interface between pieces of grammar and their connection to other parts of mind, namely the notion of Events that carry Agent-Verb-Theme information. Strict Interfaces have consequences: both the notions of Agent and Theme (or grammatical object) create an impure reflection of cognition at the point of contact with grammar.

Let's examine the notion "Agent" as it maps separately onto the lexicon, syntax and morphology. A word like *cook* is an Agent, linked to notions of intentionality, skill and responsibility. It is probably closest to the cognitive notion. The –er affix carries Agent if the verb has it as one of its thematic roles: *hitter, runner*. However, in the sentence *John is the receiver of terrible insults, John* is the grammatical Agent for *receive* just as it is for *hit*, but it does not carry most of what agency means intuitively, instead the receiver is cognitively the object of insults. Here, the interface causes a fairly radical alteration. From another angle, in the sentence *John was widely admired*, there is an implicit Agent, which is interpreted as generic or implying ignorance, but its implicit status alters its meaning: intentionality is not entailed or is at least downgraded. Similarly, *the meat was cooked* has an implicit Agent that seems different from the Agent in cook. The connection to cognition is present, but it is limited by the demands of an efficient interface. Thus, each projection through the interface narrows the cognitive content. Similarly, the TR constraint both restricts and

---

[1] "A broad characterization of UG, the latter including both task-specific and domain general properties and principles which are operative in language, understood as a cognitive capacity."

enlarges the connection to cognition. The cognate objects which the authors build upon, like *he sighed a large sigh* implies a kind of real object that is not there and thus begins to create effects that are the stuff of poetry. On the other hand, *John saw the ball under the car* can easily mean just part of the ball, but the transitive structure implies the whole ball.

This miniature treatment of Agent is a tiny echo of the authors' intricate treatment of the notion of "implicit" Theme, whose nonappearance or appearance as a clitic or a pronoun shows similar semantic and pragmatic variation. For instance, they observe this subtlety in the use of null objects, which in turn shows adult/child variation:

> If that something was a wall and someone asked you what your friend was doing you might reply with *He/she is painting Ø* or *He/she is painting a wall*. The null object answer is possible because the object is of a type that can normally be painted. Such an answer would not be expected if that were not the case, if a sofa was involved for instance. Your answer to the person's question would more likely be *He/she is painting a sofa* than *He/she is painting Ø*. It turned out that children produced overall more null objects, which we interpreted as an indication that objects are less semantically restricted than in adults. (p. 196)

If only typical objects are deletable, then the challenge for the child is to determine, perhaps culturally, what is typical. This notion of typical could have interface-specific restrictions. For instance, the idea that, where concrete compositionality fails, as it must with idioms, no pragmatic null objects are ever allowed. If you say *John is painting my friend as an enemy* and someone asks *what's John doing?*, no one, not even a child, would respond *painting* without specifying the object.

Ultimately, the authors arrive at a view that favors some important traditional ideas:

1) **Categorical knowledge:** in their words "many dimensions of syntax, semantics and pragmatics intervene in the licensing and recoverability of null elements and while their combined effect leads to the appearance of a continuum, the contribution of each factor remains categorical" (p. 189).

2) **Weak parameters:** the child must still make a deep decision on the nature of empty categories. Despite many intervening factors, is there a null *pro* object that can be referential or is null *pro* parametrically

excluded? One might therefore prefer the opposite designation "strong parameters," which are evident to the child despite pragmatics that seem to cloud the question.

3) **Multiple grammars** provide an explanation of gradient effects: if there is a process of weighing two options, with some evidence on each side, then the child maintains both sides of a parameter until one "wins." This creates the appearance of gradient effects. I have argued for Multiple Grammars: Roeper (1999), (2016), along with Yang (2002), Yang and Roeper (2011), Amaral and Roeper (2014).

The book concludes with many provocative open questions. In that spirit, we can follow its path a little further. There are at least two other domains where the TR reveals itself. Frazier (1999) has shown in parsing studies that the parser will seek to project an object after every verb, even an intransitive one, as if the core form of verbs were always transitive. In addition, productive morphology restricts newly created verbs to a transitive template, blocking double objects, complements and particles (Carlson and Roeper 1981). For instance:

Complements

John managed the store
John managed to go downtown
*John mismanaged to go downtown

Double-objects

John outKennedyed Kennedy
*John outKennedyed me Kennedy

Particles

John rethrew the ball
*John rethrew the ball out.

This is just what one would expect if an abstract form of TR defined a mentally real structure delivered by UG.

The difficulty of seeing how parameters interact with pragmatics, the lexicon and clitics has led to questioning the existence of parameters (Boeckx 2011), but Holmberg and Roberts (2014) have argued that they continue to be necessary. Once again, if the surface of grammar is complicated by pragmatics and the lexicon, then it becomes *more* important for a child to have an efficient method to make decisions, which is what a parameter provides. This book is the perfect demonstration of that perspective.

Like a small diamond, this book reflects in many directions and should be a model for collaboration in all of the fields it discusses.

Tom Roeper,
University of Massachusetts, Amherst

Acknowledgments

In the course of the last ten years or so, we have conducted, with our team at the University of Toronto, a series of experiments with monolingual and bilingual children ranging in age from three to six, acquiring French, English and Spanish. Each experiment dealt with a specific variable or set of variables involved in object omission constructions. The results of these experiments allowed us to refine our hypotheses and predictions and to see a clear picture emerge as to how to best describe and analyze the developmental sequence involved in this particular domain of language development. The impetus for this book arose from our desire to gather all of our hypotheses, experimental results and analyses and to present them as part of a unified narrative. We would like to thank Cambridge University Press for the support and editorial expertise they have provided since the submission of our initial book proposal, in particular Helen Barton, Sarah Green, Neil Smith and three anonymous readers.

One of the great rewards of academic research can be found in the opportunity to work with undergraduate and graduate assistants. We have benefited greatly from the assistance of our graduate research assistants, Maria Alkurdi-Alzirkly, Tanya Battersby, Sophia Bello, Isabelle Belzil, Ailis Cournane, Mélanie Elliott, Anna Frolova, David Fournier, Caitlin Gaffney, Monica Irimia, Meï-Lan Mamode, Joanne Markle-LaMontagne, Milica Radisic, Lynn Tieu, Danielle Thomas and our undergraduate research assistants: Samantha Andrade, Diana Dascalu, Robyn Kadoguchi, Catherine Lam, Salwa Mohi-Uddin, Kate Orgill, Aliona Rudchenko, Eric Scott, Evelina Szaczewska, Gilliam Tom and Iga Wyroba. We can only hope that they see their involvement in our project as mutually beneficial.

As will become abundantly clear throughout the following chapters, it would not have been possible to articulate the narrative developed in this book without the previous research that was available early in our project, and that has been produced since, on the topic of object omissions in L1 acquisition. Similarly, several colleagues have kindly provided tremendous comments and suggestions over the years and we would like to thank them:

Larisa Avram, Pat Balcom, Susanne Carroll, Anny Castilla-Earls, Maria Cristina Cuervo, Sarah Cummins, Anna-Maria Di Sciullo, Anna Gavarró, Brendon Gillan, John Grinstead, Maria Teresa Guasti, Theres Grüter, Aafke Hulk, Arsalan Kahnemuyipour, Tanya Kupisch, Marie Labelle, Diane Massam, Jürgen Meisel, Natascha Müller, Alan Munn, Letitia Naigles, Philippe Prévost, Liliana Sanchez, Jeanette Schaeffer, Christina Schmitt, Einat Shetreet, William Snyder, Jeffrey Steele, Nelleke Strik, Viçens Torrens, Michelle Troberg, Kamil Ud Deen and Jill de Villiers. Special thanks to Tom Roeper for having graciously accepted to contribute a preface; given the fundamental influence of his work on our own over so many years, we could not have hoped for a more appropriate preface writer!

A special thank you to all the children who contributed to this book (some of whom are now teenagers); during our many experiments, we managed to see the world and words through their eyes! We also thank the numerous day cares in the Montréal and Toronto areas; they generously made time and space available for us for testing. For the parents of all the children who participated in this study, a warm thank you for allowing your child to enchant us!

As stated previously, the nature of this book is such that some of its contents have been presented elsewhere, including the Boston University Conference on Language Development (BUCLD), Generative Approaches to Language Acquisition (GALA), the Linguistic Symposium on Romance Languages (LSRL), Generative Approaches to Language Acquisition North America (GALANA), the Congress of the International Association for the Study of Child Language (IASCL), the Romance Turn, Canadian Linguistic Association (CLA), and appeared in several journals and volumes, including *Language Acquisition, Lingua, Bilingualism: Language and Cognition, First Language, Theoretical and Experimental Approaches to Romance Linguistics* (Benjamins), *Language Acquisition and Development* (Cambridge Scholars Press), *New Perspectives on Romance Linguistics* (Benjamins), *Multilingual Individuals and Multilingual Societies* (Benjamins). We would like to acknowledge the many anonymous reviewers who have helped us improve our contributions.

Finally, this book would not have been possible without the generous funding provided by the Social Sciences and Humanities Council of Canada (410–2005–239 and 410–09–2026), and, at the University of Toronto, the office of the Provost, New College, Victoria College and the University of Toronto Mississauga.

Abbreviations

ACC	accusative case
ASP	aspect
CL	clitic pronoun
DEF	definite
DAT	dative case
F	feminine gender
IMP	imperative
IMPF	imperfective aspect
INF	infinitive
INT	interrogative
M	masculine gender
NEG	negative
NOM	nominative case
OBJ	objective case marker
PART	participle
PAST	past tense
PERF	perfective aspect
PL	plural number
PRES	present tense
PROG	progressive aspect
SG	singular number
SUBJ	subject
TOP	topic
LOC	locative
Ø	null category

1 *Missing Objects in Child Language*

1.1   General Goals

Three core premises guide this book. First is the idea, universally accepted in contemporary formal grammar, that the missing components of a sentence must be recovered. Second, that lexical knowledge, syntactic structure and contextual understanding all interact in this recoverability. The third premise is that the growth of children's grammars can be best characterized in terms of the developmental interplay of these three domains, or "submodules," of grammar. In this book, we aim to show that this interplay is especially apparent in the domain of object omission. This chapter presents the problem of missing objects in child language, explains the nature of the learning problem these missing objects represent and articulates the learnability approach, which serves as the basis for our methodology.

The following scenario happened long ago. A small boy, just shy of eighteen months, waddled into the kitchen and said to his mother, "*Want*." The mother turned away from the dishes to ask him, "*What?*" The child repeated, this time louder, "*Want!!*" This happened twice until the little boy started to cry. This conversational exchange between parent and child obviously failed. It did not fail because the sentence was spoken in bad English but, rather, because the child's conversational partner was unable to identify the referent of some missing elements in it.

When the child said, "*want*," both subject and object were left out (__ *want* __). This is an ordinary occurrence, at least if you happen to be around people under the age of two. However, for syntacticians and psycholinguists who study early language development, this is an interesting phenomenon. About the missing subject, the syntacticians would say that it was likely recoverable as referring to the speaker. In the case of the direct object, an obligatory companion of the transitive verb *want*, the content was neither easily recoverable from grammar nor from context. Specialists in language development would note that this initial stage in language acquisition is characterized by pervasive optionality of arguments (i.e., objects and subjects) and functional categories. These investigators are aware that early telegraphic speech evolves quickly into fairly well-specified sentences. The question is: How does this happen? We feel that to answer this question we must start by addressing a more basic issue: What is the difference between the grammar of this boy and that of his mother?

Returning to the above scenario, we will start by giving you a hint of how things like this happen. A speaker can delimit, from the meaning of the verb *want*, the possible interpretations of the object to the set of desirable things. The context of the utterance (the kitchen, with Mom as the interlocutor) helps to further restrict the set of desirable things to only those relevant in the specific circumstances. The child is likely to want something from the set of things available in this kitchen, at this moment, and hopefully, from the kinds of things Mom is believed to control. The problem remains, even with contextual information, that the kitchen contains many objects that this two-year-old might find interesting, even leaving aside the extra-interesting stuff that Mom will never agree to. The information in the baby's short sentence is just not sufficient and the result is a failure to communicate.

Actually, the whole field of language acquisition, or developmental linguistics, as called by some, is captivated by small sentences like these. Developmental linguistics is concerned with how children start their life with a language that comes packaged in tiny sentences that are difficult to anchor to a context, and learn to build longer sentences that include all the parts necessary to negotiate meaning and achieve grammaticality. Missing objects and subjects, such as described above, are reported again and again in the speech of young children. During most of the field's history, investigators focused on missing subjects and paid little attention to missing objects. For us, and many others, missing objects are at least as interesting as null subjects, and possibly much more mysterious. Accounts of why children omit objects are even more complicated and contentious than those proposed for missing subjects. In order to tell the story of missing objects in child grammar, we need to delve right down to the very nature of the fundamental elements that form the mental grammar and the mental lexicon, and to unravel how sentence grammar interacts with the extra-grammatical context. This trip will not resemble a tidy tour organized by a travel agency, with every stop fully planned and carefully scheduled. Instead, we hope for a rambling trek taking detours along obscure roads, occasionally backtracking to earlier points on the road and including as many stops in interesting places as possible.

We start the story of missing objects in child language with a startling admission: contrary to what has been assumed by many linguists for years, at least about languages such as English, adults do it too (Cummins and Roberge 2005). Consider the examples in (1), where the "__" indicates the missing object.

(1) a. Here, read __.
     b. I'm hungry, I want to eat __.
     c. Let's do dishes. I'll wash__, you dry__.

A keen observer will note that some of the verbs above (*read* and *eat,* at the very least) are normally characterized as "optionally transitive" verbs. However, even verbs that are often described as "obligatorily" transitive can appear with a missing object (2).

(2) a. Did you lock __? (Wife to husband, in the car, about to leave for work)
     b. There are those who annihilate __ with violence, who devour __.
        (British National Corpus; Cummins and Roberge 2004: 124)

Unlike in the child example presented earlier, English-speaking adults omit objects in ways that: a) allow interlocutors to negotiate the meaning of the missing object; and b) do not trigger intuitions of ill-formedness in speakers. Thus, such cases go largely unnoticed. When we start to pay attention to them, these implicit objects can provide crucial insights into how meaning is constructed and how speakers make sense of missing object arguments through a variety of mechanisms, including through deixis ("this thing," in 1a) and generics, from the prototypical meaning of the verb ("food," in 1b), or the discourse context ("dishes," in 1c). This book is an exploration of how children sort out the fine details of when object arguments can be omitted and when they cannot.

Explaining language acquisition becomes an even more challenging enterprise when we move beyond a single language and consider the range of possibilities observed in human languages. It turns out that across different languages there is substantial variation in how missing objects are licensed and how they are interpreted. Analyzing cross-linguistic variation represents the first step in mapping out the complexity of the learning task that children face. Here we are obliged to state not one but two obvious things. Firstly, since a child must come prepared to acquire any language, an explanation that can fit only some languages will never be fully satisfying. Secondly, the child does not know at the outset how the language she has to learn works. Therefore, our account must map out the relationship between the following three dimensions:

- What underlies children's ability to learn language (i.e., the capacity);
- What speakers specifically need to learn about implicit objects and transitivity in the target language (i.e., the representation); and
- How the language experience is configured in a specific language (i.e., the input).

In other words, triangulating from these dimensions of input, representation and capacity, language acquisition theories must be able to account for the starting point, the process of how experience leads to change in representations and the eventual outcome of language development.[1]

Our point of departure is then a learnability-based approach. Learnability approaches consider the structure of the domain to be learned in order to deduce what type of steps must be involved in the task of learning the relevant properties. It is a bit like tasting a dish and trying to imagine from its flavors what might have happened in the kitchen. In the sciences, this is known as "reverse engineering." We assume that the meaning of sentences in general (and consequently, of sentences with missing objects) is compositional in nature. A compositional view of meaning states that the meaning of a sentence results from the combination of the meanings of the parts (the lexical content, provided by words and morphemes) and the way these are combined (the syntax). Furthermore, we hold that syntactic structure defines how meaning can be tuned to context, so that syntax not only organizes words but also constrains how access to context happens. To a certain extent, sentence meaning and context interact as part of the general human ability to make inferences about context and communication (pragmatics). Other aspects of how syntax and meaning interact are specific to each language, and thus, part of the learning task. The goal of this book is to understand how children learn the specific aspects of syntax and of the syntax-discourse interface.

We take a particular view of language development where ontogenetic stages resemble the shape of potential mature states. This is known as the continuity assumption, or the strong continuity hypothesis (Pinker 1984). A bit like the little tail that appears in immature stages in tadpoles and

---

[1] On how stimuli and input interact with the linguistic system in the language acquisition process, see Carroll (2001).

human embryos, to subsequently disappear during development, but remains to the mature stages of dogs and lizards. Some readers might recognize in this a version of Ernst Haeckel's recapitulation theory ("ontogeny recapitulates phylogeny"; Haeckel 1866). In its raw form, the continuity hypothesis in language acquisition suffers from the same limitations as Haeckel's recapitulationist model: ontogeny does not replicate actual adult stages, but embryonic stages from other points in the evolutionary pathways. Leaving the biological dimension aside, in linguistics the continuity assumption has proven a useful tool to analyze target-deviant behavior in children. It happens with clear regularity that nonadult structures in the production of children learning a given language share features with adult structures in a different language.

Language development never starts with nothing, but rather starts with a variant of something. We posit that this something is a default, a minimal structure used with the widest range of meanings (Lebeaux 1988, 2000; Roeper 2007, 2008). We explore the hypothesis that "learning" consists of selecting one member of a set of predetermined hypotheses. In Fodor's (1998) language of unambiguous triggers, these predetermined hypotheses are simply pieces of syntactic tree structure. We propose that children start with the simplest representation, which is structurally the most basic and, therefore, the most flexible possible structure. With the input provided by experience, functional structure develops, giving specificity to the original default representation. From the various possible mechanisms of recoverability available for missing elements some are reinforced while others undergo attrition or blocking. The semantic representation of sentences becomes narrower, its relation to context more constrained, more precisely defined and more language-specific.

To provide a precise characterization of how this happens in the case of null objects, we propose the following steps. The first step is to consider the general analyses that have been proposed to account for missing objects in linguistics. The second is to characterize object omission phenomena cross-linguistically so as to provide a complete picture of the learning task involved. Third, we propose to examine in more depth, and with more semantic details, what children do in a few languages where null objects in acquisition have been examined carefully. As a preamble to taking this route, in this chapter we introduce some fundamental grammatical notions, a bit of the history of the field of language acquisition and make explicit our basic assumptions about how all of this should be approached.

1.2   What Are Verbs and How Are They Learned?

1.2.1   Verbs and Nouns

> Missus Gloria Pearson went to Livingstone College in North Carolina. She told me. I guess that's why she know so much about how to fix my English speaking [...] Missus Pearson say she will teach us all the rules. She say English is governed by rules of grammar, and the rules, she say, go special with nouns and verbs.

> (Verdelle 1995: 186)

Few linguists these days would agree that the purpose of grammar is to fix anybody's way of speaking. Most, however, will concede that languages are governed by rules and that grammar is but a description of speakers' rule-governed behavior. There is also wide consensus that within the rules of grammar nouns and verbs indeed occupy a special place. Nouns generally refer to entities, which can be abstract or concrete, and verbs are supposed to refer to actions, occurrences or states. Noun phrases (NPs) denote individuals or sets of individuals, whereas verb phrases (VPs) denote situations. The VP, in conjunction with the functional structure it is anchored in, establishes the association between the verb and the various participants in a situation, which are known as arguments of the verb. Such meaning-based definitions are intrinsically limited: some nouns denote actions (such as the noun *action* itself), some verbs don't. English *be*, for instance, is considered a verb but it has nothing to do with actions. Indeed, it denotes very little if anything at all: the copula verb *be* can be seen as just a linker between other contentful elements, or a placeholder for grammatical tense. In various languages, like Arabic or Irish or even some varieties of English (Becker 2004), the copula need not be present at all.

If a verb does not have to refer to actions to be a verb, what does it have to do? Since notional definitions of verbs and nouns are weak, the standard approach is to define verbs and nouns in terms of the syntactic or morphological behavior of the lexical class. Verbs are relational categories that select arguments of a given type. The main classification criterion of a lexical verb is according to how many argument noun phrases (NPs) it typically associates with. This is called the argument structure of a verb.

(3)   a. Ditransitive: [3 arguments: Subject, Direct Object, Indirect Object]
          The witch gave an apple to the girl.
        b. Transitive: [2 arguments: Subject, Object]
          Snow White ate the apple.
        c. Intransitive: [1 argument: Subject]
          She swallowed, then fainted.

Intransitives are further classified into two types, according to the role of the subject. For *swallow*, the subject is the agent. For *faint,* it is not. Swallowing is something Snow White did; fainting, instead, happened to her. The subjects of the first class of verbs (known as unergative verbs) share many syntactic properties with the subjects of regular transitive verbs. Across languages, subjects of the second type of verbs (known as unaccusative verbs) share a range of syntactic properties with direct objects.

Verbs thus play a crucial role in determining not just the number of arguments in a sentence but how those arguments are situated within sentence structure. Interestingly, children seem to know how verbs organize sentences from the beginning of their syntactic development, at the very onset of the ability for combinatorial speech. Researchers who work on this early stage of language development debate whether children at this age have mental representations for grammatical categories such as nouns and verbs. It is worthwhile to take a moment to consider the evidence pertinent to the existence (or lack thereof) of abstract categories at the earlier stages of syntactic development. Starting from the no-categories camp, researchers such as Olguin and Tomasello (1993) taught novel verbs and nouns to children aged two. This classic experimental approach allows researchers to infer what children know under carefully controlled circumstances. The method dates back to Berko Gleason (1958), who presented invented words to children in order to verify whether they understood the rules of English morphology.

(4)   Here is a wug.
        Now, there are two . . .

Since in such cases, the given words are completely new, there is no question of prior experience. For Olguin and Tomasello, the question was whether children exhibited comparable syntactic flexibility for the two core grammatical categories. These authors observed that what children learned was different for nouns and verbs. Two-year-olds treated the newly learned nouns creatively, using them in varying syntactic positions and playing different semantic roles. In contrast, when taught novel verbs, the children most often reproduced the same combinatorial pattern they had heard for each specific verb, roughly 90 percent of the time. When they did combine a new verb with a known noun, they often failed to follow the canonical word order. The implication, according to these authors, is that young children are productive with their early language in some ways, but not in others. The overall conclusion extracted in this and related work is that children are not primarily creating an abstract category for verbs for purposes of syntax, but are instead extracting lexically specific schemas (Tomasello, Akhtar, Dodson and Rekau 1997; Tomasello 2000).

There are some (rather obvious) arguments in favor of the opposite conclusion. Since verbs are distributionally more restricted than nouns, the very same data can be interpreted to say that even two-year-olds are aware of this fundamental asymmetry between nouns and verbs. It is not that babies are more cautious with verbs because they lack an abstract representation of verbs, but because they are already sensitive to the nature of verbs. It is almost as if they know that so much more is at stake when using a new verb. As Jean Aitchison tells us, "Verbs are inextricably linked with syntactic structure" (Aitchison 1994: 111). Nouns go where the grammatical context sends them. Verbs are the context. The same event can be described differently: *the hunter chases the rabbit*, or *the rabbit flees from the hunter*. Bad luck for the rabbit, in either case. For the speaker, however, the choice of verb frames the shape of the sentence. Beyond determining the number of arguments and their roles in the sentences, the verb also determines their semantic types. Snow White may be able to eat the apple, but the apple will not eat Snow White. Metaphorical extensions aside, only animate entities can perform the action of eating, and only certain things are eaten. In other words, verbs determine or "select" the properties of their subjects and objects. As a consequence, the acquisitions of verbs and their syntactic distributions are narrowly interlocked (Gleitman, Nappa, Cassidy, Papafragou and Trueswell 2005).

1.2.2   Verbs and Objects

> There is a slim but tantalizing link between a verb's [argument] structure and its meaning.
>
> (Aitchison 1994: 11)

We are now closer to the matter that interests us, which is verbs and their relationship to their objects. Verbs may be at the center of sentence structure, but one element is closer to the verb than any other: the object. The object is an inherent part of the event described by the verb and the verb restricts what can appear in the object position. As we will see, this happens even when the objects are left unpronounced. The distributional relation between verbs and objects is known as transitivity.

In Chapter 2, we will discuss a particular formal approach to transitivity, but for now, we start by introducing some basic facts. The first is that there is a range of relations between verbs and objects. On the extreme of transitivity, we have verbs whose meanings are fundamentally grammatical and for which the object is essential for the event to be fully characterized:

(5)   a. Do a dance/math/household chores/some gardening/dinner.
      b. Finish a cake/a book/my chores.
      c. Get ice cream/a headache/a car/a boyfriend/some money.

These verbs denote highly abstract properties of event structure, but express little lexical or encyclopedic meaning. Without the objects, we don't really have a clue what action or situation is actually involved. Other verbs may be lexically contentful, but still considered obligatory transitives. We still don't have a clear sense of what determines the difference between these verbs and verbs whose direct objects are variably expressed. A well-known pair is *eat* vs. *devour*. These denote fundamentally the same event. The first is neutral while the latter says something additional about manner. English speakers have fairly robust intuitions that there is a contrast between the two. Speakers know that you are as likely as not to pronounce the object of *eat*. Both options feel equally grammatical. In contrast, eliminating the object of *devour* leads to intuitions of incompleteness, or ungrammaticality (represented conventionally by an asterisk). Consider the examples in (6).

(6)   a. The dwarves were <u>eating their supper</u> when Snow White arrived.
      b. The dwarves were <u>eating Ø</u> when Snow White arrived.
      c. The dwarves were <u>devouring their supper</u> when Snow White arrived.
      d. *The dwarves were <u>devouring Ø</u> when Snow White arrived.

Yet, even the objects of *devour*-type verbs can go missing, but only given the right sort of context, as we saw in (2b). We use the Ø symbol throughout this book to represent the position where the object should have appeared. This symbol thus indicates a syntactic position that is not overtly occupied and for which it is not useful or necessary to provide a specific type of empty element for the purpose of our presentation. In the next few paragraphs, we hope to explain why it is a good idea to make reference to an empty position and, later on, we provide more specific characterizations of potential null elements for this position.

For the optionally transitive verbs such as *eat*, the encyclopedic meaning of the verb does not generally change depending on whether or not the object is included: the emphasis is on the activity when the object is missing and the sentence is more informative when the object is present (*eating some stuff* vs. *eating a cookie*). However, the presence or absence of the object does help define the type of event. In verbs with incremental objects (consumption and creation verbs fall into this category), the object defines the natural end point for activity. The dwarves' eating ends when the supper is all gone. Building a house ends when the house is finished. Drawing a circle ends when the circle is complete. Erasing a circle works the same, but in the opposite direction. When the object is implicit we say that the verb is interpreted as describing an unbounded activity. The object, when present, provides the boundary or culmination for the event. This transitivity alternation represents two different aspectual classes of dynamic events: activities (7a) vs. accomplishments (7b).

(7)   a. To write *in one summer/for months. (van Hout 2008)
         b. To write a script in one summer/*for months.

At one extreme of the transitivity continuum we have verbs that never occur without their objects, because the characterization of the situation heavily depends on it. This is the case of light verbs such as *have, get,* which have little meaning without their complements (cf., *get a book/get some money/get the flu*). At the opposite extreme we find the so-called unergatives, or agent-intransitive verbs: *dance, run, sing,* whose object is so predictable that it is seldom realized. The standard, lexical view of transitivity holds that these verbs have a single argument, the subject. We adopt an alternative view according to which unergatives are held to have implicit objects. According to Hale and Keyser (2002), these can be analyzed at the morphological level as having a hyponymic noun in the position of the object noun. The object is not a fully referential nominal phrase. Instead, the object is reduced to the lexical content of the root; basically, the nonreferential noun that corresponds to the action denoted by the verb. In other words, *to dance* means to *dance a dance.* This is not as extreme as it may seem at first. In fact, this is not that different from the earlier step we took to analyze *eat*-type verbs. Furthermore, there is evidence for this analysis. Unergative verbs commonly allow a modified cognate object, a regular DP or measure phrase to appear as their complement (Massam 1990):

(8)   a. Sleep a restless sleep.
         b. Slept the whole night.
         c. Live a good life.
         d. John ran a good race.
         e. Then he swam a mile.
         f. She danced a tango.

Therefore, if the object adds information about quantity or subtype of activity speakers are often quite happy to allow many intransitives to appear transitively. *Dance a dance* is redundant; *dance a tango* is informative. It specifies a subtype of dancing. Much like *eating spinach* is a subtype of eating, not to be confused with other types of eating activities such as *eating dessert*. Intransitives allow objects if they contribute something to the characterization of the event. The converse is also true, even stubbornly transitive verbs like *devour* allow optionality given the right context. The point is not that transitivity transgressions are an exception but that they constitute perfectly reasonable behavior. In fact, they are exactly what we would expect if the position of the object is obligatorily represented but its realization depends on the contribution of the object to the informational content of the utterance. Lexical transitivity is not a categorical property but a gradable, probabilistic concept (Merlo and Stevenson 2001).

This approach is specifically designed for unergative verbs, where the subject is the agent of a dynamic situation and the norm is that objects are not realized. It is less clear how it can apply to the second class of intransitives, unaccusatives, where the subject refers to a patient, i.e., an entity that undergoes a change of state. Semantically, the subject position of *fall, break* or *arrive* is filled by nonagentive NPs. Syntactically, across languages, these subjects possess many object-like properties. The standard analysis of this verb class is that their subjects are underlying objects that are displaced to the subject position, much like what happens to the subject in passive sentences. Unaccusatives also enter into a different type of transitivity alternation, the causative-inchoative alternation. In the inchoative alternant, the theme is subject and there is no object. In the causative construction, the theme surfaces as direct object and a causer appears as subject.

(9)   Causative/Inchoative alternation
        a. The table broke. (unaccusative)
        b. The dog broke the table. (causative)

The causative/inchoative alternation has played an important part in the language acquisition literature, both in reference to verb acquisition and in reference to object omission, as we will see at various points throughout this book. Children do not seem to treat this transitive alternation productively. In fact, in the previously mentioned studies on verb categories (Olguin and Tomasello 1993, as well as related work in Akhtar and Tomasello 1997 and others) what the evidence shows is that children do not initially generalize across causative and inchoative verb frames. This literature interprets this as the leading evidence for lack of abstraction in early grammars

(Tomasello 2000). However, it is worthwhile to reflect on the fact that the causative/inchoative alternation is not a fully productive lexical rule in English, a point already made in Wexler (2004). It is unsurprising that children would be conservative and tend to use the verb only as it is used in their input. They might have already noticed that not all verbs do the alternation. For example, the verb *roll* appears with either frame, but this is not so with the verb *fall*.

(10)   a. The ball rolled/the boy rolled the ball.
        b. The ball fell/*the boy fell the ball.

Occasionally, as observed in Bowerman (1982), children do overgeneralize. That is the most interesting point, not that they often fail to do so. Throughout most of this book, our focus is on the simpler, fully productive transitivity alternation between a transitive and an agent-intransitive frame.

(11)   Optional transitivity alternation
        a. Josh ate.
        b. Josh ate the cake.

At this point, we can summarize some basic facts about verbs and objects:

- There is a close link between verb meanings and the status of their objects; however, many questions remain concerning this relationship (Levin 2013);
- Transitivity is not a lexical but a syntactic property; verbs of the so-called intransitive classes can appear in transitive frames and transitive verbs can appear in intransitive frames (Cummins and Roberge 2005);
- Object argument NPs can have a dual purpose: one is to introduce arguments/discourse referents (*She bought a book*), the other is simply to define subtypes of activities, which can be done without making actual reference to specific entities (*She likes to collect stamps*) (Farkas and de Swart 2003; Chung and Ladusaw 2003).

The next step in building up our approach is to consider the status of missing objects. One argument in support of the view that objects are formally represented even when missing is that they possess some of the morphosyntactic properties of visible NPs. Missing objects can have gender and number features that enter into agreement relations. Rizzi's classic example from Italian demonstrates this:

(12)   Talvolta la stampa lascia Ø perplessi.
         "Sometimes the press causes-to-remain puzzled." (Rizzi 1986:533)

Here the participle takes plural form to agree with a semantically plural implicit object (i.e., a better translation for the example above would be "leaves many people perplexed"). According to Rizzi, the syntactic behavior of arbitrary null objects in Italian can be described in terms of case and binding properties. We can directly observe that missing objects appear to have fixed binding properties, according to the lexical property of the verb, as shown by Gillon (2006). Some verbs are classified as inherently reflexive or reciprocal, whereas others require disjoint interpretation reference for their objects (Reinhart and Reuland 1993). The interpretation of missing objects follows these lexically given patterns of reference:

(13)   a. John always washes/bathes Ø before going to bed.   (= "himself")
            → reflexive
         b. Hilary and John met Ø at noon for lunch.   (= "each other")
            → reciprocal
         c. Johnny is always biting Ø in school.   (= "someone else")
            → disjoint

These patterns of reference seem to fall within the prototypical scenarios associated with specific verbs: bathing is something you (most likely) do to yourself; biting, to others. An expressed object may contradict these biases, but the missing object relies on the prototypical interpretation. If the missing object were completely absent, not present in the syntax, then there would be no way of guaranteeing the right interpretation. The missing object has to associate with the right information, but this information cannot be too specific:

(14)   I ate Ø late last night.

The implicit object of *eat* means something generic, such as "dinner," or "food." It cannot denote something specific, such as, say, "fish."

   Can we get these effects in interpretation by virtue of simple, nonsyntactic probabilistic intuitions about what constitute typical situations? Can logical inference be doing the entire job? We argue this is not the case. In general, many normal, high-probability properties of situations do not become grammatically implicit meanings. Working during the day is the most typical employment scenario, but the verb *to work* does not represent in any meaningful sense the idea that the event happened "during daytime." The following dialogue is perfectly sensible:

(15)   A: She works at the corner store.
         B: The graveyard shift?
         A: No, regular hours.

Similarly, even if humans technically classify as a diurnal species, using the verb *sleep* to talk about people carries no association that it has to be done during night-time. It seems to be the general case that temporal adjuncts do not trigger grammatically stable implicit meanings, no matter how typical the behavior. However, we must note that nothing prevents us from having a specific lexical contrast that serves this purpose; *to dine* and *to lunch* come to mind here. Neither is it the case that what is typical behavior for an individual will be packaged into the meaning of an implicit object. Consider the following scenario of a dog named Lily. Lily, a stout Boston terrier, is the sort of dog who eats all sorts of stuff. What she eats does not have to be edible, nor particularly organic. In the testimony of Lily's owner, who happens to be a linguist, *She is constantly eating garbage.* Lily's garbage-eating activities occur quite frequently, at the rate of multiple times a day. However, when she is gobbling up a box of crayons, one would hardly describe her as engaged in the act of (intransitive) eating. Even among conversational partners fully aware that this eating of nonedible matter is typical behavior the following dialogue would be infelicitous:

(16)   A: Lily is eating again!
         B: Crayons?

However, nothing seems particularly impossible about this potential conversation provided that the unspecified object is lexically realized. The following dialogue sounds much more natural:

(17)   A: Lily is eating stuff again!
         B: Crayons?

The source of infelicity is the implicit object construction, which seems to go with the typical characterization of our definition of what constitutes an eating event. Inferences from our world knowledge are irrelevant except when they apply to the verbal category. To put it in syntactic terms, one of the properties of implicit objects is a typicality restriction. This restriction systematically reflects the verb's selectional properties. Selection refers to the relationship existing between the predicate and its arguments, such that the predicate is said to select certain semantic properties of the arguments that accompany it. This is how we explain what makes Noam Chomsky's famous sentence, "*colorless green ideas sleep furiously,*" nonsensical: sleep can only be done by animate entities, not by abstract concepts. This property, semantic selection or s-selection, can be equally used to describe the interpretive restrictions on missing objects in a language such as English. Just like *sleep* requires a concrete animate subject (something that can sleep, unlike *colorless green ideas*), *eat* selects objects that are concrete and edible. Obviously, s-selectional properties are lexical and thus vary from verb to verb, as illustrated in the examples in (18), based on Gillon (2006).

(18)   a. Bill read/ate Ø this afternoon.   (= "stuff")
          → quantificational (i.e., generic, indefinite)
       b. Hilary always leaves Ø early.   (= "places")
          → quantificational
       c. Hilary left Ø at noon.   (= "there")
          → ambiphoric[2] (co-text or deictic)

When an object falls outside the s-selectional properties of the verb, as in metaphorical uses, the object will be overtly realized. For example, the implicit null object of *leave* has the interpretation of "some place," but cannot have an interpretation of "something" or "stuff."

(19)   Hilary always leaves Ø when she is upset.   (≠ "things")

As a result, if what is left is a place, the speaker would opt for either (19) or the equivalent with the place spelled out. If what is left is an object, the speaker cannot use (19) but rather must use equivalent sentences in (20) with an overt object.

(20)   a. Hilary always leaves her wallet.
       b. Hilary always leaves it.

Different approaches treat missing objects differently and use different terminologies. "Object drop" implies that an object was there but was deleted. Labeling these constructions instead as involving a "null" or "implicit" object is preferable to those who believe that there is no special deletion process. It suggests the missing object is actually present and has syntactic properties but lacks phonological realization. To us these seem sensible assumptions and the facts discussed so far lead us to adopt a null object approach (Cummins and Roberge 2005; Pérez-Leroux, Pirvulescu and Roberge 2008a), which holds that all verbal roots merge with an object

---

[2]   Gillon (2006: 5) states: "Since so many expressions have both endophoric and exophoric usages, it is convenient to coin the term ambiphoric to cover those words which have both usages."

complement. The minimal expression of this object is a null nominal root, N. We propose that this basic option is available to any verb, in any language. The key fact is that languages may vary as to where it appears and how it is interpreted. While there exists a rich variety of null object constructions, the licensing and recoverability mechanisms amount to just three broad types: lexical licensing, morphological licensing or discourse licensing. The first type of licensing is what we have discussed for English. In other languages, null objects are licensed or identified through morphological agreement (object agreement markers or clitic morphemes). The null object in those cases has referential properties. These are not lexically licensed (i.e., not hyponymic, and do not exhibit typicality restrictions). These types of null objects occur across different languages families in the world: Swahili, Sora, Portuguese, Basque, etc.

In other languages, null objects do not have associated morphological identifiers and are consistently interpreted as linked to discourse. This is the case of the radical argument drop languages such as Mandarin or Japanese, where pronouns are rare and null objects freely refer to a previously established discourse antecedent (Sigurðsson 2011).

(21)   Japanese (O'Grady et al. 2008)
         Toshi-ga   hon-o   mita. Watashi-mo mita.
         Toshi-NOM book-ACC saw-1SG I-too   saw-1SG
         'Toshi saw the book. I too saw.'

The diversity of null object constructions is truly astonishing. We attempt to do it more justice in our presentation in Chapter 2. In subsequent chapters, we will show how within these differences between languages lie some of the clues we need to explain children's developmental path. For now, we review some of the basic facts we know about direct objects in acquisition.

1.3   A Brief History of Objects in Acquisition

Long ago, Roger Brown pointed out that many of the sentences uttered by young children appear very similar to those uttered by adults, but with several portions of them deleted. Let us return to our initial observation about the boy who cried in the kitchen. Under Brown's approach (22a) and (22b) would be variable realizations of (22c).

(22)   a. Want.
         b. Want cookie.
         c. I want that cookie.

The obvious question is why do children omit these arguments? Is it simply because little children lack the capacity to make longer sentences? Throughout the eighties, studies of argument omission in young children occupied a prominent position in theories of language acquisition. Some authors argue that omissions can be explained in terms of performance limitations, or output constraints, as in work by Bloom (1990) and Valian (1991), which we discuss below in more detail. Alternatively others wonder whether children omit objects because they have a different representation of sentences, one that allows optionality of the object. Hyams (1986) and Radford (1990) proposed representational accounts, using radically different assumptions. Radford (1990) attributed argument omission to the maturation of functional categories. According to his approach, the functional architecture of sentences has not yet matured and functional categories are absent. Therefore, the story goes, children's utterances are not constrained by the same functional conditions as those of adults and for case-theoretic reasons arguments need not be realized. This type of approach is discontinuous because it holds that children's grammar is substantively different from that of adults. In contrast, the continuity approach considers the great range of variation across languages and makes a bet that what children are doing is, in fact, exercising one or several of the other options given by Universal Grammar (UG). Hyams' influential work relied on alternative parameter settings, as she proposed to analyze early child English in comparison to null subject languages.

Ideas in the wild can take interesting paths. In this case, the paths of objects and subjects bifurcated. Hyams' representational account of early subject optionality became one of the best-known ideas in generative acquisition. The performance approach, that argument drop was the result of performance limitations, became the dominant view of children's object omissions. This difference arose, in part, because of the magnitude of the phenomena reported. Authors such as Hyams (1986), Bloom (1990), Valian (1991), Wang et al. (1992) all pointed out that argument drop is asymmetrical: subjects were being dropped by English-speaking children at much higher rates than objects. Ungrammatical missing objects in English-speaking two-year-olds were reported at around 8–9 percent (Bloom 1990). In Wang et al. (1992)'s comparative study of the acquisition of English and Chinese, missing objects in English were less than 4 percent, whereas missing subjects were close to 33 percent if gerunds and infinitives were included, and 15 percent, if they were not. These data were gathered from English-speaking children aged 2;05 to 4;05. The much younger children in Valian (1991) also had low rates of target-deviant missing objects.

Performance limitation accounts have a direct, intuitive appeal. It is not surprising that many see this as the first line of explanation; after all, at the age of two or three, children's utterances are rather short. Versions of this approach were discussed as early as the early seventies by Lois Bloom, at the inception of the field of language acquisition as we know it. It solidified into the standard assumption for objects when Paul Bloom, in an analysis of the three children in the Brown corpus (Brown 1973), noted an inverse relation between VP length and subject realization (Bloom 1990). The longer a VP, the more likely the sentential subject was to be omitted. Bloom very reasonably concluded that young children produce arguments inconsistently because their utterances are constrained in length.

Valian (1991) added an interesting twist to the characterization of missing objects as the result of performance limitations. While replicating Bloom's results on VP length, she also found that the overall increases in object realization had little relation to grammaticality. Young children produced few errors with transitivity overall. Valian noted that increases in object realization centered on verbs with optional direct objects. Children seldom made errors with strongly transitive verbs. Children in her study left objects empty for optionally transitive verbs. Object realizations with pure transitives were quite high, within a range over 93 percent, but for optionally transitive verbs the range was 50–60 percent. In contrast, subjects started at a low of 23 percent realization in obligatory contexts (with a concomitant 77 percent of complementary omissions), with clear increases. Object realization was highest in children with high MLUs (who produced 77 percent realization, 23 percent omission). Considering the developmental path, Valian noted that with age and increased utterance length, children's expression of direct objects increased for optionally transitive verbs. At the same time, the overall representation of intransitives and optional transitive verbs in the children's vocabularies decreased, while the frequency of use of obligatorily transitive verbs increased. Valian drew two conclusions from this. First, children are tracking parental lexical use closely, since they are able to distinguish between pure transitives and optional transitives. Second, children manage to drop objects but avoid ungrammaticality. Valian attributes great sophistication to children, proposing that they make more frequent use of optional transitive verbs because they are trying to balance their performance limitations with an awareness of the patterns of argument realization of the individual verb items.

Since Valian's study, lexical conservativity has been a recurrent finding in studies of children acquiring English (Tomasello 1992; Theakson et al. 2001;

Ingham 1993/1994). Tomasello (1992) reported that children show a strong preference for using verbs in the sentence constructions in which they have heard them. He highlighted the fact that half of the early verbs in young children's lexicons are used in a single frame. He proposed the Verb Island Hypothesis: when children learn a new verb they do not know how to mark syntactic participant roles. Instead, they need to hear how parents use each verb individually. According to this hypothesis, early verb uses do not reflect abstract syntactic categories, but are lexically stored. Tomasello concluded that early linguistic competence in children was item-based (Tomasello 2001: 169). In other words, the little phrases of little children are not produced by means of a combinatorial grammar, where utterances would be produced by means of a rule that could create constituents from categories (verb + object). Instead, according to Tomasello, children's utterances are part of a long list of lexical chunks. Under this view, children have a lexicon of idiomatic phrases (*eat-cookie, drink-milk, sun-shining,* etc.) but no abstract grammar *per se*.

   Theakston and colleagues published a 2001 article that examined Valian's arguments against further analysis of a similar dataset, this time collected in England. They contend that if early production is examined at the lexical level, the evidence that children favor null objects, in their view, disappears. In their study, in similarly collected data of spontaneous speech, children used most optionally transitive verbs in a single frame. According to them, this suggests that children are unaware of the optional status of a given verb. Since verb frame selection is fully predicted by parental use, they concluded that children do not select syntactic frames on the basis of complexity. Instead, they followed the approach that posits that young children operate with limited-scope lexical formulas, without awareness of optional transitivity nor of the category "verb." The link of early verb choice to performance in Valian's analysis, they claim, is an "overinterpretation of the data," and any performance theory that assigns syntactic categories to children is "essentially analyzing data at the wrong level" (Theakson et al. 2001: 149). Input, these authors emphasize, is the thing to consider, not categories. So let's do just that.

1.4   The Nature of Experience

As it turns out, children's data on categories looks much more like their parents' than anyone expected. Charles Yang, a computational linguist at the University of Pennsylvania, proposed to submit children's data to a quantitative comparison of productivity with adult data (Yang 2013). While most of the debate has taken place with regard to determiners and nouns, those results match those of the analysis of verb frames reported by Kowalski and Yang (2012). This was a small study on verb usage by children and mothers from the classic Harvard corpora, which contains Roger Brown's data from Adam, Eve and Sarah. Their analysis confirms all previous observations that children use most verbs with a single frame. However, their data also reveals that this also happens to be true of parental speech. Kowalski and Yang conclude that these findings confirm that children's language closely matches adult input, but are inconsistent with the claims of limited productivity (Kowalski and Yang (2012: 10).

The story is that the explanation for why most lexical items occur with a single frame is the same for both groups of speakers and has little to do with absence of abstract categories. As Yang (2013) explains, the distribution of frames is one more instance of a mathematical pattern known in psychology as Zipf's law. Zipf's law describes a peculiar but well-known statistical property of the lexicon, namely, that the frequency of a word tends to be approximately inversely proportional to its rank in frequency. The consequence is that relatively few words are highly frequent, while many more occur rarely or only once in a linguistic sample. Graphing the number of times a word appears in a corpus against the cumulative percentage of word types at that frequency produced in a corpus yields a characteristic long tail (Yang 2013). Most lexical items have limited frequency. If a verb shows up only once in a corpus, it can hardly display syntactic variety:

> In light of the distributional reality of language, it is impossible to expect anything other than Verb Islands, especially when we deal with much smaller sample sizes as is usually the case with child language.   (Kowalski and Yang (2012: 9))

The conclusion is that children's utterances are made of the same stuff as adult utterances. Children are lexically conservative, but then, by this criteria, once the input is carefully examined, so are adults. The results are consistent with the idea that children's morphosyntax is continuous with adult forms, and inconsistent with claims of limited productivity from the usage based literature (Kowalski and Yang (2012: 9)).

Does saying that children's grammar reflects the same syntactic categories and mechanisms as adults' mean that we expect the grammar of a child to be identical to their parents'? Not necessarily. It simply means that we can characterize the two forms of linguistic expression with the same substantives categories. More generally, the continuity perspective represents the developmental dimension of the uniformity hypothesis, which holds that unless there is evidence to the contrary we assume that languages are underlyingly uniform, with variety across languages restricted to "easily detectable properties of utterances" (Chomsky 2001: 2; see Matthewson 2013 for discussion on the methodological implications of these ideas, and discussion in Chapter 4, for its implications in acquisition). Our interest is in one easily detectable difference between adult language and child language, namely, that young children allow objects to remain implicit in places where an adult would not. Processing accounts are quite reasonable but we find them less than fully satisfying. That children omit constituents because their sentences are short is right in some sense. Does it tell the complete story? We think not. Many important questions are left unaddressed. What representation do children have when they leave the object out? The processing account tells us little about something that we will introduce briefly below and discuss in more detail in Chapter 3, namely that children extend the object omission stage longer in some languages than in others. It likewise does not explain, as we will show in Chapters 4 and 5, why developmental null objects interact systematically with their syntactic and semantic context. If children's departures from the target are systematic, then we must look deeper into the representational question.

If this is correct, language development is grammatically based but performance driven: nontarget consistent properties observed in language development correspond to "genuine UG options, but the factors determining their temporary adoption by the child lie in the growth of performance systems, outside the grammatical system proper" (Rizzi 2005: 42). Therefore, our plan is to focus on the question of the grammatical representation of the object omission stage.

1.5   The Conclusion of the Introduction

The main goal of this book is to account for pervasive patterns of missing objects in child language. Across many languages, such as French, Greek, Spanish and English we find many instances of the same phenomenon.

(23)   French (Müller et al. 1996)
         Adult: On peut   le   manger, l'oeuf?
                 we can-3SG it-CL-ACC eat-INF the.egg
                 "Can we eat it, the egg?"
         Ivar: Tu peux   manger Ø, oui. (target: Tu peux le manger, oui.)
                 you can-2SG eat-INF, yes. (target: you can it eat, yes)
                         "You can eat, yes."   (Ivar, 2;10;23)

(24)   Greek (Tsakali and Wexler 2004)
         Sikose Ø. (target: Sikose to.)
         Lift-SG-IMP (target: Lift-SG-IMP it-CL-ACC)
         "Lift.". . . (Mary, 1;09)

(25)   Spanish (Fujino and Sano 2002)
         PAR: Pero dime qué frutas me voy a comer.
               "But tell me what me what fruit I am going to eat."
         CHI: Te   voy   a pelá Ø.
               you-DAT go-1SG to peel
               "I am going to peel for you."   (Maria, 2;02)
         PAR: ¿Pero qué me   vas a pelar?
               but what me-DAT go-2SG to peel
               "But what are you going to peel for me?"

(26)   English (Pérez-Leroux et al. 2006)
         *FAT: what did he do?
         *CHI: he cut Ø. (Ross, 3;02; MacWhinney 2000)

The missing object stage occurs in all the languages we have been able to examine, albeit with varying degrees of intensity and for different durations. Although it is extremely challenging to compare across methodologies, children and languages, it seems that in some languages developmental object omissions disappear early on, while in others the missing object stage is longer. In this book, we devote quite a bit of attention to the cases of French and English, where there is a substantive amount of comparative work, including our own. The evidence is very clear that French children continue to exhibit missing objects until much later than English-speaking children (Pérez-Leroux, Pirvulescu and Roberge 2008a). In fact, missing objects in French children occur robustly until the age of four. At this age the length of children's utterances is not particularly constrained. Hence, the output constraints explanations proposed for English-speaking two-year-olds do not retain validity in this wider research context. Specific performance limitation accounts have been proposed for French, which we discuss in Chapter 4.

Our goal is to answer three questions:

- What is the nature of the missing object stage?
- In what sense do different languages offer different conditions such that their missing object stages are different in duration and intensity? In other words, what qualitative and quantitative properties of the input determine the timing of development? And finally,
- What drives the developmental process that takes the baby from the missing object stage to the mature state in grammar?

We should first further clarify how we are defining the key terms. We have so far used the term "missing objects" pretheoretically. For us, it has a somewhat neutral and more descriptive flavor. As we have seen, more commonly used in the field are terms such as "object drop," "empty objects" and "null objects." The first of these terms hints heavily at a process and aligns metaphorically with performance views. The other two seem to suggest that sentences with missing objects contain an object position, so that the object is there but not pronounced. This seems to align with a representational view. We will use these terms mostly for discussion internal to representational approaches, and the term "missing objects" when we are comparing approaches.

The basic observations above (the pervasiveness of missing objects in acquisition and the difference in expression of the stage across languages, even between languages of similar types) have lead us to propose that object omissions by children should be studied from a "null object" perspective. Based on the potential richness of null object constructions in the input (see Section 2.2.2), we propose that UG prepares the child to handle and make sense of this variety. As a result, we hypothesize that during the null object stage the child extends the use of the default null object option to various contexts, until all target missing object options are "learned." For us, learning consists of restricting the missing objects to those contexts where interlocutors, in the specific language, are able to produce an interpretation for them. In this view, children rely on the broader tools provided by UG more freely than is allowed by the adult grammar and during development they narrow the system down to the target possibilities.

Our null object approach relies on the assumption that direct objects are merged independently of the lexical properties of the verb. The object can be null or lexical; the phonological realization of the object does not necessarily depend on the verb. Actually it does a little bit, but only in a probabilistic sense, such that some verbs are more likely than others to allow the object to be left unpronounced. If the realization of the object is not fully determined by the verb in a language like English, the interpretation of the missing object is. For a null object, the default option corresponds to a null bare noun (N) that is semantically selected by the verb (Hale and Keyser 2002). S-selection of N by V leads to a generic, nonreferential prototypical interpretation as discussed above.

From an acquisition perspective, we can take the null cognate object representation proposed by Hale and Keyser as the initial setting in UG. However, as will be discussed in detail later, we have reasons to believe that the representation relies on a full null noun phrase instead of simply N. This null object representation is the point of departure for L1 acquisition in the domain of verbal complementation (Pérez-Leroux, Pirvulescu and Roberge 2006a, 2008a). When children are dropping objects they rely on just such a minimal representation. This transitivity approach predicts the existence of a null object stage in L1.

The null object approach represents a shift when compared to previous approaches to object drop in child language. Object omissions in children are not a "deficit," rather they are indicative of developmental steps on the way to the adult system. These steps are unavoidable as the child only has the input but no foreknowledge of what it means. Our approach also represents a shift from approaches that posit categorical verbal transitivity. We will show that simultaneous consideration of formal issues and acquisition issues on the question of implicit objects leads directly to a null object approach.

We will call this particular approach the "transitivity requirement" approach. The transitivity approach is acquisition-driven, cross-linguistic and modular. The first two properties are technically within the basic goals of generative grammar. The latter is a fundamental feature of our approach. We argue that any treatment of implicit objects across languages and of the presence of a missing object stage in child language must take into account the separate dimensions of narrow syntax, the lexicon and discourse representation, in addition to explaining how these interact.

Why acquisition-driven? A formal analysis that can characterize how children learn language is inherently more profound than an account that describes the facts well but waves a hand at language learning and assumes it happens by magic. The ability to describe how languages are learned is what Chomsky refers to as explanatory adequacy and this is the explicit goal of theories based on Universal Grammar, although not always uniformly taken to heart by theoreticians (Chomsky 1986).

Why cross-linguistically based? It should be possible to extend any proposed analysis to other languages. A theory that can successfully characterize the range of observable variation in the languages of the world is a superior, more general theory of language, as opposed to one that is limited to characterizing one language. A comparative approach is even more crucial in acquisition: language learning is an ability that is general while the actual language to be learned is an accident of the environment. The child faces learning challenges that are different in different languages. The linguist and the psychologist must provide an explanation as to how any and all of those challenges are met by children. A story that works for English but fails for Korean provides not just an incomplete picture of language learning but a misleading one.

Why modular? It must be modular because experience is integrated across dimensions that have different properties. Discourse plays a role in the availability of transitivity transgressions. The interpretation of missing objects is sensitive to configurational factors not only cross-linguistically, but as we will show, also in development. It is crucial that our acquisition model take into consideration the parallel contributions of lexicon, narrow syntax and discourse. This is necessary not only for explaining the missing objects themselves, but most importantly, to also explain how children learn what they need to learn to become adult-like. Why can we not make do with only one of these dimensions of language representation? Because the experience of the child conflates the three: the child is simultaneously learning a lexicon, learning to interpret utterances in context and analyzing a formal distribution for grammatical categories. An approach that considers only the task of lexical learning (verb learning) has little to say about the interesting facts concerning the discourse contexts that are associated with object drop in children. Formal learning is relevant for a child to successfully integrate lexical learning across constructions, like when a patient argument has been displaced or realized in some other syntactic function, as in the case of passives. At the same time, the formal dimension presents an incomplete picture if lexical and discourse factors are not integrated in the evaluation of the missing object stage. All three dimensions are crucial to determine, across languages, when missing objects occur and how they are understood.

As stated above, we adopt a learnability-based approach, one that emphasizes the structure of the learning domain in order to deduce what type of learning steps must be involved. We assume the meaning of sentences in general (and consequently, of sentences with missing objects) to be compositional in nature, i.e., to result from the meanings of the words (the lexicon) that are part of them and the way they are combined (their syntax). Furthermore, we hold that syntactic structure determines how meaning can be tuned to context, so that syntax not only organizes words but also constrains the linguistic access to context in specific ways. Some ways are general to communication (pragmatic principles), others are very specific to each language, and thus, part of what is to be learned. Our goal is to understand how children learn the specific aspects of syntax and of the syntax-discourse and lexicon-discourse interfaces.

Our proposal is steeped in the continuity assumption mentioned above. As we said, language learning never starts with nothing, but with a variant of something. We explore the hypothesis that "learning" consists of selecting one member of a set of predetermined hypotheses. In grammar, this translates into selecting from a reduced set of minimal structural patterns that merge themselves in increasingly complex recursive configurations at both micro and macro levels of sentential structure. The child starts from the simplest representation, which is also structurally the most basic and flexible. With the input provided by experience, this representation becomes narrower and more language-specific.

To provide a precise characterization of how this happens in the case of null objects we propose the following steps. In the next chapter, we first consider the general analyses that have been proposed to account for null objects in linguistics, and to characterize object omission phenomena cross-linguistically so as to provide a complete picture of the learning task children face. The second step is taken in Chapter 3 and consists in situating what we know about missing objects in children within this broader cross-linguistic picture, and to articulate the specific details of our acquisition proposal. Step three in Chapter 4 is to concentrate on the question of discourse-based recoverability and extend our inquiry into the question of how children interpret missing objects. The fourth and final step is to offer a detailed exploration of the lexical semantics component from both a variation and an acquisition perspective; this is the subject of Chapter 5. Our progress through those steps inescapably entails increased level of technicality in our presentation such that readers who are not familiar with the field of language acquisition and theoretical syntax may find it daunting. With this in mind we designed a concluding chapter that summarizes our main findings and analyses in an accessible style; it should therefore be possible for anyone to read Chapters 1 and 6 in order to understand the big picture of our work. They can then elect to peruse through Chapters 2–5 in order to dig deeper.

2   *From the Missing to the Invisible*

2.1   *Introduction*

As our point of departure for this chapter we suggest that missing objects in young children's production do not necessarily correspond to a complete absence but rather to a special syntactic representation. We argue that the variety of adult systems in the treatment of null and overt direct objects is such that a rich general system must be postulated in the initial stages; learning amounts to constraining possibilities. Under this view, missing objects are actually represented in the structure but their properties make them seemingly "invisible." In other words the syntactic domain, whose development we are exploring in this book, does not lend itself to an approach in terms of an initially simple or deficient system that develops in complexity.

The objectives of this chapter are: 1) To present matters related to the input that are relevant for the development of transitivity in child L1, to illustrate the complexity of the task at hand and to debunk the myth that a child simply has to be exposed to the behavior of a particular verb to learn how to use it; 2) To provide a preliminary description of null object representations in adult systems; and 3) To link the premises introduced in Chapter 1 to the adult input, which leads to Chapter 3, where we return to the acquisition process to examine the L1 developmental path and discuss the existence of a null object stage.

We argue for the centrality of the adult input for the issue at hand. We start with preliminary and simple examples, progressing to more complex ones, to show the complexity of verbal transitivity from the perspective of the many modules that can contribute to it (Section 2.2). The variety of cross-linguistic input, with respect to null versus overt direct objects, can only be revealed by a presentation of the wide range of grammatical constructions involved. While some patterns appear to be quite simple, others are more complex, with very specific restrictions. We use this presentation to illustrate the variety of input based on the different types of null object constructions available across languages and within one language. A dozen different types of null object constructions are presented. Our aim is not to offer a complete account of the acquisition paths leading to these different adult systems, but rather to motivate our hypotheses with respect to the nature of the starting point or initial state.[1] After all, children's initial grammar must be ready to accommodate all possibilities or types of null object constructions. The initial grammar must be general enough to permit any of these possibilities and yet restricted enough as to allow its acquisition.

With this initial conclusion in mind, in Section 2.3 we turn to null objects in child production, which raise significant methodological issues because detecting licit and illicit null objects in child language can be tricky. Decisions about how to interpret child production must be based on a grammatical perspective of the central concept at stake, namely verbal transitivity. We discuss this concept and its integration into a model of competence such that various types of null object constructions can be accounted for. This leads to the formulation of the concept of a Transitivity Requirement (TR), a strong hypothesis according to which a structural complement position is obligatory in all VPs.

Assuming that verbal transitivity is a given, then there must be a "minimal instantiation of transitivity" (MIT) and we must also assume that what a child needs to learn is not that a given verb can appear with an object or not, but rather the conditions under which the object is overtly realized as well as the recoverability mechanisms at play when it is not. Those conditions crucially include the particular (semantic) relation that holds between that verb and the object position. In other words, what kind of object is compatible with a particular verb? Then the question of determining whether an object can be lexical or empty becomes secondary to determining the type of restriction imposed on it by the lexical semantics of the verb.

The minimal instantiation of transitivity thus becomes the initial setting in universal grammar in this particular grammatical domain (see Section 2.4). And since MIT includes a null object we argue that object omissions in children should be studied from a "null object" perspective. From this perspective, on their way to restricting the system to the target possibilities only, children use the tools provided by UG more freely than is allowed by adult grammar.

---

[1] We also stress the important point that there is not a commonly accepted "null object parameter" in the theoretical literature. This is discussed in more detail in Chapter 4.

The null object approach represents a shift when compared to previous approaches to object drop in child language. Object omissions in children are not a "deficit"; rather they are indicative of a particular developmental path leading to the adult system.

2.2   *Null Objects and Transitivity in Adult Systems*

The objective of this section is to broadly, and cross-linguistically, delineate the complexity of input in the domain of direct object realizations, in order to arrive at a reasonable hypothesis as to the learning task that infants face. After all, it is only through being equipped with a thorough understanding of the end state that we can hope to discover the path needed to reach it.

2.2.1   *Null Objects Are Not Null Subjects*

As established in Chapter 1, children's early language production includes various missing elements of diverse natures. Although we concentrate here on null internal arguments and more specifically null direct objects, external arguments (subjects) are also often missing in child language and recent work by Bello (2014) presents evidence of indirect object drop in French L1 acquisition. Previous studies have examined null subjects in child language in detail. In fact, some of the earliest studies in L1 acquisition within the generative paradigm were done using null subjects as their empirical basis. The reason for this is the hypothesized existence of the null subject (or prodrop) parameter (NSP). Essentially, the NSP is based on the empirical observation that some languages require an overtly expressed subject (e.g., English) in tensed clauses while others do not (e.g., Italian).

(1)   a. He speaks English.
         b. * Ø speaks English.

(2)   a. Lui   parla italiano.
            he-NOM speak-3SG Italian
            "He speaks Italian."
         b. Ø parla   italiano.
              Speak-3SG Italian
              "Speaks Italian."

From an L1 acquisition perspective, Hyams (1986) argues that the optional nature of null subjects in Italian means that the initial setting of the NSP must be based on the impossibility of null subjects, which then gets negated by the input. In other words, children start out with the assumption that their grammar does not allow null subjects. Exposure to English does not provide evidence that this is incorrect and the NSP remains in this setting. Exposure to Italian however provides direct evidence (such as 2b) that the minus setting of the NSP is not valid for Italian and the NSP gets reset to a positive value. Now, although the semantic selection of the subject or the specific role it plays as an argument of a given verb is determined by that verb, its presence as an external argument is due to the Extended Projection Principle (EPP) and its overt or covert realization involves morphological considerations linked to the tense/agreement system.

We do not take a position here on whether or not a prodrop parameter exists, and if it does, on its nature; see Biberauer et al. (2010), particularly the introduction by Ian Roberts and Anders Holmberg, for an extensive discussion. The crucial point is that a null object parameter has not been proposed due to the differences between subject drop and object drop in adult language. The general account of the development of null subjects in child language as just described cannot be used to characterize null object systems and their development for the simple reason that null object constructions appear to be cross-linguistically more diverse than their null subject counterparts. Languages of the world do not seem to easily accept classification based on a binary value (+ or –) for a property like [null object]. As we will see below, while most would agree that English is [–null object], many constructions exist in this language where a direct object remains "understood" (3a) or is quite simply dropped (3b).

(3)   a. I bought a sandwich and I ate Ø on the train.
        b. Break eggs into skillet. Cook Ø until done as desired.

In Mandarin, on the other hand, it is perfectly natural to drop an object (and a subject) that has been previously mentioned in the discourse. In fact, in (4), "the object gap must be interpreted as referring to a specific, referential item, i.e., a previously mentioned or visible book" (Tieu 2007: 2).

(4)   wo zai   du __
        I   PROG read
        "I am reading."

It would then be tempting to classify Mandarin as a [+null object] language; however, contrary to what would be expected based on a language like English, a Mandarin sentence meant to express only the activity of reading (i.e., one without a referential object, or specific book or reading material) contains an overt generic object form as in (5) and this is true for many verbs (Tieu 2007).

(5)   wo   zai   du   shu
         I   PROG   read   book
         "I am reading."   (Tieu 2007)

These basic observations only serve to illustrate that languages of the world are not easily classifiable as null object or nonnull object languages, a fact we return to in Chapter 4. While this does not solve the learning problem, we can at least assume for the remainder of this book that a high-level binary parameter is not at stake. In other words, it is very unlikely that children merely have to determine the value of an overarching parameter, and then set it to that value so that they can then speak a null object or a nonnull object language. From a minimalist perspective, everything seems to function as if UG only cares about the presence of a direct object, not its realizations. In fact, null objects can be found in a wide variety of grammatical constructions; some patterns appear to be quite simple, others are more complex with very specific restrictions, so it is necessary to examine a wide range of the possibilities observed in the languages of the world.[2]

2.2.2   A Cursory Look at Adult Systems

How do we map the lay of the land for null objects cross-linguistically? Right from the onset, we are faced with two important issues. First, how do we define null objects? This is important, of course, in order to determine what counts as part of the adult system (which in turn establishes the target of the learning process). Does sentence x in language y involve a null object? And if it does, what is the nature of the null object and what accounts for its presence?

We define a null object construction as one in which an object is left unpronounced. Although this definition would include examples of displaced direct objects, our work concentrates on "base-generated" null objects. Stated differently, we focus on instances of null objects in which the object is not found elsewhere in the sentence, setting aside the null objects found, for instance, in interrogatives (6), passives (7), unaccusatives (8) and topicalizations (9) as they involve a displaced object.

(6)   <u>Who</u> did John see __?

(7)   <u>The robber</u> was arrested __ yesterday.

---

[2] See also Luraghi (2004) for an insightful contribution on this topic from a typological and language reconstruction perspective.

(8)   <u>Mary</u> arrived __ before everyone.

(9)   <u>This book</u>, I read __ when I was a kid.

To simplify for the moment, in a structural representation of the relationship between a verb and its complement, a null object occupies the canonical internal argument position, that is, Obj as the sister of V in languages like French and English.[3]

(10)   VP
           /\
          V Obj

The second issue has to do with verb classes. Verbs have traditionally been classified in terms of their transitivity as reflected in dictionary entries, which typically use a binary approach to define a given verb as either transitive or intransitive. We return to this important issue later in this chapter but for the sake of the presentation at this point let us concentrate on verbs that are optionally transitive, that is, verbs that alternate between uses with an overt object or not. We assume, as most researchers do, that even when optionally transitive verbs are used intransitively, an object is understood to be involved.[4] If John ate, some unspecified thing was eaten. In some languages though, a verb, even when used transitively, can appear without its object. In Portuguese or Russian for instance, if one says the equivalent of *John ate*, it may be the case that one is actually telling you about what he ate.

   For the sake of argumentation, we explore different types of null object constructions attested cross-linguistically, keeping in mind that the examples presented would potentially appear in the input received by a child and would therefore serve as the basis for grammatical development. This nonexhaustive list is meant to illustrate the cross-linguistic variety of null object possibilities and the inherent ambiguity of such constructions within certain languages.

   In many languages, null objects are licensed or identified through morphological agreement or clitic morphemes. The null object then clearly has anaphoric referential properties. These are not lexically licensed and do

---

[3] Note that the order of the verb and object is irrelevant. Also, it may be the case that this fragment of structure is not as basic as it seems, a fact that is discussed below and in Chapter 4.

[4] What is controversial is whether or not the object is grammatically, structurally or semantically present and, if so, what the appropriate grammatical representation is; see Chapter 4.

not exhibit typicality restrictions, as noted in Section 2.3.3.1. Both the cases in (11) and (12), with agreement and an accusative clitic, respectively, exhibit nonlexically licensed empty canonical object positions, illustrating these common options across the world's languages.

(11)   Sora; Stampe (1993)
        nyen gij-t-Am
        'I   see-pres-2OBJ
        "I see you."

(12)   French
        Jean la   connaît.
        Jean her-CL-ACC knows-PRES-3SG
        "Jean knows her."

Note however that such constructions are not, strictly speaking, considered to be null object constructions as it can be said that the object is represented in the sentence. Whether or not this is an appropriate view remains to be seen, but the fact remains that they constitute a portion of a child's input without an overt object in the canonical object position.[5] While these two patterns appear to be relatively well understood, others seem more complex, with very specific restrictions. Consider the case of Baule, a language from Ivory Coast, whose null objects combine lexical, featural and positional restrictions:

> The verb *non*, "drink," is a so-called Object Drop verb, which means that its subcategorization requirements specify that it occurs with a null object pronoun, whenever possible. Object Drop verbs are required to drop any pronominal object with an inanimate singular referent that occurs at the end of a clause. Pronouns which have animate or plural referents or pronouns that do not occur at the end of clauses are always overt.   (Larson 2002: 3)

(13)   A   nonni   nzue'n?   Een, n   nonni
        2SG-SUBJ drink.past water.def yes 1SG-SUBJ drink-PAST
        "Did you drink the water?"   "Yes, I drank it/some."

---

[5] The parallel with subject clitics is worth noting here as their presence in a language leads many researchers to conclude that that language is not a null subject language. As a result, French is most often classified as a nonnull subject language. Other researchers disagree with this approach and argue that French (and other subject clitic languages) is a null subject language; see Roberge (1990), Auger (1994), Culbertson and Legendre (2008), Culbertson (2010), among others.

(14)   Een, n   nonni   (*i).
       yes 1SG-SUBJ drink.past (*3SG-OBJ)
       "Yes, I drank it/some."

Null objects can also be licensed through discourse linking in the case of discourse-oriented/radical argument drop languages such as Mandarin or Japanese, where pronouns are rare and null objects freely refer to a previously established discourse antecedent (Sigurðsson 2011).

(15)   Japanese; O'Grady et al. (2008)
       Toshi-ga   hon-o   mita. Watashi-mo mita.
       Toshi-NOM book-ACC saw   I-too   saw
       "Toshi saw the book. I too saw (it)."

Hungarian represents a somewhat intermediate case. According to Luraghi (2004: 251), null objects are widespread in this language: "Hungarian has no weak pronouns for the third person; in sentences where anaphoric reference is made by the direct object, if the latter is not strongly accented for pragmatic reasons, a n[ull] o[bject] occurs in conjunction with the definite conjugation, which alone points toward the existence of a definite direct object." She provides the following example to illustrate:

(26)   Ismered   a   nyelvet? Igen, ismerem
       Know-PRES-DEF-2SG the language yes know-PRES-DEF-1SG
       Do you know (are you familiar with) the language? Yes, I know it (Yes, I do).

Slavic languages also represent a fertile ground for null objects constrained by the aspectual specifications of the verbs. For instance, Frolova (2013) cites the following excerpt from Forsyth (1970):

> A potentially transitive verb, when used in its perfective forms, requires an object (expressed or implied). It makes sense to say, *včera ja pisalIMP* "yesterday I wrote," but in isolation the sentence *včera ja napisalPF* is meaningless. The latter demands an object such as *pis'mo, sočinenie* ("a letter, a composition") etc. In conversation, of course, it is common to answer such a question as *vy napisaliPF pis'mo* ? ("did you write the/a letter") by saying simply *napisalPF* ("ØNOM wrotePF ØACC"), implying the object already referred to. (Forsyth 1970: 91)[6]

---

[6] Here IMP=IMPF (imperfective aspect) and PF=PERF (perfective aspect).

(27)   Russian – Gordishevsky and Avrutin (2003: 1)

> A: Chto ty sdelal so stulom?
> "What did you do with the chair?"
> B: Ø slomal Ø. / Ja slomal   ego.
>   broke-M   I broke-M him
>   "(I) broke (it)." / "I broke it."

Other languages possess both pronouns and discourse-identified null objects. For instance, in Portuguese, anaphoric null objects (without clitics) are quite freely allowed (a) despite the availability of accusative clitics (b) (Raposo 1986: 373).

(28)   a. A Joana viu Ø na   TV ontem.
            the J.   saw on+the TV yesterday
            "Jane saw on TV yesterday."
         b. A Joana viu-os   na   TV ontem.
            the J.   saw-them on+the TV yesterday
            "Jane saw them on TV yesterday."

French, on the other hand, only allows some referential null direct objects without clitics (Lambrecht and Lemoine 1996; Larjavaara 2000; Cummins and Roberge 2005, among others).

(29)   Noailly (1997: 100)

> Et la tête qu'il fait le jour où on rapporte au logis un store décoré d'une photo de Marylin ... S'il déteste Ø vraiment, on le case dans la salle de bain ...
>
> "And the look on his face the day you bring home a blind decorated with a photo of Marilyn (Monroe) ... If he really hates Ø, you stick it in the bathroom ... "

The term "clitic-drop" is often used to refer to this type of construction because it appears to be exactly the same as the corresponding equivalent with an overt clitic. This construction in French is not fully generalized, but is restricted to some registers and appears to have special pragmatic functions, which is not the case in Portuguese.

In the literature on null objects, many examples of null objects are described in what can be generally referred to as an instructional context, much like recipes (3b above). This occurs in English as well as other languages (Massam and Roberge 1989; Haegeman 1987; Bender 1999; Ruda 2014, among others).

(30)   Cook Ø in plenty of boiling salted water until "al dente." Drain Ø and serve Ø
         with a sauce of your choice.

All the preceding examples have a referential or definite flavor but not all null objects do. In fact, one of the most widely accepted typologies of null objects gives two types: referential (or definite) and nonreferential (or indefinite). The nonreferential type can be described roughly as one that does not refer to a specific entity. In such cases the verb is interpreted with an activity reading so emphasis is placed on the action described by the verb, and as such, the object implicated becomes irrelevant in the discourse. One of the earliest works that provides a detailed description of this type of null complement is Fillmore (1986); see Lambrecht and Lemoine (1996), for French. Familiar examples of such understood objects are:

(31)   a. Are you going for lunch? No. I ate already.
         b. What do you do for a living? I write.
         c. I read all night.

In fact, as speakers of English, we are so accustomed to this use that a brief metalinguistic reflection is sometimes needed to even realize that the verb's meaning implies the existence of an object. Within this general type, Rizzi (1986) discusses a particular interpretation found in Italian, the arbitrary plural human null objects, which he argues must be syntactically represented.

(32)   Talvolta la stampa lascia [Ø perplessi]
         "Sometimes the press causes-to-remain puzzled." (Rizzi 1986: 533)

It is important to note – and we come back to this below – that there are instances where a nonreferential null object, such as in the English examples in (33) and (34), has the appearance of referring to an antecedent. This is not a truly anaphoric use of null objects, however. Cummins and Roberge (2005) propose that this interpretation is the result of pragmatic inference. The contrast between (34) and (35), in fact, shows that when a truly referential reading of the null object is forced, the result is unacceptable in English. In (34), the understood null object provides an activity reading, which inferentially applies to the dishes. However, such implicit objects fail as answers to object focus questions, as shown by (35).

(33)   While I wait for you, I'll buy a newspaper and I'll read ...

(34)   A: We have to get rid of all the ugly dishes before your date arrives.
         B: Okay, you wash and I'll dry. (Goldberg 2001: 515)

(35)   A: What did you do with the dirty dishes?
         B: * I washed and dried.

While this cursory look at null object constructions in adult grammar is far from revealing the extent of the variety found in the languages of the world, we believe it is sufficient to draw the following conclusion. Based on the potential variety found in the input, we conclude that a child's initial grammar must be ready to accommodate all these possibilities; it therefore must be general enough to permit them and yet restricted enough as to allow their acquisition. In the present research we adopt the general approach proposed in Cummins and Roberge (2005), which takes into account the contributions made by various modules (syntax, semantics, pragmatics) and to which we return in the following sections.[7]

2.3 *Transitivity in Adult Systems: The Grammatical Perspective*

It follows from our presentation so far that what we are really exploring here is the general concept of transitivity and its structural representation. So, we suggest that an analysis of object drop in child language must be incorporated into an account of this central concept. In fact, we argue that an independently motivated, very specific and universal approach to transitivity coupled with observations on the development of nominal elements provides an effective approach to the L1 facts.

Complements of various types and transitivity alternation phenomena have received a lot of attention in the generative literature, and the concept of transitivity itself has been central to general linguistics (Hopper and Thompson 1980), and to the development of various approaches to diachronic change (Blinkenberg 1960). It is fair to assume that descriptive and prescriptive grammars postulate the reality of this concept as a property of certain classes of verb and this also holds, although indirectly, for studies in lexical semantics that sort verbs according to classes such as transitive, intransitive or unergative, defined on the basis of their capacity to appear with or without objects. Any dictionary search for a verb such as *to eat* will return entries containing a variety of labels meant to express the fact that this verb is optionally transitive: "used with object," "used without object," [I/T], "with object," "no object," etc.

Although transitivity is often taken for granted and simply assumed, there are many definitions of this concept. The traditional descriptive approach is to say that it is the expression of a relationship between two elements (a verb and,

---

[7] A null object approach can also be fruitfully applied to the study of diachronic change as demonstrated in Lavidas (2013: 1016) .

say, a DP) such that the meaning of the verb would be incomplete in the absence of the DP. Transitivity, according to this view, exists as a lexical property of some verbs whose argument structure is such that a semantic role must be assigned to an object. It is the essence of the verb to involve an object. Transitivity can be reflected in a variety of ways, for example morphologically through case marking, but we are especially interested in the syntactic expression of this relationship in a structure since this is what is at stake in the development of transitivity in young children.

2.3.1 Basic Concepts

Our grammatical analyses rely on the most basic concepts developed within generative grammar over the last 50 years, more specifically the Minimalist approach of Chomsky (1995) and subsequent work. Our analyses are broad enough to be easily understood by nonlinguists and, we believe, adaptable to other models of grammar. Nevertheless, a description of the components of the grammatical analyses as they are done in minimalism is in order.

Lexical entries contain the idiosyncratic properties of lexical items, including meaning and phonological form(s). The set of lexical features may also include categorial and ϕ-feature specifications (gender and intrinsic numbers). Alternatively, the lexicon only includes roots, as proposed in Distributed Morphology, with further specification occurring in the course of the derivation with vocabulary insertion at a later stage based on those specifications. Although this represents two quite divergent views of the lexicon and its interface with syntax, for our purposes nothing crucial initially hinges on the differences.[8] The lexicon also includes functional heads.

Lexical items drawn from the lexicon are merged and create structure through projection and further applications of Merge. Merge is a simple but powerful operation that can be applied externally – when an item drawn from the lexicon is merged to another element; or internally – when the merged element is part of an already created structure.

With respect to transitivity, we explore the role of the lexicon in the next section. Structurally speaking, transitivity can be expressed in its simplest form as the merging of a verb and another constituent, which becomes its complement, as in (10) above, repeated here as (36).

---

[8] However, the Distributed Morphology approach offers more flexibility with respect to means of satisfaction of a Transitivity Requirement since the requirement could be one related to a property of the root or the lexicalizing head (v). Refer to Section 2.3.3.2 for an example of this possibility.

(36) VP

Obviously, further structure (applications of Merge) and lexical differences will lead to drastically different surface realizations. For instance, although both *dance* and *give* may appear with a complement (obligatorily so, as argued in Section 2.3.4), the elements merged as their complements receive very different interpretations: a dance in one case, a relation in the other.

It follows from this that the transitive/intransitive/unergative/unaccusative/inchoative/etc. distinction is essentially construction-based, and as argued in the next section, has little to do with lexical specifications beyond the semantic restrictions imposed by the verbal root.

2.3.2   Lexical Analysis

It is a well-known fact that many transitive verbs can be used unergatively. It is possible for a traditional lexical approach to handle such verbs. Given the verb *to eat*, one could postulate two lexical entries, as illustrated in (37).

(37)   Fellbaum and Kegl (1989)
  a. *Eat$_1$*, unergative, "eat a meal," incorporates an object component.
  b. *Eat$_2$*, transitive, "ingest food in some manner," incorporates a manner component which forces the presence of an object.

This approach states, in effect, that when an object is overtly realized it is syntactically present, but when it is not overt then it is not syntactically present. Crucially, therefore, the presence of an object is itself attributed to the lexical semantics of the transitive verb. In other words, the fact that a verb can assign a certain semantic role to the object is a necessary and sufficient condition for the presence of an object. For instance, Levin (1999) defines the cross-linguistic class of Core Transitive Verb (CTV) as having the causative event structure in (38). Linking rules ensure that the *y* participant is realized as the object.

(38)   Levin (1999: 231)
    $[[x \, ACT_{<manner>}] \, CAUSE \, [BECOME \, [y \, <STATE>]]]$

This lexical structure can be read as x acts in a manner that causes y to become in a certain state. However, transitivity as a grammatical concept is also often dissociated from lexical semantics, that is, verbs are not in themselves transitive or intransitive, but can or cannot appear in a transitive construction. For Levin (1999), other verbs besides the CTVs can appear with two participants and thus in a transitive structure but they typically involve a single event with a pure constant participant required by the idiosyncratic meaning of the verb – y in (39) – which then links to the object position; as such they are noncore transitive verbs.

(39)   Levin (1999: 235)
        a. Leslie swept the floor.
        b. [x ACT $_{<sweep>}$ y]

Thus, the simplest way to characterize this view is to say that some constructions are transitive and some verbs have semantic properties that make them compatible with this construction. This partly explains why transitivity is often described as a continuum from verbs that almost always appear with an object to verbs that almost never appear with one (Blinkenberg 1960; Desclés 1998; Hopper and Thompson 1980; Lazard 1994). Note however that such a continuum refers, not to the property of being able to appear with an object, but rather to whether or not an object is overtly realized. Extensive research has thus been done on the semantic and pragmatic factors that can affect the "use" of a verb as transitive or intransitive. However, in this kind of approach very little is said about the structural aspects of transitivity. The question we need to ask is: What allows for the presence of an object if this presence is dissociated from lexical specification? Note that under this view, even when an object is not syntactically present it is still assumed to be active in the compositional interpretation of the sentence. This is expressed in (37a) through incorporation of the object component into the lexical entry of the verb. Paradoxically, this leads to the view that the unergative interpretation (37a) does involve an object (see García Velasco and Portero Muñoz 2002).

   Now turning to L1 acquisition, we see that the participation of an object must somehow be internalized by children. How is this possible? It could be that the entry in (37b) systematically implies the entry in (37a). This would essentially mean: 1) A transitive verb can "automatically" be used unergatively or, stated differently, that the transitive nature of a verb subsumes its potential unergativity, and, 2) Transitivity for a particular verb must be learned before unergativity. We are then back to square one: How can the transitivity of a verb be learned unless the child somehow starts out with the assumption that transitivity comes first? Therefore, we propose that this assumption be integrated into UG.

   Another problem with a purely lexical approach is that it has been argued convincingly that at least some instances of transitive verbs with unexpressed objects can be shown to involve syntactically represented null objects (Rizzi 1986; Raposo 1986). For example, in (40a), the unexpressed object of *eat* is available for a parasitic gap interpretation much as in the classic example with *read* in (40b). The sentence in (40a) is ambiguous and can have the (frivolous) interpretation that the filed article has been eaten, in addition to the one whereby the activity of eating something happened after the filing of the article.

(40)   a. <u>Which article</u> did he file __ before eating__?
         b. <u>Which article</u> did he file __ before reading__?

The point here is that this can only be accounted for if an empty element is present in the object position of *eat* to act parasitically on the trace in the object position of the verb *file*. In order to maintain a lexical account, one would have to add a third option, namely that of a syntactically represented unexpressed object. There would therefore be three possible representations for the same verb: overt object, null object, no object. In L1 acquisition, it would then be necessary to explain how these options are learnt and under what circumstances each of the three options can be used. We propose instead that the no object possibility is subsumed under the null object representation as just one of the possible null object constructions.

Returning to our discussion of null object constructions, if the lexicon is assumed to represent idiosyncratic properties of lexical items, it must be concluded that lexical representations do not constitute the best option for the locus of the transitive-unergative alternation – or the possibility of being used with a null object – as this alternation simply does not appear to be an idiosyncratic property of only certain verbs. Rather, it is a pervasive possibility, not only within a particular grammar but also cross-linguistically; see Cummins and Roberge (2004) for a comparison between French and English. From a language acquisition point of view, if the transitive-unergative alternation is not a property of certain verbs it must be a property independent of lexical choice. Consequently, a transitive verb that appears without an object is not actually unergative; it is simply transitive. Whether the object is expressed or not is independent of the status of the verb with respect to overt transitivity. The simplest acquisition path for a child is to assume that transitive verbs are always transitive whether an object is overt or not; in other words, transitivity is best viewed as a (universal) grammatical property, not a lexical property.

Returning to Levin (1999), there is no one-to-one correspondence between the existence of an "object" participant in the event structure of a given verb and its overt presence in the clause. Linking rules associating the CTV's event participant y or the noncore transitive verbs' pure constant participant y to a structural object position are thus necessary. The question remains: Do the linking rules themselves create the structural object position or is the position merged independently of the linking rules?

2.3.3   Structural Transitivity

In this section we examine structural transitivity, that is, the idea that transitivity is expressed grammatically, not solely as a reflex of a lexical property or as the fulfillment of a lexical requirement. In other words, it is not because a verb x requires or accepts an object that one is expressed in the sentence.

We briefly present well-known facts from various languages, beyond the null object facts presented in 2.2.2, as convergent evidence indicating that the presence of a direct object position in a structure is to be attributed to more than just the semantics of the verb heading the verbal complex. In other words, the facts enumerated below all point to the centrality and obligatoriness of verbal complementation.

2.3.3.1   Cognate Objects and the Like

As is well-known, verbs traditionally classified as unergative appear quite freely with objects in English and other languages (Blinkenberg 1960; Jones 1988; Massam 1990; Larjavaara 2000). The object can be etymologically cognate to the verb as in (41) or not, as in (42). In this last case, the object behaves as a "transitivizing object" (see Massam 1990).

(41)   a. John smiled a wicked smile.
        b. Vivre   sa   vie.
           live-INF own life
           "To live one's life."

(42)   a. Tosca sang an aria.
        b. Elle grimaça   un rictus résigné. (Larjavaara 2000: 32)
           she grinned-3SG. a grin   resigned
           "She grinned a resigned grin."

Unaccusative verbs generally do not accept cognate or transitivizing objects, as shown in (43) for French and English.[9] If the superficial subject of unaccusative verbs is an underlying object then the direct object position is not available for a cognate or transitivizing object (see Section 2.3.3.2).

---

[9] There are a few apparent exceptions to this generalization, such as in (i) and (ii). In (i) the apparent direct object involved is more likely the end point or the path of movement expressed by the verb. This might also be the case for (ii).

(i)   a. Aller son petit bonhomme de chemin.
           "To go one's own way."
        b. To go it alone

(ii)   He died a good death.

(43)   a. *Il   venait   souvent son chemin.
         he-NOM came-3SG often his route
         "He often went his route."
       b. *He arrived an early arrival.

Note further that the object is without a doubt an internal argument and it behaves as such. In (44a) for instance, the transitivizing object is relativized as an ordinary direct object. In (44b), it is pronominalized as an accusative clitic just as an ordinary direct object would be.

(44)   a. Face aux grands événements que nous vivons.
            "Given the important events that we are living."
       b. On sentait là, sous sa poitrine, de gros battements qui la haletaient.
            "You could feel, in her chest, a deep beat panting her."

Verbs traditionally classified as unergative can thus appear with a referential direct object. As stated in the case of unexpressed objects, a lexical account can be offered (e.g., as an extension of meaning from *to live*$_1$ = unergative to *to live*$_2$ = transitive). But inasmuch as this is not an idiosyncratic property of certain verbs, it would seem counterproductive to attribute it to a special behavior of specific lexical items. Moreover, if the presence of an object position is to be attributed to the semantics of the verb then we have no other choice but to assume that the semantics of all unergative verbs is potentially sufficient to license an object position. The unergative/transitive distinction loses all value.[10] Something more general must underlie the property. Under a structural transitivity approach, the availability of a structural object position must be dissociated from the fact that the verb can give it a semantic interpretation. The unergative/transitive distinction can thus be maintained but reduced to the ability of a given verb to provide interpretations for the object, not to its ability to provide the projection and the interpretation of that object.

   Hale and Keyser (1991, 1993, 2002) argue that unergatives have a transitive lexical relational structure universally. In their earlier work, they propose that conflation (or incorporation) of a cognate object to a light verb results in an unergative verb; so, *to dance* would have a structure corresponding to "to do a dance." In their later work, Hale and Keyser (2002) abandon the hypothesis that conflation is the lexical operation responsible for the representation

---

[10] This is not an original conclusion. For instance, Luraghi (2010: 136) points out that Croft (1991) "suggests that activity verbs all have an understood direct object: while this view is shared by other authors regarding those activity verbs which have a transitive counterpart, such as *eat* or *paint*, Croft extends the analysis to other verbs." As pointed out, different frameworks offer different implementations of this suggestion.

associated with unergatives. Rather, they propose that the unergative verb enters into a relation with a null N complement as in (45). This relation is one of classificatory licensing whereby "the verb identifies the complement to some sufficient extent" (p. 92). They use the term "hyponymy" to refer to this selectional relation and notate it with braced indices as in (45).

(45)   V   Hale and Keyser (2002: 93)

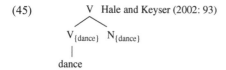

As pointed out by Dobrovie-Sorin (1998: 408), Hale and Keyser's representation is clearly lexical in nature; in fact, she states that "this view of the lexical representation of unergatives does not oblige us, and perhaps does not even authorize us, to assume that the traces of the incorporated cognate objects are projected in the syntax." However, it is quite possible to reinterpret their representations as syntactic. Dobrovie-Sorin (1998: 408) herself states the necessity of this: "What we need is a theory of the representation of unergatives at S-structure rather than in the lexicon." To do so, she suggests that unergatives and transitives may both take a direct object optionally. Her approach thus consists in unifying transitives and unergatives as verbs that can take direct objects. We go a step further in forcing the presence of an object position with all verbs and in claiming that the variable behavior observed in unergative verbs is directly attributable to this requirement.

2.3.3.2   Unaccusativity
Most existential and movement verbs are assumed to be members of a class of unaccusative verbs. The main property of such verbs is that their surface subject originates from an internal argument position (object) and then moves to the external argument position (subject).

Consequently, an important number of clauses exhibiting a Subject-Verb order are in fact underlyingly Verb-Object. Given the EPP, these clauses are in fact S-V-O, with O moving to the position of S. Therefore, all instances of S-V clauses in a language such as French or English, can potentially involve an unaccusative verb, an unergative verb or a transitive verb. But given the preceding discussion, none of them can truly be argued not to involve a direct object position. Under this view then, there are no S-V clauses in those languages; they are all S-V-O.

This discussion naturally extends to the causative alternation observed in many languages with certain verbs such as *break*. Indeed, Rappaport Hovav (2014) argues that all alternating verbs are lexically associated only with the internal argument(s) (objects), and that the conditions under which an external causer argument (subject) is used must be determined independently based on other factors (including pragmatics). For Cuervo (2014), there are two types of anticausative constructions (unaccusative constructions) depending on the position of the internal argument (object) involved. In other words, the internal argument of alternating verbs is not necessarily merged in the canonical direct object position. Cuervo represents the two possibilities as:

(46)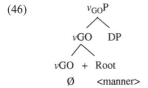

(47)　Se salieron　tres　clavos
　　　SE came-out three nails
　　　'Three nails came off.'

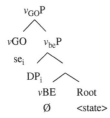

Unaccusatives and the causative alternations point to the centrality of the internal argument position as the starting point or origin of further constructions, as well as to a certain flexibility in terms of the exact position occupied by the argument (see Section 2.3.4).

2.3.3.3　Lexical Inventory

As further support for the view that the nature of the unergative/transitive distinction should not be based on the availability, or not, of a direct object position on a verb by verb basis, it is worth pointing out that Blinkenberg (1960), in a corpus-based study, found that only approximately 20 percent of French verbs behave mainly as unergatives. The relevance of this finding is in diachronic (not synchronic) terms and a number of researchers argue that it is a reflex of the status of transitivity as a grammaticalization process (see Bréal 1897; Bernard 1991, among others). If the distribution of verbs in terms of the transitive versus unergative distinction were purely random this imbalance would be difficult to account for. Therefore, it would again seem justified to assume that the distinction is not lexical but syntactic in nature. Given such a view, verbs always appear with an object (overt or not). Verbs differ in the interpretation that they can assign to that object position. Blinkenberg establishes a clear distinction between semantic transitivity and syntactic transitivity; the numbers he gives thus reflect semantic differences among verbs and not their status as being able to project an object position or not.

2.3.3.4   Expletive Objects

Expletive subjects (48) have played a central role in the development of linguistic theory in many frameworks. The obvious reason for this is that they can be seen as showing that a subject position is structurally necessary even when the event does not involve a semantically necessary subject (agent, causer, etc.).

(48)   It would appear that the problem is solved.

Expletive objects have received much less attention in the literature and, indeed, there is no consensus on their very existence (see Rosenbaum 1967; Postal and Pullum 1988; Runner 2000, among others). The following examples represent the type of construction we have in mind here for English:

(49)   a. We demand it of our employees that they wear a tie.
         b. I take it then that you won't be joining us.
         c. I expected it, correctly, to be hard to teach that stuff.
         d. Really dance it!
         e. To battle it out.
         f. Beat it!

Our purpose is not to provide an account of this construction but many previous analyses involve either two different base-generated internal argument positions (one for the expletive and the other for the sentential complement in examples 49a, b, c) or a landing site for the extraposed sentential complement. One of the questions raised is why the sentential complement seems to be dispreferred in what appears to be the regular object position (presumably occupied by the expletive pronoun). Note that the sentential subject construction counterpart does not show this effect (50).

(50)   That they won't be joining us (*it) will be a problem.

If expletive object constructions have something to do with structural transitivity, then we can interpret the facts as showing that sentential complements are not as likely to be compatible with the basic complement position, albeit for reasons that remain obscure for the moment. However, the contrast with sentential subjects indicates that the resistance may be of a semantic nature such that the selectional restrictions imposed by the verbs are not directly satisfiable by sentential complements. This would mean that the expletive pronoun in object position has more semantics than when it occupies the subject position. In support of this, we note that the equivalent construction in French has recourse to the pronoun *ça*, which has a strong deictic flavor.

(51)   J'aime pas (ça) quand tu pars en voyage.
         I like not (that) when you go-2SG on trip
         "I don't like it when you go on trips."

In Quebec French, that same pronoun is used to satisfy the transitivity requirement of the ethical dative construction with unergative verbs (Roberge and Troberg 2007):

(52)   a.   Elle t'   a   dansé   *(ça)!
              she you-CL-DAT   has danced it
              "She really danced!"
         b.   Son bébé lui   a dormi *(ça).
              her baby her-CL-DAT has slept   it

2.3.4   The Transitivity Requirement

In this section, we develop the concept of a Transitivity Requirement (TR) as the key to understanding the facts enumerated above and the developmental path followed by children in their acquisition of transitivity. It is a strong hypothesis according to which a structural complement position is obligatory in all VPs.[11] We discuss possible implementations of this requirement mostly based on a parallel between TR and the Extended Projection Principle (EPP), which in its original formulation requires an externalized structural subject position. It is argued that effects similar to, but crucially different from, that of the EPP on the subject position exist for objects. Since TR applies in the thematic layer of the clause (the VP shell), its minimal instantiation involves broadly defined semantic recoverability based on the "constant" component of a verb. In contrast, since the EPP applies in the functional layer (IP) it involves morphological recoverability conditions. Despite these obvious differences

---

[11] We take the term "strong" to mean that the hypothesis is formulated in such a way as "to guide research and theory for particular cases in interesting directions, even if it may not tell us the whole story of these fundamental processes." (http://academic.brooklyn.cuny.edu/education/jlemke/webs/wess/tsld013.htm)

between the two, viewing TR as an EPP in VP remains a useful heuristic for a better understanding of TR.

In minimalist terms, TR corresponds to a simple application of external Merge of the verb and another constituent. When no complement is overtly expressed, an empty constituent (ec) must be used. External Merge of an empty constituent to a verb can be seen as necessary even under Krivochen and Kosta's definition of Dynamic Full Interpretation (2013: 73), according to which "any derivational step is justified only insofar as it increases the information and/or it generates an interpretable object."[12] Merge in this case allows for the projection of V as a VP; whether the element merged with V is associated to phonological features or not is irrelevant. In other words, the application of Merge (V-OBJ) creates a VP and defines V as V_{min}, a necessary condition for head-to-head movement of V to higher functional projections. This implies that Merge applies independently of lexical content of V. The tricky question then arises of determining what motivates this particular application of Merge and how to implement it in syntax. Let us assume that TR essentially means the merging of a constituent to V. There are four basic options, from stronger to weaker:

1. Obligatory merging of a structural internal argument position that is not necessarily thematically active; in other words, TR is postulated as an independent universal principle (analogous to the EPP, but for objects);

2. A variation on Option 1 that preserves the possibility that the merge operation does not apply systematically in all languages; stated differently, TR is a parametrized independent principle;

3. Optional merging of the constituent where the two options (presence or absence of the object) must be constrained by some other component such as satisfaction of selectional features; TR is thus viewed as an optional independent operation with constraints;

4. TR does not exist as an independent operation or principle but its effects derive from other grammatical principles.

---

[12] Specifically applied to Merge, Krivochen (2013: 22) states: "our position is that if Merge is considered to be an operation and we assume also D(ynamic) F(ull) I(nterpretation), that is, the assumption that application of any operation must either lead to a legible object or increase the informational load, to apply Merge to a single object is trivial in any faculty. If {a} is already legible in the relevant interface level, then why apply Merge in the first place? It would be computationally redundant and therefore far from Minimalist. We maintain that binary Merge is the minimal-maximal nontrivial option and therefore reject any proposal of unitary Merge on interface grounds."

Besides offering potentially fascinating new possibilities for analyzing facts relating to transitivity in natural languages, Option 1 is the most radical (or strongest) and should therefore be adopted and explored first. Option 2 should only be considered once the validity of Option 1 for certain languages but not others has been demonstrated, a possibility we reserve for future research. Option 3 amounts to a weaker version of Option 1 and corresponds to most of the current approaches to transitivity; as we will see, it is insufficient to account for acquisition, a point we shall return to later. Option 4 (deriving TR from independent principles) should ultimately be considered as the optimal outcome. This is true in most frameworks, including Minimalism, but two remarks are in order. First, this option assumes the existence of TR effects and thus of the corresponding descriptive generalization, stated in (53) (Roberge 2002).

(53)   Transitivity Requirement (TR): A complement position is always included in the projection of V, independently of lexical choice of V.

Stated differently, the direct object position is given by Universal Grammar and is not dependent on lexical features of the verbs.[13] As such, trying to understand the generalization is a step towards eliminating it as a stipulation. Furthermore, as previously noted, our approach is very reminiscent of the type of research that has been produced on the EPP since its inception, namely that the principle first appears as a postulation, which then gives rise to attempts at deriving it. As is likely still the case for the EPP, it is not clear whether we are currently in a position to derive TR. We thus maintain it as a postulate and discuss the reasoning behind it.

One way to look at TR is through a comparison with the EPP since TR looks like the internal argument counterpart of the EPP. The EPP is clearly a requirement of the clause, in the functional layer of a clausal structure and its intuitive basis is the concept of predication, which appears to be a universal requirement. In the Government and Binding framework, a distinction is established between 2 types of selectional requirements:

> We will say that α θ-marks the category β if α θ-marks the position occupied by β or a trace of β. Note that α subcategorizes a position but θ-marks both a position and a category [...] Clearly, θ-marking is closely related to subcategorization. The notions are not identical, however.   (Chomsky 1981: 37)

---

[13] This does not entail that the lexical entry of a verb does not play a role in the interpretation of the direct object; Chapter 5 explores the role of the lexicon in detail.

This last provision is made in reference to sentential subjects, leading to the EPP, since a verb can θ-mark a subject but does not subcategorize it in this framework. Our hypothesis is that this is also true of the object position within VP. In the same way that the subcategorization component of the presence of a subject is the EPP, the subcategorization part of the presence of an object is TR. This requirement is thus decoupled from idiosyncratic lexical specifications.[14]

Recalling Option 4 above, the proposals that are made to eliminate the EPP as a postulate, and derive it from other independently needed mechanisms or operations, are too numerous to present in detail here. Many of these proposals amount to the satisfaction of a feature of a functional category through the merge of an element in the Spec of that functional category. According to this view, the EPP has an interpretive nature, in that it serves to eliminate an uninterpretable feature on a functional category. Yet other proposals maintain that the EPP is purely structural and not based on interpretive requirements (see Lasnik 2001). As Epstein and Seely (2006: 51) put it: "The EPP has in its many varying and unclear forms been deemed not only mysterious, but to the extent that it is clear, 'highly' redundant with other principles of Universal Grammar." The similarity with the equally mysterious TR is striking and we can easily extend the general approach to TR, by stating that a feature (of a nature to be determined) on V (lexical) is checked at Merge by a DP (or other types of complements). Yet we have seen that TR is not narrowly lexical but rather seems generalized to V as a category. TR would thus be a categorial requirement on Merge and transitivity would be interpreted as a property of V, possibly, as a defining feature of [+V] categories.

Di Sciullo and Isac (2008: 268) argue that the ordering of Merge operations follows from the assumption that Merge is asymmetrical in nature and applies to elements "whose sets of features are in a proper inclusion relation." For the specific case we are interested in here, they propose that it is the categorial features that are relevant for the search for inclusion relations (they specifically exclude semantic features from the search). They assume the following feature specifications for verbs, where μ means uninterpretable:

(54)   unergative V: [V]
          transitive V: [V]
                             [μD]
          unaccusative V: [V]
                             [μD]

---

[14] A similar separation can be found in Chung and Ladusaw's (2003) saturation vs. restriction, to which we return in Chapter 5.

Assuming the analysis of unergatives adopted here (based on Hale and Keyser 2002) it is likely that unergative V would also have, if not a [μD] feature, then at least some other nominal feature, which means that all Vs have the same feature specifications, at least those pertaining to the application of Merge. Practically speaking, if all Vs have an unvalued nominal feature, then all Vs must merge with an element capable of valuing that feature and this is the state of affairs described by TR. In Chung and Ladusaw's terminology, this would amount to stipulating that all Vs can and must be restricted via Merge. Although, we obtain the right outcome, Di Sciullo and Isac's approach is not quite compatible with our assumptions so far since TR appears to have a semantic flavor. In addition, applying a feature such as [μD] to all Vs defeats the purpose of introducing the feature in the first place since it no longer serves to distinguish classes of Vs and types of VPs (i.e., those with or without a complement).

It turns out that various researchers have put forward proposals that closely resemble TR. According to Erteschik-Shir and Rapoport (2004), a verb always projects as a verb-complement structure, a predicate, and the merged complement realizes a meaning component of the verb. They state: "Syntactic structure is constrained by the requirement that lexical verbs be typed (by merging a complement) and by a principle of Full Interpretation: that all meaning components be interpreted according to the structure projected." (2004: 218). Yet other approaches separate the object requirement from V through the introduction of a functional projection above VP, the Spec of which hosts the object, which in turn must be present to check some feature of the functional head. For Bowers (2002) the projection is a Transitive Phrase (TrP). Tr assigns accusative Case to the object and, interestingly, the object moves up to Spec TrP to satisfy an EPP feature of Tr. Basilico (1998) also proposes a functional category (also Tr) between the two VPs of a VP shell. An object can be merged directly in the Spec, Tr position or in the inner VP. In this approach, there are two object positions, each corresponding to two interpretations (thetic versus categorial; see Kuroda 1972). The thetic interpretation, provided by the inner position, gives emphasis to the event involving the object but does not single out the object. The categorial interpretation in the outer position ascribes a property to the object. For her part, Borer (2004) offers a line of reasoning similar to the one we follow in this book. She states:

> To the extent that it can be established that the projection of arguments is independent of the properties of substantive vocabulary items,

clearly some syntactic structure must exist such that it represents the unique linking between structural positions and argument interpretation. The specific properties of that structure could then be the subject matter of a separate debate.   (Borer 2004: 293)

In her exoskeletal approach, an aspectual functional projection hosts the direct object. Hill and Roberge (2006) suggest that objects can occupy both the complement and specifier positions within VP, thereby achieving a result similar to Basilico's representations, without recourse to an extra functional projection.

Pesetsky and Torrego (2004) represents, to our knowledge, the approach that most closely matches the one introduced here. For them, "the architecture for clauses whose main predicate is verbal must be (16) [(55)] (omitting the base position of the external argument, which is Spec, vP for all but unaccusative clauses)."

(55)   Verbal predication structure (Pesetsky and Torrego 2004: 503)
        SUBJ T_s [$_{vp}$ v T_o [$_{VP}$ V OBJ]]

For VPs without overt DPs, such as the ones illustrated here:

(56)   Pesetsky and Torrego (2004: 511)
        a. Mary arrived.
        b. The boat sank.
        c. A bell sounded.
        d. The dog barked.
        e. They worked hard.
        f. The victim screamed.

they suggest that unaccusatives and unergatives all contain a null DP, an assumption we have also adopted here. We thus see that despite the lack of specificity as to what exactly is responsible for the (obligatory) presence of an object in VPs, many researchers converge on the need to separate the transitivity requirement from lexical specification.[15]

As an important consequence of TR, only two frames are possible (order irrelevant): SVO (transitive and unergative verbs), and VO (unaccusative verbs) which extends to SVO with the EPP. As discussed above, Hale and

---

[15] It is fascinating to note that the authors of the Port Royal grammar (1780) offer a postulate that closely resembles TR to account for the use (in Latin) of cognate objects with unergative verbs: "On peut résoudre par-là cette question; si tout verbe non passif régit toujours un accusatif, au moins sous-entendu." (We can solve this question in this way; if all nonpassive verbs govern an accusative, at least an understood one.)

Keyser (1993) have already proposed this for the lexical structure representations of denominal verbs.

Thus, all basic VPs turn out to include only the possibilities in (57a, b) and crucially not (57c):

(57)   a. VP   b. VP   c. VP

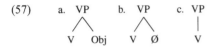

Without TR, it is far from obvious why this should be so. Now, to be sure, this cannot be the end of the story and given the nature of human languages and the extensive variation they exhibit, we expect particular grammars to differ in how they handle TR. Again, a parallel with the EPP imposes itself, as pointed out in Roussou and Tsimpli (2007): "The TR is often matched to an EPP property regarding the object. Thus, in parallel with the subject EPP, one would expect the modes of object EPP satisfaction to vary." We submit that the various proposals from other researchers presented above may turn out to correspond to different modes of TR satisfaction, a possibility that deserves its own expansion but one that is beyond the scope of this book.

2.3.4.1   Further Indirect Evidence for TR

We have taken the strongest position: the internal argument position is there, even if thematically inactive. Some recent psycholinguistic studies have yielded behavioral evidence that implicit objects are present in the mind of speakers. These studies pursue different types of implicit objects, in different languages and using different methodologies. What they have in common is that they address important questions about the representation of implicit objects. Is the object present, in a syntactic sense, even though it is not phonologically realized? Are unergative verbs processed in a similar way to optionally transitive verbs? How does degree of transitivity interact with the expectations of an object?

Shetreet, Friedmann and Hadar (2010) present an fMRI study that seeks evidence regarding the representation of verbs with optional complements based on Hebrew. They compare verbs with optional complements such as *eat* to three other types of verbs, namely one-frame[16] verbs with no complement (*sneeze*), one-frame verbs with obligatory complement (*punish* with DP) and two-frames verbs with obligatory complement (*discover* with DP or CP). They compared the cortical activation of the optional complement verb, with

---

[16] In their terminology "frame" is essentially equivalent to subcategorization contexts.

and without an object, to the other types of verbs, through a comprehension task in which the subjects were asked to listen to sentences and decide whether the activity described was more likely to happen at home or not. When no activation is found in the comparison, it can be concluded that the verbs are processed in a similar way and that, by extension, their representations are similar. Diverse activations on the other hand suggest different representations. They found no activations in the comparisons of the optionally transitive verb (say, *eat an apple*) with one-frame verbs (*punish someone* or *sneeze*) and diverse activations in the comparison with two-frame verbs (*discover something* or *discover that something*). They conclude that "verbs with optional complements are more different from two-frame verbs than from one-frame verbs" (p. 782), and have one complementation frame. Interestingly, they also observed an absence of activations in the comparison between verbs with optional complements in the omitted form to verbs with no complements, and that "such pattern suggests that verbs with optional complements in the omitted form are probably similar to verbs with no complements" (p. 782). Using our terminology, we would say that their results show that optionally transitive verbs are similar to unergative verbs in the cortical activations they involve. But they go a step further and conclude: "these findings suggest that verbs with omitted optional complements have a similar number of complements as verbs with no complements, i.e., zero" (p. 779). However, we believe this conclusion is not warranted in light of the previous discussion on the nature of transitivity and the treatment of unergative verbs; all their evidence shows is that both types of verbs are similar. If Hale and Keyser are correct, then the neurolinguistic evidence can be used to support representations with null objects for both unergatives and optional transitives used without a complement, that is, the representation in (57b).

Psycholinguistic research on priming also offers tantalizing results providing indirect evidence for TR. Structural priming studies are based on the observation that exposure to certain structures facilitates the use of the same structure. Thanks to the amodal nature of priming, it is possible to test whether hearing and processing certain constructions primes the production of the same constructions. Cai, Pickering, Wang and Branigan (2015) designed a study comparing prepositional object (PO) constructions (*John gave a book to Mary*) to double-object (DO) constructions (*John gave Mary a book*). The language used was Mandarin Chinese, in which as we saw previously, it is possible to omit subjects and objects and which allows the relevant PO/DO alternation.

The DO construction with an omitted direct object is illustrated here (Cai et al. 2015: 259):

(58)   Niuzai mai-le   yiben shu hou song-gei-le shuishou
        cowboy buy ASP a book   later give-ASP   sailor
        "The cowboy bought a book and later gave the sailor."

The recourse to a priming setting allows them to test whether the omitted object is syntactically represented or not. In their first experiment, they asked whether DO prime sentences with a missing object behave similarly to DO primes with an overt object, and the results provided a positive answer. The second experiment aimed to determine if PO prime sentences with a missing object behaved similarly to PO prime sentences with an overt object. Again, the results showed that they do. In their words: "We found that comprehending sentences in which one argument was omitted affected people's subsequent syntactic choices in production in the same way as comprehending sentences in which all arguments were overtly expressed" (p. 263). As to what this means for mental representations, the authors specifically argue against an analysis of missing arguments (as in 58 above) that assumes no syntactic representation for the missing argument and recoverability through context: "Our results do not support the alternative syntactically nonrepresented account, according to which comprehenders build syntactic structures that represent only overtly realized arguments (i.e., "incomplete" syntactic representations), and use context to instantiate a semantic representation of any missing arguments" (p. 264).

   The work by Cai and colleagues thus gives us important evidence that anaphoric null objects (in the kind of language that supports these) are syntactically represented. How about nonindividuated null objects of the type found in unergative constructions? A somewhat different type of evidence on this issue, for English, comes from a study exploring the contrast between VP ellipsis and VP anaphora. VP ellipsis involves retrieval of the elided structure and should coactivate, in addition to the target object, semantically related items and phonologically related words since surface structure is involved. On the other hand, VP anaphora should only trigger semantic retrieval and coactivate only semantically related lexical items. This was established in work by Snyder and Runner (2011), who measured the number of looks to the target object (cake) at the point of processing the portion of the input related to ellipsis (*did* (*it*), in 59b).

(59)   a. Margaret baked a cake, and Martin did too.
         b. Margaret baked a cake, and Martin did it too.

Runner and Baker (2015) sought to further test for the presence of structural activation effects alone, so they proposed to examine whether subcategorization preferences could be tested for reactivation during VP ellipsis and anaphora. To this effect, they manipulated transitivity in the antecedent clause: whether the object was present or not (usage) and whether the verb was biased towards expression of the direct object or towards leaving it implicit (bias). *Kick, bake* and *read* were considered high-transitivity verbs, whereas *order, answer* and *forget* were considered to have low-transitivity biases. Their prediction was that transitivity bias should lead to higher numbers of fixation to the target objects and related terms when the verb is reactivated. They predicted that high transitive bias verbs should trigger higher expectations of an upcoming object in VP ellipsis (but not in VP anaphora). This prediction proved correct: participants gave significantly more fixations to target object in VP ellipsis (compared to intransitive controls) than in VP anaphora.

This study also provides support for the psychological reality of null objects. The results included more fixations to the semantically related object with transitive bias verbs (specific to the VP ellipsis construction) as well as an intriguing three-way interaction for predictive fixations (verb bias x usage x construction), so that the magnitude of the effect was larger for transitive bias verbs presented transitively in the antecedent clause, and for intransitive bias verbs when presented intransitively. This latter result is striking, and particularly important in the context of our assumptions regarding transitivity. While the "transitive bias + transitive use" effect would be predicted in any account, the "intransitive bias + intransitive use" effect would not. In fact, it only makes sense if one assumes that optionally transitive verbs that frequently appear in intransitive frames strongly represent their implicit objects.

Now, we do not suggest that the neurolinguistic and psycholinguistic results reported here validate TR conclusively. We do suggest that they represent pieces of evidence that are part of a larger puzzle. By putting the pieces together, a picture reveals itself and that picture, to us, looks a lot like TR.

2.3.4.2   Interim Conclusion

We have argued for the existence of a Transitivity Requirement as a syntactic condition based on structural requirements relating to V. The facts described in

Section 2.3.3 are interpreted as reflexes of TR. This requirement in its minimal instantiation gives rise to a generic interpretation of the predicate (emphasis on the activity, not on the object itself) regardless of the particular verb used. The predicate is then open to further interpretation based on lexical choice of V and the functional make-up of the clause giving rise to further null object possibilities.

2.4   The Learning Task

As we reach the end of this presentation of the types of adult systems that represent the input to which children are exposed, let's have a first look at the learning task involved. If TR (however it is formulated and ultimately derived) is part of UG, then we predict that all null object constructions that are found in the input, actually or potentially analyzed as such, play a central and indispensable role in how children arrive at their target grammar and the developmental path they follow. TR predicts that verbal transitivity does not have to be "learned," and that the intuitive approach discussed above, according to which children learn verb by verb whether each is transitive or not, cannot be true.[17] The presence of overt objects with particular verbs in the input only serves to help the child establish the conditions under which complements are "pronounced" or not in their language. Stated differently, we hypothesize that the learning task boils down to establishing the null object possibilities and if this is true, we expect to observe "issues" in child production and comprehension data attributable to the variety of the input as presented in this chapter.[18]

The question we ask in the next chapters of this book is thus: What do children produce with respect to null objects and does their production differ from the input? This is not a simple task for the same reason that leads us to the formulation of our hypothesis in the first place, namely the diversity found in the input. Methodologically speaking, given the diversity of grammatical constructions that can be analyzed as null object constructions, it can be quite tricky to distinguish target-like from nontarget-like null objects in children's spontaneous production (see Pirvulescu 2006a). This can be illustrated with the following scenario: Imagine a situation where someone is eating an apple and a child says, "*Look. She is eating.*" There is

---

[17] As stated repeatedly in this chapter, this does not mean that we deny that lexical learning is involved, quite the contrary as we will see in Chapter 5.

[18] In the next chapter we examine the impact of this diversity on the language-specific input for the child learner and, more specifically, the fact that the input includes sentences that are not directly informative as to the transitivity status of given verbs.

nothing wrong or nontarget-like with this sentence and we may have no reason to assume that it contains anything that is not equivalent to what would be available in the input. But this reasoning is only valid if the intent of the child was to describe the activity involved in the situation (for instance in answer to something like *What is your friend doing?*). However, we would have to conclude that the sentence is nontarget-like if the child meant to say that her friend is eating an apple. For instance, if as adult speakers of English, you were asked, *"What is your friend doing with the apple?"* you would not answer, *"She is eating."* That kind of null object is not attested in English. The problem is that child production data do not always provide sufficiently unambiguous situations for the researcher to decide if a given null object construction is licit or illicit. We address this issue in the next chapters.

2.5   *Conclusion: Transitivity from the Acquisition Perspective*

We have argued that verbal transitivity is best viewed as a universal requirement imposed on all verbal predicates and, as a consequence, a minimal instantiation of transitivity must be postulated as the initial setting in UG. This, in turn, provides a starting point for L1 acquisition in the domain of verbal complementation in interaction with the input. In other words, TR "prepares" a child to handle and make sense of the cross-linguistic richness of types of null object constructions as well as the inherent ambiguity of many of those constructions when they are uttered in real-life situations. We formulated the hypothesis that the existence of nontarget-like null object constructions (i.e., object omissions) in child production corresponds to an artifact of the learning task involved, as children use TR as a tool to restrict their grammatical system to the target possibilities. If this hypothesis is on the right track, then we should observe a null object stage in all children, regardless of the language learned.

Object omissions in children should therefore be studied from a null object perspective. This represents a shift when compared to previous approaches to object omissions in child language: They do not correspond to a deficit, rather, they are indicative of a developmental step on the way to the adult system. In Chapter 3, we review available evidence to assess this hypothesis and elaborate on the inherent ambiguity of the input.

3 Rome Leads to All Roads

3.1   Introduction

The null object in child language presented in Chapter 2 is the starting point for all adult grammars. This approach predicts the same starting point across languages with differences in the developmental timeline depending on the specific grammatical options the child has to acquire. The acquisition of transitivity and null object constructions, from our perspective, is guided by the TR, departs from MIT and unfolds at a pace dictated by language-specific properties. We proposed in Chapter 2 that the initial null object category is a minimal representation of the transitive relation, based on a constant component of the verb. All other considerations that enter into the transitivity relation (i.e., the lexical verbal types and language-specific recoverability mechanisms) have to be learned. We will revise and make this proposal more specific in Chapters 4 and 5.

By postulating a universal Transitivity Requirement under the form of a basic application of Merge we are committed to the availability of such representation as a tool that children can use to learn language-specific properties. It follows that until those language-specific properties are learned we should expect an overgeneralization of the minimal structure within and across languages: within languages, we should see uses of null objects in contexts where they are not permitted or where they are severely restricted in the adult grammar; across languages, a null object stage should be detected. Accordingly, the child's grammar should differ from the adult's grammar not in the availability of null objects but in how they are used. This view commits us to take a careful look at properties of null object constructions in the input. Since an object position is universally available, the absence of an overt object with a given verb in the input does not indicate that this verb is used intransitively but rather that a null object of a certain type has been merged with it. What type of null object? This is the acquisition question. The answer to this question depends, in each language, on the language-specific constraints on the instantiation of different types of objects. Cross-linguistic differences are therefore predicted according to language-specific null object configurations. As it involves learning in different modules (lexical, syntactic), this model also predicts that development from target-deviant object omissions to target-like overt objects should be gradual rather than categorical. These ideas are explored in this chapter in the context of the various studies available in the literature on the acquisition of the verb and its direct object complement. The goal of this chapter is to provide evidence that:

- a null object stage is detectable cross-linguistically;
- there are similar developmental paths across languages but different resolution times;
- the implications of the null object stage extend to acquisition in different contexts, such as bilingual acquisition.

In pursuing our goal, we touch on several current debates relevant to the question of object omission: discussions focusing on cross-linguistic differences with respect to (pronominal) object omission, the question of methodological differences, object omission beyond clitic languages and the intersection with null object varieties. On the methodological side, we focus on comparability, which is more readily achieved in elicited production experiments. Our discussion closes with a section on pronominal omission in bilinguals, a population for which our approach makes a specific prediction: since qualitative as well as quantitative characteristics of the input play a role in the timing of acquisition, we predict higher omission rates in bilinguals in comparison to monolinguals.

3.1.1   What Omissions Tell Us

In children's production omissions, as with their innovations, are the grammatical breadcrumbs that show us the path the child takes through the language maze. Omissions are apparent before children begin to join two words together. Holophrases are the first cases where production is reduced, but meaning is considerable. From an utterance, such as "Birdie!" through a rich interpretation in the situational context, the adult infers that a child's intended meaning might be something much more elaborated, like "the bird flew out from the branch."

As soon as children add two words together the omissions of elements, especially grammatical ones, become more obvious: an utterance such as "apple mommy" with two lexical words is typical of early productions. Are omissions symptomatic of biomechanical constraints or limits in working memory? Probably, but there is more. Children are "omitters" in the sense that generally, even when presented with consistently produced elements in the input, they will tend to omit more than adults. Children overextend or prefer to omit both grammatical and lexical elements. An artificial language experiment by Hudson Kam and Newport (2005) shows that when presented with consistent input (100 percent use of artificial determiners) children with a mean age of 6;04 produced determiners at around 60 percent. In contrast, adults did not omit at all.

In the same vein, Ingham (1993/1994) shows that while children learning verbal complementation patterns generally follow the input they still present with more omissions than in their input: examination of the spontaneous production of a child showed that she omitted 8/30 of the direct objects with the verbs that appeared only as transitive in the input, but 4/7 of the direct objects with the verbs that appeared as optionally transitive. Moreover, an experimental task with novel verbs showed that children creatively omit direct objects with transitive verbs presented consistently with direct objects in the input (see more detailed discussion in Chapter 5).

Why do children omit? What Hudson Kam and Newport (2005) observed was that children regularize patterns in the input and at the same time impose new patterns (often, categorical use or omission). They conclude that children possess a language learning mechanism that is different from the one possessed by adults because children show a preference for the regularization of optionality patterns whereas adults are more likely to match probabilities. For us, the learning mechanism must connect to the initial abstract representation the children have.

Omissions in young children suggest that children are at the same time innovators and conservative learners. What does this mean? Within a universal grammar approach, one needs early abstract rules and representations to make sense of the input itself. At the same time, results from different domains generally show omissions to both reflect and go beyond the input patterns. In other words, depending on the particular grammatical structure presented in a given language, patterns of omission can either approximate the input or lead to differences from the target. This may vary across grammatical domains and implicitly across languages, and can yield evidence of how representational systems for language develop.

Additional insights emerge from those who look at omissions from the perspective of a parametrized grammar. Snyder (2007) put forth an interesting proposal whereby omissions of grammatical elements reflect a conservative stance on the part of children as language learners. According to Snyder, children will refrain from producing new grammatical constructions until they "have both determined that the construction is permitted in the adult language, and identified the adults' grammatical basis [i.e., the relevant rule] for it" (Snyder 2007: 8). The result of this grammatical conservatism is that omissions are prevalent in child speech and errors are circumscribed.

Let's review Snyder (2007)'s view of developmental omissions more closely. He notes that the passage from omission of grammatical elements to their production could be quite abrupt. This seems to be the case for the acquisition of verb-particle constructions in English. A child can go from utterances such as *box up* with verb omission to more adult-like constructions such as *lift up the box* within three to four months (these examples are from Snyder (2007). Snyder proposes that during these quick transitions children go from the unmarked setting of a parameter to a language-specific marked one. This description does not match what is observed in cases such as the omission of sentential subjects, object pronouns or determiners. In these domains, we do not observe abrupt changes but rather protracted and gradual development. What is more easily observable is a period of optional omission, when a grammatical element is either used or not, within the same context, by the same child. The examples in (1) concern the production of subjects and are taken from the Grégoire corpus, CHILDES database, from a recording when the child was 1;09.

(1)　　　a. Subject omission
　　　　　　＿veux plus.
　　　　　　"Want not."
　　　　　b. Lexical subject
　　　　　　Veut monter <u>Grégoire</u>.
　　　　　　"Wants go up Grégoire."
　　　　　c. Subject clitic
　　　　　　<u>J</u>'ai mis.
　　　　　　"I have put."

Optional omission gradually phases out but at different rates across domains. For example, even within the same language some forms of optionality can give way to an adult-like production pattern early on, such as in the case of the acquisition of French determiners and subject omission in French;

alternatively, optionality can persist for a prolonged period of time, such as in the case of object clitic omissions in French. In Section 3.4 we return to the different approaches that have been proposed to interpret differences in the timetables of resolution of the omission stages.

Both naturalistic and experimental data have been used in the study of omissions. These two approaches often yield different results. This might not be readily apparent since few studies include both spontaneous and elicited production tasks with the same participants, or because the language of young children is often investigated in naturalistic settings and the language of preschool children by means of experiments. Snyder (2007) points out that errors of omission abound in spontaneous speech while errors of commission mostly become apparent in experimental settings. As an example, he points to the acquisition of left-branch extraction (Snyder 2007). Experimental results show that children seem to allow movement of an element in the left-branch position without pied-piping, which runs contrary to adult grammar (example from Gavruseva and Thornton 2001: 257):

(2)   Who do you think 's drink the baboon tasted?
        Adult correct sentence: Whose drink do you think the baboon tasted?

Snyder shows that in contrast, in spontaneous production data collected from three children matching the age of the children who participated in the study by Gavruseva and Thornton (2001) (4;03 to 6;00), these types of questions are absent in two out of three children and the examples from the third child (very few) all involve correct pied-piping. The elicited data then provides examples of errors of commission involving left-branch extraction while the spontaneous production data show omission of this structure altogether. Focusing on these types of contrasts, Snyder argues that children's naturalistic data is a more stable reflection of competence; children may make mistakes conditioned by the experimental settings themselves: "It appears that children are grammatically conservative by preference, but that the demands of controlled experimental tasks (in contrast to passive observation) can overcome this conservatism" (Snyder 2007: 73). The point is that in these situations children may make true errors – performance errors such as disfluencies – which do not reflect underlying knowledge and seem not to conform to the standard continuity assumption that children's innovative output reflects a grammar allowable within UG.

The discrepancy between different types of production modes (spontaneous and elicited production) also appears in the domain of object omission.

This is different from the cases on which Snyder (2007) builds his argument, where the choice seems to be between error and avoidance of a structure (rather than functional or argumental omission proper). For objects, the contrast between elicited and naturalistic data is one of more vs. less omission. Compare the report from the study of spontaneous or controlled production data of young English-speaking children (Bloom 1990 – early stages, and Wang et al. 1992 – two-year-olds) where it was found that children omit direct objects at an average of 8–9 percent to the report in Pérez-Leroux et al. (2008a) where in an elicited production task omissions as high as 35 percent were found for two- to three-year-old children. Similar comparisons exist in French (Jakubowicz et al. 1996; Pirvulescu 2006a,b). Are the high omission rates in experimental settings the result of a task effect in the sense of Snyder (2007)? Some investigators indeed propose that specific task characteristics (such as prompt type or saliency) might lead to higher omission rates in elicited production studies (Jakubowicz et al. 1996; Moscati 2014; Mateu 2015).

While not denying this fact (context, after all, is one of the key ingredients in the recoverability process), we question the particular interpretation that omissions are merely an artifact of the task, or a performance effect. First, we side with Roeper (2004), who states, "misleading contexts only mislead if the child has a grammar that allows it" (Roeper 2004: 502). In other words, for any misinterpretation triggered by a biased context, there has to be some grammatical representation supporting that interpretation. In this sense, even if children are led by specific task features to omit more objects, the underlying grammatical representation has to accommodate these omissions. Second, with respect to problems in methodologies, the shoe might also fit the other foot. The asymmetry between results in spontaneous vs. elicited production highlights a methodological difficulty with naturalistic data that is seldom acknowledged explicitly. For complex, multidimensional phenomena, identifying and coding the context in a much noisier domain can be a tricky undertaking. Results might differ in spontaneous vs. elicited production because the actual linguistic structures involved are not identical. In the case of object omission, detecting pronominal omission in a naturalistic setting is the result of a complex, less-than-reliable bundle of decisions. Compare, for instance, the sophisticated schema for coding the contexts where the direct object argument can be omitted (Allen 2000; see Chapter 4.3.1), based on informativeness or accessibility features, and the general transitive approach at the basis of the detection of illicit omission employed in many naturalistic studies of omission (see Section 3.2.1.1).

Another difficulty with the coding context appears when we compare the differences between coding subject omission versus object omission. Subject omissions are much more easily handled: the subject is either present or not. Judging whether a missing object is illicit or not, when lexical transitivity is implicated in the decision, can easily become an exercise in mind reading. To make a judgment as to whether or not an utterance is illicit with a missing object requires the corpus analyst to go beyond the linguistic context: they must also know things about the physical scenario, the child's gaze and his intent. Not the safest bet, at least at the current level of methodological practice. The moral of the story is that naturalistic data is not sacrosanct. When experimental and naturalistic data differ from each other it could be because, in the latter, more is going on all at once. One of the best illustrations of this methodological problem is the work done on the acquisition of direct object clitics. We take this up in detail in the next section, showing that the discrepancy between spontaneous and elicited production is only apparent: when a rigorous definition of the denominator is used, the results from the two production modalities are fully comparable.

3.2   *A Cross-Linguistic Object Omission Stage*

The challenge we take up in this section is to show that, despite the existing variation across methodologies and across languages, we can be confident that object omission is indeed uniformly found across languages. One of the predictions of the transitivity approach is that we should find evidence of similar development – a distinct null object stage – regardless of the specific grammatical instantiation of the complementation structure. If omissions are not a performance phenomenon, driven by properties of some grammatical markers (such as low prosodic saliency, certain config- urational properties or morphosyntactic deficiencies), we expect to see significant omissions not only in clitic languages such as French but also in strong pronoun languages such as English. The proposal we explore is that languages exhibiting relatively more diversity in null object construc- tions (such as French) will have their relevant object properties acquired later than in languages where omissions are more restricted in the target grammar (such as Spanish).

We start our discussion with the phenomenon of object clitic omission because research on object omissions in acquisition was, for a certain period of time, based on the assumption that this phenomenon happens only in languages with pronominal object clitics. Object omissions were thought to be marginal in languages with strong pronouns and totally uninteresting in null object languages. The examination of object clitic omission across languages presents several challenges. First, a methodological one: data reported so far, mostly from production, distributes between naturalistic observation and elicited production and the results differ in some cases leading to different interpretations of the causes of omissions. Second, object clitic omission seems to partition clitic languages into two patterns: some languages show early or no clitic omission while others display considerable rates of clitic omissions (cf., Wexler et al. 2004). We tackle these challenges in the following sections.

3.2.1   *Clitic Omission Within and Across Languages*

3.2.1.1   Spontaneous and Elicited Production Data

Data from spontaneous and elicited production methodologies lead in some languages to contradictory results, calling into question the very existence of an omission period in these languages. One of the best examples, for some time now, is French. On the one hand, the rate of omissions in spontaneous production has been found to be low and children seem to use mainly lexical nouns (Hulk 1997; Jakubowicz et al. 1997; Jakubowicz and Rigaut 2000; van der Velde 1998; van der Velde et al. 2002). On the other hand, an asymmetry seems to exist between spontaneous and elicited production data (Pirvulescu 2006a,b). One of the first studies to notice this asymmetry is Jakubowicz et al. (1996) who considered the high rate of object omission in elicited production compared to the preference of lexical nouns in spontaneous production:

> We believe that the high percentage of object omissions [...] is a by-product of the task itself. If these children assumed that French allowed object deletion, they would have omitted objects also in spontaneous interaction data. As shown [...] this did not happen.   (Jakubowicz et al. 1996: 384).

The root of this asymmetry, however, proved to be a methodological problem linked to the question of how to correctly consider a baseline or denominator (Pirvulescu 2006a,b). In an experimental setting, the baseline is clear: the number of trials where the context was set up to elicit a pronominal object. The question is more complicated in the analysis of spontaneous speech since most environments of object use do not require obligatory pronominalization. In general, early spontaneous production studies on the acquisition of Romance languages considered the omission of object clitics from the more general perspective of "illicit object omission" based on the lexical status of the verbs used: obligatory transitive verbs vs. optionally transitive verbs. For instance, in their study of spontaneous production, Müller et al. (1996) and Müller (2004) give the following example as a case of illicit object omission:

(3)   Il met __ dans le bain.
         "He puts in the bathtub."

In (3), the verb *mettre* is considered an obligatory transitive verb and therefore should not appear without an object. In this approach, the context in which omission is identified is of little import while the lexical categorization of the verb is crucial. These initial studies thus cite as denominators obligatory/ optional transitives (Müller et al. 1996; Müller and Hulk 2001), the complement context (Hamann 2003) or the objects of transitive verbs (van der Velde et al. 2002; Jakubowicz et al. 1996, 1997).

   For some other studies, the scarcity of object clitics seems to be complemented by the use of lexical nouns. However, here again the contexts not requiring the use of a pronominal clitic seem to have been included in the count, as the following example illustrates (from van der Velde et al. 1998: 122):

(4)   Situation: Hugo's mother is preparing the animals to construct a farm.
         Child: Je fais une ferme. "I'm making a farm."   (Hugo, 2;05,05).

A clear statement of how omissions were calculated comes from van der Velde et al. (2002: 118): "The percentage for accusative and reflexive clitics was calculated dividing the actually produced cases by the number of transitive and pronominal verbs, respectively" (this also holds for works such as Müller et al. 1996; Müller and Hulk 2001; Jakubowicz et al. 1996, 1997). The percentage of omissions in spontaneous production, calculated under the denominators mentioned, is low, varying between 10 percent and 15 percent (van der Velde et al. 2002; Jakubowicz and Rigaut 2000).

   However, while the production of overt lexical elements in object position is interesting in comparison to pronominal elements, the fact remains that pronouns and nouns are entities governed by different licensing and recoverability requirements. Considering both types of objects together can lead to a two-pronged methodological problem. Pirvulescu (2006a) reconsiders this asymmetry in light of the methodology used to calculate the percentage of omissions. The question of pronominal omission is essentially related to the discourse context and not to verbal transitivity because clitics are required by a certain discourse situation. A pronominal clitic must have an antecedent in the preceding discourse and, while it can have a token-reading or a type-reading, it must correspond to an entity that can be presupposed (Lopez 2003). Therefore, the context relevant for the omission of pronominal clitics is the following: "in the clitic-context the referent is definite; it is the topic of the discussion; and it is contained in the immediately preceding discourse" (Pirvulescu 2006b: 227; see also Tsakali and Wexler 2004).

An example from spontaneous production is provided in (5a) from the York corpus, Mona and Para files, CHILDES database. This context is the same as the one used to design most elicited production studies, an example of which is given in (5b):

(5)   a.   Spontaneous production : clitic context
              Adult: tu ne veux   pas   le   mettre dans l'eau [le canard]?
                     you not want NEG it-CL-3SG-ACC put in the water [the duck]
                     "You don't want to put it in the water?"
              Child: __ mettre ici.
                     "Put here."   (Max, 2;00,14; example from Pirvulescu 2006a)
         b.   Elicited production: clitic context
              Experimenter: Qu'est-ce que le père fait avec la balle ?
                            "What is the father doing with the ball?"
              Child: Il la   frappe.
                            he it-CL-3SG-ACC hit-3SG
                            "He hits it." (Nathaniel, 2;08; Pérez-Leroux et al. 2005)

As a consequence, in French, when the omission of pronominal clitics is distinguished from the omission of lexical nouns, the results of spontaneous production show a high rate of omissions (around 60 percent at the highest) while the use of lexical nouns drops drastically, as is the case in elicited production experiments (Pirvulescu 2006a,b).

Discrepancies between results from spontaneous vs. elicited production are not limited to French; they have also been found, so far, in Spanish, Romanian and Greek. Data from Spanish and Romanian present an interesting mirror image of the asymmetry between spontaneous and elicited production found in French. In some studies, elicited production seems almost free of omissions, while spontaneous production gives us at least some qualitative indication that there is omission in early child production in these languages.

Analyses of naturalistic data for Peninsular Spanish show a discrepant picture. Lyczskowski (1999), an unpublished MA thesis cited in Wexler et al. (2004) reports no omissions on Spanish. Fujino and Sano (2002) analyzed the same several child recordings from the CHILDES database. One of the children, Maria (aged between 1;08 and 3;11) comes from a similar linguistic background as the children in Wexler et al. (2004). Fujino and Sano (2002) report omission rates varying between 7.7 and 92 percent between the age of 1;7 and 2;5. The small number of tokens in this study makes the results vulnerable, however, the examples provided convincingly show that omission is an option in early Spanish; one such example is provided here:

(6) Father: Pero dime qué frutas me voy a comer.
              "But tell me what fruit I am going to eat."
     María: No sé.
              "I don't know."
     María: Te voy a pelá.
              "I am going to peel you ___"
     Father: Pero me vas a pelar el qué?
              "But what are you going to peel for me?" (María, 2;02)

These sources show again the low reliability of corpus analyses when it comes to object omissions. Turning to elicitation, Wexler et al. (2004) was the first and, until recently, the only study documenting clitic production in children from Spain. The children in this study are grouped in three age groups, ranging from 2;06 to 4;11 years old. In the Spanish present tense condition, the omission pattern is nonexistent. Clitic omission is more visible in the present perfect condition for the youngest group, but older children do not omit, again showing that many factors determine omission rates.

(7)		Clitic	Clitic omission	Full DP
	2-year-olds:	26/32	5/32	1/32
		(81.25 percent)	(15.62 percent)	(3.12 percent)
	3-year-olds:	39/40	0	1/40
		(97.5 percent)		(2.5 percent)
	4-year-olds:	40/40		
		(100 percent)		

Elliott and Pirvulescu's recent results (2015) confirm that by age three Peninsular Spanish children no longer omit clitics (0.03 percent omissions for three-year-olds and none for older children in an elicitation task where infinitival verb and clitic were the target). However, Elliott (in progress) shows that younger children (two-year-olds) omit direct object clitics at 11 percent, fully replicating the results from Wexler et al. (2004).

In the case of Romanian, the results also diverge widely across studies. Avram (2001) shows that in an elicited production task children aged 2;05 to 4;00 have an omission rate of 27.5 percent (however, the children were not grouped by age, therefore we can only infer from this study that perhaps the omissions are due to the younger children). Moreover, Avram and Coene (2007) analyzed two longitudinal corpora of monolingual Romanian (A. 1;05 to 2;10, B. 1;09 to 3;05). The data reveals early emergence of third person object clitics (at 1;09 and 2;00, respectively), high omission rates in obligatory contexts for a short period of time (between six and eleven months) but an early convergence to the target – over 90 percent clitic production around 2;10 at an MLU under three.

(8)   Adult: Da' ce -ai   făcut   cu ea?
                but what have-2SG do-PART-PAST with it
                "But what did you do to it?"
       Child: Am   dezlipit   *[o] aşa.
                Have-2SG - taken-PART-PAST off __ like this
                "I have taken __ off like this." [A. 3;05]

Babyonyshev and Marin (2005) offer results from an elicitation task using act-out props with children aged 2;00 to 3;10, which differs to some extent from the ones in Avram (1999).

(9) Exp: "Look what else I have here, a bad dinosaur and a snake and look, the
             snake is swallowed, he is in the dinosaur's mouth."
             Ce   i-   a făcut   dinozaaru l   la şarpe?
             What him-CL-3SG-DAT has done-PART-PAST dinosaur-the to snake?
             "What did the dinosaur do to the snake?"
     Child: L-   a-   nghiţit
             him-CL-3SG-ACC has   swallowed-PART-PAST
             "He swallowed/ate him." (child aged 2;04; Babyonyshev and Marin,
             2005: 15)

While two-year-olds had significant omissions (60 percent), Babyonyshev and Marin chose to focus on the results from three-year-olds, with only 6.5 percent omission rate, and contrast their results with those obtained by Avram (2001).

The authors argue that a limitation on production of phonological words could be responsible for the high omission rate in two-year-olds: results divided by MLUw lower and higher than 2.0 reveal that for MLUw lower than 2.0 the omission rate is 86 percent while for MLUw higher than 2.0 the omission rate is only 16 percent. However, the low number of participants in the MLUw lower than 2.0 (seven children) weakens the results. Second, the rate of 16 percent in participants with MLUw higher than 2.0 shows that there are some object omissions in Romanian children that perhaps cannot be accounted for in terms of production limitation. Lastly, a look at longitudinal corpora results in Avram and Coene (2007) shows that children reach 50 percent direct object production when their MLU is still below 2.0. We can contrast this with French, where children reach this rate at 2;05 and 2;10, respectively, when their MLU is approximately 3;05 (Pirvulescu 2006b). Therefore, MLU limitations cannot tell the whole story.

Finally, work on Modern Greek shows again the same incongruence between results from elicited production (Tzakali and Wexler 2004) and spontaneous production (Marinis 2000 and references cited therein). While elicited production is free of omissions, results from spontaneous production seem to indicate that there might be some omissions in the early stages (up to or around age 2;00); however, as Marinis (2000) puts it, there is "no unequivocal evidence that children omit clitics and not full DPs" (Marinis 2000: 18). Tsakali and Wexler (2004) report virtually no omissions in the elicited production task at the youngest age. However, the authors also analyze several spontaneous files and show that there is a discrepancy between spontaneous and elicited production for two-year-olds: in spontaneous production, Greek children have a much higher rate of omissions, between 5.6 percent and 19 percent across children.

Overall, these results raise two issues. The first has to do with the interpretation of early omissions. Early omission followed by early resolution of grammatical elements has often been interpreted as the result of production limitations, with no reference to the underlying grammatical makeup of the utterances involved. For an MLU value around 2.0, factors such as sentence complexity, place of the element in the surface string and its prosodic status play an important role in the omission of grammatical elements (Bloom et al. 1975; Bloom 1990; Demuth and Tremblay 2008). All these factors are related to production limitations in very young children or to processing of syntactically complex constructions or derivations (see Grüter and Crago 2012; Mateu 2015). Yet the interpretation based on production limitations is not as clear as it could be, at least when looking more closely at the spontaneous data we find in the Romanian studies. In this case, Romanian children reach high levels of clitic production when their MLU is still below 2.0 (Avram and Coene 2007). At the same time, an MLU higher than 2.0 does not result in a total disappearance of omissions (Babyonyshev and Marin 2005). In addition, as we will discuss below, omission of the clitic is rarely absolute, the most frequent pattern being optional omission, which depending on the language, extends well beyond the age where processing limitations can be invoked (e.g., for French, children still omit when they are four years of age, albeit less extensively). The simple fact that pronominal clitic omissions do not have a resolution time that is uniform across languages casts doubt on a single explanation in terms of processing limitations.

The second point is that the pattern of cross-linguistic variation emerging from acquisition data across the various clitic languages (including the "early languages" such as Spanish, Romanian and Greek, where clitics appear early and omission recedes rapidly) leads us to suspect that clitic omission is not a uniform phenomenon across clitic languages. Could we conclude that there are indeed two distinct patterns with respect to clitic omission and its development, as proposed by Wexler et al. (2004) and others? Our arguments on this matters are presented in detail elsewhere; see for instance Castilla and Pérez-Leroux (2008a) and the subsequent reply by Gavarró, Torrens and Wexler (2010). For now, let's state our view: an answer to the null object phenomena in acquisition cannot be found by only looking at the acquisition of direct object clitics, rather a look at the more general development of direct objects and verbal transitivity is needed. But first, we attempt to clarify the pattern of omissions observed across languages via the controlled setting of elicited production.

3.2.1.2   Cross-linguistic Diversity in Clitic Omission

The topic of pronominal clitics is an obligatory stop for any linguist working on the Romance languages and the present book will not make an exception. We focus here on results from controlled elicitation studies because they allow the most comparability. As we will see, there is considerable cross-linguistic variation in the resolution time across the languages that have been investigated. Nevertheless, a common core lies at the heart of the differences: there is omission across languages for young children. The results we present and discuss were obtained with very comparable methodologies. Specifically, in these elicitation studies, the preceding story included an explicit mention of the direct object with the goal of introducing it as a possible discourse antecedent.

This is the "clitic-context" we discussed in the Previous Section, where the target element to be used is the pronominal clitic. The elicitation prompt is a VP emphasis question (*What is X doing ...*) that includes an additional mention of the target object. This limits the set of possible responses to answers that directly involve the target object.

An example of such experimental task is provided in (10):[1]

(10)	Context:	Le père veut que son fils joue bien à son premier match de baseball. Regarde, il montre à son fils quoi faire avec la balle.
		Le père frappe la balle.
	Question:	Qu'est-ce que le père fait avec la balle?
		"What is the father doing with the ball?"
	Expected answer:	Il <u>la</u> frappe.
		he it-CL-3SG-F hits
		"He hits it." (Nathaniel, 2;08; Pérez-Leroux et al. 2005)

Table 3.1 shows a detailed description of clitic omissions across languages with respect to age and adult baseline.

We can see from this table that at the earliest age (two-year-olds), clitic omission is attested across languages with the exception of Greek. However, we have already noted, there are two possible complicating factors: first, with an MLU of up to approximately 2.0 we have to take into consideration the factor of production limitations; second, at this early age the discrepancy between results from elicited production and spontaneous production is the greatest. Moreover, Table 3.1 shows that it is at this age that there is the highest variability for the availability of cross-linguistic data as well as for success of the elicitation method. This leads us to concentrate on age 3;00, as indeed most of the studies have done. Table 3.2 isolates results from elicitation studies at the age of three, categorizing them by type of direct object used.

We can draw a certain number of observations from Table 3.2. First, the results across different studies for the same language (e.g., French, Italian) are highly congruent. For French for instance, all four studies show a high rate of omissions as well as high rates of use of DPs; there is also dialectal congruence, since two of the studies (Pérez-Leroux et al. 2008a and Pirvulescu et al. 2011) use data from Québec while the others present data from France. Second, as discussed in the section on naturalistic data analysis, three languages stand out with low or virtually no omissions: Romanian, Spanish and

---

[1] Note that there are several variants of this type of elicitation task.

Table 3.1 *Omissions in the clitic-context across different ages with adult baseline in percentages – elicited production*[2]

Language	2-year-olds	3-year-olds	4-year-olds	5-year-olds	Adult baseline
French (Zesiger et al. 2010)	N/A	N/A	21.0–8.5	6.4–3.8	N/A
French (Pérez-Leroux et al. 2008a)	N/A	34.5	25.7	11.5	0.014
French (Müller et al. 2006)	44	30	N/A	N/A	N/A
Colombian Spanish (Castilla and Pérez-Leroux 2010)	N/ N/A	25	13.7	11.5	4
Peninsular Spanish (Wexler et al. 2003/2004) (present and present perfect tasks)	0 15.62	2.5 0	0 0	N/A N/A	N/A N/A
Peninsular Spanish (Elliott, in prep.)	11	3	0	0	0
Catalan (Wexler et al. 2003/2004) (present and present perfect tasks)	74.2 83.9	25 19	4.2 6.4	N/A N/A	N/A N/A
Italian (Müller et al. 2006; Schaeffer 1997)	67 64	22 15	N/A N/A	N/A N/A	N/A 0
Romanian (Babyonyshev and Marin 2005)	60	6.5	N/A	N/A	N/A
Avram et al. (2015)	N/A	12.88	N/A	N/A	1.5
Bulgarian (Ivanov 2008)	60.8/49.4	24.8/6.4	N/A	N/A	0

[2] Other studies reporting production data that deviate significantly from the elicited production method in (10) were not taken into consideration. This is the case of Grüter (2006) for example, who used a controlled production task and included pronominalization contexts as well as contexts where a lexical object is appropriate. This is also the case of Avram (2001) where the results for children age 2;05 to 4;00 were not grouped by age.

Table 3.1 (*cont.*)

Language	2-year-olds	3-year-olds	4-year-olds	5-year-olds	Adult baseline
Polish (Trzyna 2015)	N/A	61 (2;05 to 3;05 year-olds)	32	22	N/A
Greek (Tsakali and Wexler 2004)	0.8	0	N/A	N/A	0
Portuguese (Costa and Lobo 2007)					
Null object context (optional clitic) enclisis	68.29		76.19		50
Null object context (optional clitic) proclisis	71.79		68.18		22.2
Island context (obligatory clitic)	41.86		34.78		0

Table 3.2 *Experimental data from elicited production across languages by different syntactic type of direct objects in obligatory environments at around age three (clitic languages)*

Languages	Direct object clitics (percent)	Full DP object (percent)	Omissions (percent)
French (Jakubowicz et al. 1997)	10	30	60
French (Schmitz et al. 2004) (Group 2)	21	45	30
French (Pérez-Leroux et al. 2008a)	13.2	50.7	34.5
French (Pirvulescu et al. 2012)	16.1	39	28
Peninsular Spanish (Wexler et al. 2003/2004)	97.5	0	2.5
Peninsular Spanish (Elliott, in prep.)	95	2.0	3.0
Colombian Spanish (Castilla and Pérez-Leroux 2010)	33	1	25
Catalan (Wexler et al. 2003/2004)	68.2	6.8	25
Italian (Schaeffer 2000)	62	23	15
Italian (Müller et al. 2006) (Group 2)	~30	~45	~18

Table 3.2 (*cont.*)

Languages	Direct object clitics (percent)	Full DP object (percent)	Omissions (percent)
Romanian (Babyonyshev and Marin 2005)	93	0.5	6.5
Romanian (Avram et al. 2015)	82.9	0	12.88
Bulgarian (Ivanov 2008)	75.2	0	24.8
Greek (Tsakali and Wexler 2004)	100	0	0
Polish (Trzyna 2015)	43	7	32
Portuguese (Costa and Lobo 2007)	7.31/12.82	19.5/15.38	68.29/71.79

Greek. Third, there seems to be dialectal variation with respect to the acquisition of Spanish: very low omission in Peninsular Spanish and fairly high omission in Colombian Spanish. This variation is of interest: why do children acquiring Peninsular Spanish omit minimally while children acquiring Colombian Spanish have a substantial rate of omissions? Another noteworthy point is the higher rate of omission in European Portuguese (Costa and Lobo 2007), when compared to the other languages. European Portuguese allows null objects in some syntactic contexts (main clauses) and bans them in others (strong island constructions). Omissions are attested at higher levels than in adult controls across contexts. However, the rate of omissions in strong island constructions was lower than in contexts where null objects can be used, showing sensitivity to syntactic restrictions – see Table 3.1. These results were corroborated by Costa et al. (2008), who found lower rates of omissions with reflexive and first and second person object clitics (a context that does not permit null objects) than with third person object clitics (alternation with null objects permitted), but still at higher rates than in adult controls. In addition, as Costa and Lobo (2010) have shown, omissions last longer in European Portuguese than in other languages.

The review of these various studies allows us to make some inferences worth emphasizing. There is evidence of object clitic omission across languages and the timing of acquisition of direct object clitics varies across languages. It is our take that the data cannot be interpreted as a categorical divide between two patterns (languages with object clitic omissions and languages with no object clitic omissions), as proposed in Wexler et al.

(2004), who attributed this divide to independent properties of the object system (the need, or lack thereof, to check off participle agreement). First, languages such as Spanish and Romanian do show clitic omission, though the omissions occur only at very early stages. Therefore, in a system that attributes late omission in French to some properties of the syntax of objects in this language, we would need separate explanations for the two types of omission stages. Second, in these languages the spontaneous production data, even though sometimes difficult to analyze and rely on quantitatively, show at least qualitative examples of omission. Third, the intersection between clitic omission and the availability of null objects in certain languages such as European Portuguese reveals that the differences between rates of omissions across languages are relative rather than categorical. What we see when we look across languages is gradience in the rates of omissions with languages ranging from those where omissions subside very early (Romanian, Spanish) to languages where omissions remain longer (Italian, French) or much longer (Portuguese). We also see gradience across constructions, something to which we will return at various points in our argumentation. These are all important points, deserving further examination. We should start by comparing clitic languages to nonclitic languages.

3.2.2   Is Object Omission an Omission of the Clitic?

An examination of pronominal clitic languages might lead to the conclusion that object omission is a consequence of the clitic status of the pronominal; however, interesting results from nonclitic languages have emerged. These will lead us to propose that indeed the clitic is part of the problem, but not its cause. A crucial piece of evidence comes from studies of languages with strong direct object pronouns as well as from contexts in which pronominals are not possible and in which lexical DPs are either optional or obligatory.

The omission of direct object strong pronouns in obligatory contexts in nonclitic languages has been attested. Pérez-Leroux et al. (2008a) show that English-speaking children have pronominal omissions at rates comparable to those of French-speaking children, in the same type of experimental obligatory context – but only at the age of three. In this study, children were presented with the familiar scenarios (shown in (10)) with equivalent optionally transitive verbs in the two languages. In this context, the omission rates for three-year-olds are 34 percent for French children and 35 percent for English children. Different rates of omission can be seen for older children in French vs. English, suggesting different developmental timelines, much in the same way as in the case of clitic omission across different clitic-languages: omissions drop to 25 percent for four-year-olds in French and to 0.8 percent for the same age group in English.

Object omission also extends to contexts in which a lexical noun phrase is obligatory: higher rates are seen in child production than in adult production. For example, direct object omission is attested in Russian, a language with strong pronouns and null topics, in studies by Gordishevsky and Avrutin (2003, 2004). According to these authors, omissions are not possible in the target grammar, i.e., when the antecedent or the contextual referent is not present and a lexical DP should be used. They show that in these contexts children between 1;08 and 2;06 years have omission rates between 11 percent and 24 percent in spontaneous speech. In (11) we see an example in which Zlata, the child, speaks about a woman who took her sandals (cf., Gordishevsky and Avrutin 2004: 7–8).

(11)   Adult: Zlata, kakaja tëtja?
                   Zlata, what woman?
          Child: _   zabrala _ (1;09,24)
                   Ø-NOM take-PERF Ø-ACC
                   _ took _

Frolova (2013) corroborated this in a controlled experimental setting in Russian. Her data show that children omit significantly more objects than adults in simple transitive clauses in obligatory nonindividuated contexts where object omission is not allowed in the target grammar. Russian allows for the optional use of direct objects in most transitive contexts. However, with telic verbs, the transitive context obligatorily requires an overt lexical object.

(12) Posmotri, ètot porosënok očen'   ustal.   On xorošo porobotal.   Čto
      on sdelal ?
      Look, this small   pig-NOM Øis   very tired. he well   worked-PERF What
      he did-PERF ?
      Look, this little pig is very tired. He worked very well. What is he doing?
      On postroil   dom. / *On postroil Ø.
      He built-PERF house-ACC
      He built a house. / He built ___. (Frolova 2013: 152)

In this context, children omit the obligatory object at 24.7 percent while adults produce them categorically. In the same study, Frolova finds that children also prefer omissions more than adults in contexts where omissions are allowed: in imperfective nonreferential contexts (where null objects and object nouns are permitted) and in imperfective referential contexts (where null objects and pronouns are permitted). This is not an isolated finding; other studies have found that in contexts where the realized object is an option among others children produce sentences with object omissions at a higher rate than adults.

Applying a comparable experimental procedure to two languages that allow null objects as alternatives to pronominals, Mykhaylyk and Sopata (forthcoming) show that in both Polish (a clitic language) and Ukrainian (a strong pronoun language) children at three and four years old prefer null objects at higher rates than adults in contexts where the targets are: null, clitics and (less acceptably) lexical DPs (for Polish); or null, strong pronouns and (less acceptably) lexical DPs (for Ukrainian). Specifically, data analysis showed similar development of clitics and strong pronouns and did not uncover a clitic effect when comparing omissions across the two languages. In other words, children do not seem to omit more in the clitic language. Therefore, as the authors argue, the clitic/full pronoun difference is likely to be irrelevant in the acquisition of direct objects in such languages (Mykhaylyk and Sopata, forthcoming: 27).

Similarly, Mykhalkyk et al. (2013) shows that in experimental settings that elicit both indirect and direct objects in Russian and Ukrainian, children omit significantly more direct object arguments than adults (adults do not have omissions in Russian and omit 15 percent in Ukrainian, while children omit much more frequently, at 55 percent in Russian and 52 percent in Ukrainian). In these contexts, a lexical noun should have been the preferred answer (13).

(13)   Experimenter: [. . .] "What is Peter doing now?"
          Child target answer: On dajet kurice červjaka. (Russian)
                                 Vin daje kurci červjaka. (Ukrainian)
                                 "He is giving the hen a worm."

Omission of lexical and pronominal direct objects is therefore not restricted to contexts where an overt object is obligatory but appears in context where an overt object is optional and in such cases children omit at a higher rate than adults. This higher preference for omissions in optional contexts in not restricted to those languages that are traditionally classified as allowing null objects; Pérez-Leroux et al. (2008a), comparing French and English child performance in optionally transitive contexts, found that in a context

Table 3.3 *Percentage of object omissions in individuated and nonindividuated contexts in French and English for three-year-old children (adapted from Pérez-Leroux et al. 2008a)*

Age/Language	Individuated context	Nonindividuated context
French: 3-year-olds	34.5	33.2
French adults	1.4	27
English: 2- and 3-year-olds	35	40
English adults	0	26.4

where an optional lexical noun phrase can appear children also omit the direct object more than adults (14b). Compare the individuated context (14a, pronominal required) to the nonindividuated context (14b, optional lexical noun):

(14)   a.   Individuated context: What is the girl doing with <u>the flower</u>?
                                          She is smelling <u>it</u>.
        b.   Nonindividuated context: What is Clifford doing?
                                          He is eating (the bone/something).

The percentage of omissions in both contexts is highly comparable across French and English and within each language the same children have higher omissions than adults, as shown in Table 3.3.

Object omission seems therefore to be of a more general nature: clitics, strong pronouns and lexical DPs are omitted in obligatory contexts. Children also omit more direct objects than adults in optional contexts. In addition, omission is present in null and nonnull languages alike. Interestingly however, differences in the resolution time appear across languages irrespective of the type of direct object. We find that in some languages developmental object omissions disappear early, while in others the object omission stage is longer.

What the previous sections show us then is essentially the variable nature of the phenomenon of direct object omission: diversity across languages, across methodologies (spontaneous vs. elicited production, different types of elicited production) and across the more general typology of strong pronouns vs. pronominal clitic languages. In light of this, we claim that it is wrong both to characterize object omission as clitic omission as well as to maintain the categorical distinction between languages with omission and those without omission. What we see instead is generalized omission and different resolution times across languages. In addition, as we address below, omission of the direct object generally alternates with the expected type(s) of objects within the same contexts.

3.3   *Object Omission and Optionality*

By focusing on omission, we should not neglect one point: children use all the options available to them for the expression of direct objects. Along with omissions, and depending on the type of language, we also see a range of overt objects. For pronominal clitics, children have been observed to variably drop the clitic in the clitic-context. M, one of the French-speaking three-year-olds in Pirvulescu et al. (2011) produced the responses in (15a), (15b) and (15c) in response to various trials for the same type of context. This suggests that clitics can be in free variation with null objects and lexical DPs within the same speaker.

(15)   a. Prompt: Dis à Kermit ce que l'ourson fait avec les framboises.
                    tell to Kermit what the bear does with the raspberries
                    "Tell Kermit what the bear is doing with the raspberries."

              Child: Il les   mange. (object clitic) (M., 3;06)
                       he them-CL-3PL-ACC eats
                       "He eats them."

        b. Prompt: Dis a Kermit ce que Sébastien fait avec le verre de jus.
                    tell to Kermit what Sebastian does with the glass of juice
                    "Tell Kermit what Sébastien is doing with the juice."

              Child: Il boit Ø. (omission) (M., 3;06)
                       he drinks
                       "He drinks."

        c. Prompt: Dis à Kermit ce que la fille fait avec les rideaux.
                    tell to Kermit what the girl does with the curtains
                    "Tell Kermit what Sébastien is doing with the curtains."

              Child: Elle découpe les rideaux. (lexical DP)
                       she cuts   the curtains
                       "She is cutting the curtains." (M., 3;06)

Group data in Table 3.2 also confirms that while three-year-old children omit their clitics fairly often, omission is not the only type of answer. For French, object omission seems best characterized as optional omission. For example, Pérez-Leroux et al. (2008a) shows that no child omitted at 100 percent. Thus, children are capable of producing (some) pronominals in the appropriate context from the earliest age. For elicited production this starts around age two. Table 3.1 shows that no study reports 100 percent omissions. Some of the studies with spontaneous data, on the other hand, sometimes show (close to) 100 percent omissions in the very early stages. This was the case of Coene and Avram (2011) for Romanian for one child aged 1;11. Fujino and Sano (2002) found 92.9 percent omissions for one child aged 1;09. However, as we have shown, in spontaneous data the type of context that was taken into consideration when counting direct objects was often unclear.

As in clitic languages, omission is not the only response type children provide in languages with strong pronouns, both in contexts where strong pronouns are target and in contexts where lexical DPs are the target. For example, in English in obligatory contexts with strong pronouns, three-year-old children omit at 35 percent, use pronouns at 35 percent and use lexical DPs at 25 percent (Pérez-Leroux et al. 2008a). In Russian, in obligatory contexts with lexical DPs, three-year-old children omit at 30 percent and use lexical DPs at 69 percent (Frolova 2013).

Young children might prefer omissions but they can also use overt objects in a task-appropriate way (in the sense that they would only use a pronominal as an overt object in a task eliciting a pronominal). This is also true of languages or contexts where omission is an option alongside overt object(s). Across all languages investigated, we have found evidence for this preference for omissions but with different resolution times for different languages. Omissions might be more salient in pronominal clitic languages, but this is in part because only in these languages has omission been investigated in a highly systematic way.

How should we interpret these findings? The diversity of the phenomenon under study is nearly matched by the diversity of inferences made about it. Yet, given the multifaceted nature of object omission and the richness of variation in this domain it is not surprising that such varied theoretical analyses have been proposed. It is our take that all of them have something to contribute to our understanding, but obviously that does not mean that they can all be right. Each explanation works if we look at the data from a fixed point, i.e., such as for a single language or for a cluster of languages. In the next few pages we show that, ultimately, these accounts are insufficient and that we need to develop an explanation that can capture the diversity observed.

3.4   *Object Omission in Different Theoretical Approaches*

Explanations for direct object omission each bear the mark of our understanding of the phenomenon at a certain point in time; they are also the result of looking through a particular lens at a particular type of language. On the one hand, we have the numerous works that looked mainly at the phenomenon of clitic omission. These works have naturally exploited various properties of clitic constructions, leading to a variety of explanations. These range from syntactic to semantic-pragmatic; prosodic and processing-based accounts are also involved. On the other hand, we have work on languages with omission of strong pronouns and lexical DPs, where proposals are often based on the development of some aspects of pragmatic competence or simply linked to growth on utterance length.

Again, we start with accounts of object omission in pronominal clitic languages. These accounts understand omissions to result from the problematic development of the clitic construction itself and usually compare, within the same language, either normal vs. impaired language development (SLI), object clitics with other types of clitics (subjects, determiners) or omissions with respect to different features of the object clitic (person, case, gender). The way of framing the main question is clearly articulated in Jakubowicz and Nash (forthcoming: 58): "Why is object pronominalization avoided in Romance language development?" The general proposal is that while child grammar makes use of the same principles and features as the adult grammar, limitations on the child's working memory interact with some of the most complex computations – such as complex dependencies, steps in movements, levels of embedding, noncanonical merge and feature structures. As such, the child's grammar is deficient in some sense as it cannot accommodate some types of complexities (Jakubowicz et al. 1997; Jakubowicz and Nash to appear; Prévost 2006; Chillier-Zesiger et al. 2001; Hamann et al. 2007; Tuller et al. 2011; Grüter and Crago 2012). For example, when comparing object clitics with other types of clitics in French (subject clitics and determiners) Jakubowicz and Nash conclude that what is problematic for children is " … projecting as arguments 'noncanonical' or category deficient constituents such as clitics … " (Jakubowicz and Nash, forthcoming: 72). Based on the same comparisons, Zesiger and colleagues identify complex dependencies as the locus of difficulty, since subject and object chains cross each other in contexts with subject and object cliticization (Zesiger et al. 2010: 573). Other proposals integrate the configurational and featural property of clitics with their semantic-pragmatic properties. Based on object scrambling in child Dutch and clitic omission in child Italian, Schaeffer proposes that child grammar is underspecified for specificity. Under this view, young children lack the pragmatic feature that forces consideration of the common discourse background. During the period when specificity is absent from the syntax children determine referentiality directly from the discourse rather than through the grammar (Schaeffer 1997, 2000). This is an interesting notion that we will attempt later to integrate.

A broader perspective in evaluating clitic omission was offered in the work of Ken Wexler and colleagues (Wexler 1998; Wexler et al. 2003; Tsakali and Wexler 2004). Their goal was to investigate " [...] whether clitic omission is a universal stage that all children speaking a clitic language go through or this holds only for some languages." (Tsakali and Wexler 2004). Indeed, they were the first to highlight the fact that clitic omission is differentially distributed across clitic languages. This is evident when one compares Catalan and Italian to Spanish and Greek in Table 3.2. Wexler and colleagues proposed the Unique Checking Constraint (UCC), a complexity constraint on the computational system of the early grammar that restricts the movement computations the child is capable of in a given derivation. The UCC was initially proposed in order to account for the Optional Infinitive stage: a maturational constraint explaining the delayed emergence of some morphosyntactic aspects (Wexler 1998). This constraint states that the D-feature of DP can only check against one functional feature (Wexler et al. 2003, 2004). According to the UCC, in the case of clitic constructions, some languages require the object to pass through multiple checking operations, as in the case of French, Italian or Catalan. The common factor for such languages is that they all have overt past participle agreement that leads to the necessity of multiple checking. The UCC warrants that one checking can take place (for the past participle agreement) but no subsequent checking can take place (for the object clitic) and as such the object clitic is omitted. In languages without past participle agreement double checking does not occur and therefore the clitic will surface (Spanish and Romanian). The model predicts a categorical divide between languages displaying object clitic omission and languages without, and a crucial correlation is established with the availability of past participle agreement in languages with omission.

Indeed, for languages with past participle agreement, a uniform observation is a high rate of omission. This has been documented in a series of separate studies in European and Québec French, Italian and Catalan (Jakubowicz et al. 1996, 1997; Schmitz et al. 2004; van der Velde 2003; Pérez-Leroux, Pirvulescu and Roberge 2008a; Tedeschi 2008; Wexler et al. 2003/2004). However, the results of languages without past participle agreement do not support this dual categorization. Subsequent research demonstrates substantial variation in varieties of Spanish as to clitic omission (de la Mora, Paradis, Grinstead, Flores and Cantú 2004; Bedore and Leonard 2001; Castilla 2008; Castilla et al. 2008a,b). While there are fewer studies, this may also be true of Romanian (Avram 2001). The existence of variation in languages without participle agreement weakens the explanatory power of the UCC considerably, because now two accounts for developmental omissions are needed: one for languages with omission and another for those without. There is an additional challenge coming from French. The proposed link between past participle agreement and object omission presupposes that children have mastery of agreement, or are at least aware of it. Pirvulescu and Belzil (2008) tested children's knowledge of past participle agreement in Quebec French. A group of children aged three to four, who still significantly omit object clitics, seem unable to control past participle agreement even though their performance with adjectival and verbal agreement is at ceiling. It is not clear that an argument can be made that these children are even aware of participle agreement. Pirvulescu and Belzil (2008) conclude that participle agreement is at best a marginal feature in the early grammar of French and, therefore, too weak to be considered as controlling or constraining the realization of the direct object clitics in child production.

Computational complexity approaches suffer from a range of problems, some general, some specific. The hypothesis that children have difficulties merging the clitic because of the complexity of the derivation involved predicts that children will avoid clitic structures in French and instead prefer merging lexical DPs, as this would be less computationally taxing than a clitic. However, merging a lexical DP, as we have seen, is one strategy along with object omission; even in Jakubowicz and Nash (forthcoming), three-year-olds had a rate of 15.7 percent omissions and other studies obtained even higher omissions (see Tables 3.1 and 3.2). In the case of the proposal according to which crossing chains between subject and object clitics is problematic for children, one would need to explain, as pointed out by Grüter (2006), why chain crossing affects only object clitics and not also subject clitics in these constructions.

An important component of any computational complexity approach, which is much less discussed, is the nature of the child's representation when the clitic is not used. One proposal (Prévost 2006) suggests that children resort to null objects when processing limitations prevent their production of the computationally more complex clitic construction: processing limitations could, as Grüter and Crago (2012) put it, "interact with computational complexity at the level of syntactic representations" (Grüter and Crago 2012: 544). This seems to entail that in such cases the avoidance strategy consists of using one of the two representations available in the child grammar: a null object or a lexical object. Grüter (2006) and Grüter and Crago (2012) show results that seem to indicate that the omission of clitics is limited to language production only. According to their study, children do not seem to be able to assume a null object representation in the interpretation of an utterance lacking an overt object (we will pursue this with greater detail in Chapter 4). Thus, according to these authors, utterances lacking clitics would only indicate a problem with the syntactic encoding of the clitic for production but not a null object representation.

While a problematic encoding of the clitic structure is plausible, a model that can account for problems with clitics in comprehension as well is needed, as some recent studies have shown that children do have difficulty with the interpretation of object clitics. Children have more trouble with the interpretation of direct object pronouns than reflexives (van der Velde 2003; Zesiger et al. 2010) and also struggle to correctly use the morphosyntactic information that is part of the clitic in order to retrieve the proper antecedent (Grüter et al. 2012 for Spanish; Pirvulescu and Strik 2014 for French). For example, an online study on the comprehension of Spanish clitics by Grüter et al. (2012) found that four-year-old children have difficulties in using the gender of object clitics to identify the correct referent; these were the same children who did not consistently produce object clitics, exhibiting instead a higher rate of omissions. For French, Pirvulescu and Strik (2014) show that children have difficulties comprehending the features of object clitics in that they are not fully able to rely on their featural content for antecedent retrieval. Moreover, the youngest age group appears to not use the featural information of pronominal clitics at all: children in this group choose clitic forms based on the recency of the noun phrase listed in the description. One interesting outcome of this study is the evidence that children have general problems with the comprehension of pronominals since their performance with strong pronouns in adjunct position also shows deficits (albeit less severe than in the case of clitics). Clitics are therefore not the only locus of difficulties.

A production model focused on clitic encoding or a computational model based on the complexity of the clitic construction can only partially explain omission results. For example, models such as Jakubowicz and Nash (forthcoming) or Zesiger et al. (2010) can account for differences between various types of clitics (i.e., direct object clitics being acquired later than subject and reflexive clitics) and for the preference for lexical direct object DPs. Recent results showing that children also omit strong direct object pronouns are not accounted for within these approaches. These models can bring regular and impaired language development (SLI) in line together as part of a continuum but in doing so these approaches have often focused exclusively on a "deficit" approach to the development of object clitics. The focus on computational difficulties has marginalized the fact that constructions including object clitics are multifaceted and involve a convergence of syntactic, pragmatic, lexical and phonological constraints. In addition, one crucial feature of omissions has been overlooked: while children prefer omissions they are also able to provide clitics in the required contexts. We propose to rephrase the initial question – why do children avoid clitics? – by asking instead: Why do children prefer omissions?

The beginning of an answer can be found in work on languages that allow (in their adult version) both the overt pronominal and null object options. Joao Costa and his colleagues (Costa and Lobo 2007; Costa et al. 2008; Costa et al. 2012) have extensively investigated European Portuguese, a clitic language that allows null objects (see also Mykhaylyk et al. 2013; Mykhaylyk and Sopata, forthcoming, for null object languages with strong pronouns). In Portuguese, as we have seen, the rate of omissions found in contexts where the clitics freely alternate with null objects is higher than in contexts where there is no such alternation. Overall, children also omit more than adults. These authors propose that higher rates of clitic omission and a longer omission period are a consequence of two factors for Portuguese: the existence of both null objects and object clitics, and the variable placement of object clitics. In some contexts, several options are freely allowed in European Portuguese – null object and clitics, both preverbal and postverbal; the authors suggest that "the choice between multiple convergent derivations may yield problems in production" (Costa et al. 2008: 4). In other words, it is the availability of options and the fact that the conditions for choosing one or the other option partially intersect at the discourse and syntactic level that leads to an overextension of the null object option.

So, null objects are a developmental problem both in languages traditionally not thought to have null objects and in the so-called "null object languages."

In Chapter 2 we examined the diversity of null constructions across languages, and came to the conclusion that all languages have null objects but vary as to their type. In some languages, referential object omission is restricted to some contexts or to some verbs (the case of French). In our previous work, we identified these cases as "clitic-drop" (Cummins and Roberge 2005) and insisted that they were important for figuring out how the acquisition process works (Pérez-Leroux et al. 2008a; Pirvulescu et al. 2014; see also Tuller et al. 2011). In the next section, we will try to clarify how certain input characteristics can pose a problem in the acquisition of direct objects.

3.5   *Input Effects: Ambiguity and Diversity*

Input complexity, understood as the diversity of relevant constructions as well as their ambiguity, could play an important explanatory role for the question of timing in the acquisition of direct objects. This idea has floated around various contributions in the literature but has never been fully scrutinized (Pérez-Leroux et al. 2009a; Costa and Lobo 2010; Tuller et al. 2011). Chapter 2 highlighted the extent of the diversity of null object constructions across languages. From our theoretical perspective, this typological exercise was meant to show that the initial minimal default null object representation should be both general enough and restricted enough as to accommodate such a variety and allow for its acquisition. But variation exists not only across languages and varieties of languages, but also within a single E-language (Chomsky 1986; Roeper 1999). Faced with variation in the input, how can the child interpret evidence of implicit objects? Is it possible that optional lexical transitivity provides the child learner with ambiguous data with respect to the interpretation of missing objects? In this section, we focus on showing how constructions involving null objects can be ambiguous in the input.

Probably the most obvious example of input ambiguity is found in languages that allow both overt and null direct objects for the same transitive structure and with a similar interpretation, as for example in the case of European Portuguese, Ukrainian or Polish (Costa and Lobo 2007; Mykhaylyk and Sopata, in press). The Polish example provided in (16) shows that three types of answer are possible in the classic referential elicitation scenario: pronouns, omissions and lexical DPs, the latter being somewhat superfluous from a pragmatic point of view but nevertheless grammatically licit (Mykhaylyk and Sopata, in press: 15–16):

(16) Context: Teraz spójrzmy na ten obrazek i opowiedz Dragonowi, co się stało.
"Now let's look at this picture and tell Dragon what has happened."

Question: Co Piotru's zrobił kotkowi?
what Peter did to-cat
"What did Peter do to the cat?"

Possible answers   Pronoun: On go umył.
he him washed
"He washed him."

         Null object: Umył.
"Washed."

         Lexical DP: (On) umył kota.
(he) washed cat
"He washed the cat."

As Mykhaylyk and Sopata (forthcoming) show, children approximate the options present in the input (pronoun, null, lexical DP), with a strong preference for omissions when they are younger (up to five years old). Interestingly, this is precisely what children do in English, French and other languages normally not considered to be null object languages! Reviewing (yet again!) Table 3.2 we see that in general the three types of answers to the standard elicitation scenarios are found across languages. This leads us to suspect that even in languages where null objects are highly restricted, the evidence in the input might be ambiguous for children. The leading view within learnability studies is that ambiguous input does not move the acquisition process along (Fodor 1998; Sakas and Fodor 2012).

We can consider some candidate cases. Contexts where direct objects cannot be omitted generally, but only under certain circumstances, minimally provide evidence for the child that null objects are allowed, at least in principle. For example, Tuller et al. (2011) list as one relevant property of third person direct object clitics the fact that they can be omitted under certain discourse circumstances, as in (17). English could also present the child with cases where the direct object pronoun can be optionally omitted, as in (18) (from Ingham 1993/1994: 96).

(17)   A: Voulez-vous que je vous donne mon numéro de téléphone?
want-you   that I   you give   my number of telephone
"Do you want me to give you my phone number?"

B: Non, je (le) connais ___.
no,   I (it)   know
"No, I know (it)."

(18)   John aimed at the target and missed (it).

Constructions that can be ambiguous between generic activity and referential readings as in (19) might also contribute to a null object interpretation (from Yip and Matthews 2005).

(19)   The chef-in-training chopped and diced all afternoon.

For clitic languages, constructions in which a pronominal clitic is present but found preverbally (instead of in the canonical postverbal position of full DP direct objects) may lead to a failure on the part of the child to recover the features from the clitic, resulting in the clitic construction as evidence of null objects.[3] The following examples from Müller and Hulk (2001: 8) for French and Italian illustrate this case:

(20)   Il le voit [ec] / Lo vede [ec]
         he it sees
         "He sees it."

Finally, constructions where the referential object is displaced, resulting in an empty postverbal position, can lead to an object drop interpretation. For example, in Hulk and Müller (2000: 230), it is mentioned that a child could interpret a construction such as (21) as a case of a referential null object.

(21)   Ça j' ai   vu *ec*.
         that I have seen
         "That, I have seen." (*ec* = empty category)

In one of the few studies investigating how transitive constructions appear in child-directed speech, Pérez-Leroux et al. (2006b) looked at spontaneous data from the CHILDES database (MacWhinney 2000): MacWhinney (English), Sachs (English), York (French) as well as an additional French corpus (the Pupier corpus). We extracted all utterances with the following six verbs: *build*, *cut*, *draw*, *drink*, *hit* and *eat*, and their French equivalents *construire*, *couper*, *dessiner*, *boire*, *frapper* and *manger* (these verbs, frequent in naturalistic settings, were then used in our elicitation experiments). It was recognized that these verbs differ in their likelihood to appear with an expressed object. The focus of the analysis was on object omission: all instances of omissions with these verbs in adult production were classified as either individuated (if there was a potential antecedent to the object in the linguistic context) or nonindividuated (if this was not the case). Examples provided are taken from Pérez-Leroux et al. (2006b: 11):

---

[3] Recall that in comprehension, young French children seem to be oblivious half of the time to the featural information on the clitic; cf. Pirvulescu and Strik (2014).

(22)   Examples of nonindividuated interpretation (underlined)
    a.   French
        *COL: Ça écrit pas très bien. Ah! c' est bien mieux. Qu'est-ce que tu écris
             this writes not very well.   it is much better. what is it that you write
             Cynthia?
        *CYN: C'est cassé ça, han?
             it is   broken this huh
        *COL: C'est cassé?
             it is   broken
        *PAU: C'est pas bon hein?
             it is   not good huh
        *CYN: Est pas bon
             is   not good
        *MOT: <u>Tu écris ou tu dessines chérie?</u>
             you write or you draw   dear
             "Are you writing or drawing dear?"
        *CYN: E [:je] dessine
             I   draw
        *MOT: <u>Tu dessines,</u> qu'est-ce que tu dessines?
             you draw   what is it that you draw
             "You are drawing, what is it that you are drawing?"
        *CYN: E [:je] veux dessine
             I   want draw
        *MOT: Qu'est-ce que c'est le dessin?
             what is it that it is the drawing
    b.   English
        *FAT: you just made that one up that's sort of a nice song though Mark.
        *MAR: it's not a song either.
        *FAT: you know you could be a music man too.
        *FAT: mommy says that you have a very good voice.
        *FAT: you could be a singer.
        *FAT: <u>you could be a guy who sings while he builds.</u>
        *MAR: very funny.
        *FAT: it's true.

(23)   Examples of (potentially) individuated interpretation (underlined)
    a.   French
        *CYN: Emmanuel!
        *MOT: Emmanuel, et   c'est qui l'autre?
                          and it is who the other
        *CYN: Emmanuel encore.
                          again
        *MOT: Oh, c'est qui ça?
                   it is who that
        *CYN: Des cailloux, xxx.
             some stones

        *MOT: Donne le gâteau, c'est fini peut-être les xxx là,
            give   the cake it is done maybe the xxx there
            tu mangeras tout à l'heure.
            you eat-FUT later
            "You will eat later."
        *CYN: Photos Cynthia. [?].
            photos
        *MOT: Il faut pas que ça l'excite   trop.
            it must not that it him-excite too much
        *CYN: C'est Emmanuel peut-être? [?].
            it is Emmanuel maybe
        *MOT: Et ça, qui c'est ça?
            and that, who it is that
        *CYN: Pipi.

  b. English
     *FAT: you wan(t) (t)o come up?
     *FAT: he's hitting me in the belly.
     *FAT: trying to climb up.
     *FAT: ok.
     *FAT: no, no!
     *FAT: you can't [!] have the papers.
     *FAT: you have to go down again.
     . . .
     *FAT: ok.
     *FAT: now (are) you going to do + . . .
     *CHI: what?
     *FAT: mhm.
     *CHI: ok.
     *FAT: <u>I wish you'd stop hitting</u>

Our analysis revealed that all the verbs under study show some degree of omission and, more importantly, that examples of the type in (23) (potentially individuated interpretation) are as prevalent as those of the type in (22) (potentially nonindividuated interpretation). Crucially, the examples of omission of the type in (23) are the ones compatible with an object drop grammar. In other words, these represent the type of ambiguous input that could prolong a null object stage. How are such examples ambiguous? Consider a statement such as (24), uttered by an adult.

(24)   I wish you'd stop hitting.

The null object of the verb *hit* can be interpreted generically as in "I wish you would stop hitting people." However, the availability of a potential referent in the preceding discourse or extralinguistic context can also signal to the child that the null object is being recovered through the discourse, as would happen in a null topic language. The utterance in (24) would then mean "I wish you would stop hitting me (or him, her, etc.)." This particular corpus analysis was not, quantitatively speaking, robust enough to settle the question of whether one language had more input ambiguity than the other. However, it does serve to illustrate with real-life examples what the problem is.

Why do omissions linger in certain languages, such as French, yet disappear quite rapidly in sister languages with much of the same configurational properties?

We must start by making it clear what we mean when we say that the input is diverse, or more ambiguous. Input can be considered more diverse if constructions with a pronominal in object position alternate with or add to constructions where the object can be omitted. The range of constructions where the direct object can be interpreted as a potentially referential null object is quite large in French, as illustrated in (25).

(25)   a.   Omission of referential null objects (Larjavaara 2000: 39):
                Mais t'as pas à lui filer le tournevis. J'étais où quand tu lui as donné __ ?
                "But you shouldn't let him have the screwdriver. Where was I when you
                gave __ him?"
    b.   Fronted topicalized object:
                (Parce que) ça je sais __
                "Because, this I know."
    c.   Clitic construction:
                Marie le   voit __
                Mary him-CL-3SG-ACC sees
                "Mary sees him."

The source of diversity lies in word order as well as in contextual licensing. In contrast, English has a more restricted repertoire of constructions potentially interpreted as involving a referential null object, corresponding essentially to utterances of the type in (26). The input is rather unambiguous with respect to the possibilities of null objects.

(26)   John aimed at the target and missed (it). (Ingham 1993/1994: 96)

On the basis of what we have seen so far, we advance the hypothesis that the availability in the input to children of constructions that could be interpreted as having a referential null object is likely a feature shared by most languages. It is reasonable to then assume that differences in input pertaining to the diversity/ambiguity of direct object constructions involving (seemingly) referential null objects, coupled with the availability of a null object default, are linked to the observed differences in the timing of acquisition. What we now need is a learning model that can make explicit the link between input and acquisition timing.

Some theoretical proposals have explicitly considered qualitative variations in the input and some of them link these to timing in the acquisition of certain properties. Roeper (1999) proposes that general optionality in syntactic constructions (which could also be linked to lexical types) could be captured by the proposed notion of "theoretical bilingualism." This refers to a system where grammars can coexist and where one of those grammars is a "minimal default grammar," i.e., it follows the principle of economy of representation (less structure and shorter movement rules). This model has inspired several accounts in language acquisition, notably the influential proposal of Müller and Hulk (2001) for bilingual delays. These authors aimed to explain differences in the timing of acquisition of direct objects between monolingual and bilingual children. The gist of the proposal is that with the availability of an acquisition default (the null object representation) and under indirect influence from a null object language, bilingual children are expected to remain in the default stage longer than monolingual children. The facts of null objects in bilingual contexts deserve a special treatment, so we will devote the next section to them. For now, we still need a solution for the problem of monolingual children's omission across languages. Linking the availability of the acquisition default to different resolution times across languages requires an additional mechanism.

Yang (2004) pushes the idea of grammars in competition further by linking it to token frequencies of the relevant input data. His goal is to explain the gradual nature of changes in grammatical development as well as differences in acquisition timing for constructions within a language and across languages. In his variational model of learning, the actual rate of language development is a function of concurrent changes in the probability of selecting one particular grammar within a competition model of multiple grammars (Yang 2002, 2004). The starting point is a UG-defined hypothesis space where all possibilities are available to the child:

> each grammar G_i is paired with a weight p_i, which can be viewed as the measure of prominence of G_i in the learner's language faculty. In a linguistic environment E, the weight [...] is determined by the learning function L, the linguistic evidence in E, and the time variable t, the time since the outset of language acquisition.
>
> (Yang 2002: 26)

The linguistic evidence relevant for the selection of a specific grammar over its competitors is called a "signature" and consists in a set of sentences analyzable only with the target grammar. For example, for French children to converge towards a verb raising grammar the occurrence of a sentence such as (27a) in the input is crucial while (27b) is not relevant (examples from Legate and Yang 2007):

(27) a. Jean voit souvent Marie.
      Jean sees often Marie.
      "Jean often sees Marie."
    b. Jean voit Marie.
      "Jean sees Marie."

In (27a), the ordering of the verb with respect to the adverb provides evidence that the verb raises in French and thus constitutes a structural "signature." According to Yang (2010), the frequency of utterances such as (27a) in the input is approximately 7 percent. Acquisition of finiteness in French is early (acquired by twenty months old); such a frequency of unambiguous data in the input must therefore be sufficient. In contrast, an example of late acquisition would be verb-second in German, with an unambiguous input frequency of approximately 1 percent (acquired by thirty-six–thirty-eight months).

Our take is that such a variational learning model, together with a null object acquisition default, can explain the observed differences in the timing of acquisition of direct object across languages. The possibility of using this model for objects was hinted at in Pérez-Leroux et al. (2008a) in the context of observed timing differences in the acquisition of direct objects in French and English. It has been implemented in more detail in Pirvulescu et al. (2014) for bilingual children.[4] This approach can also be applied to the issues raised by the differences observed in the acquisition of direct object clitics in different varieties of Spanish. More specifically, we advance that the difference between object omission in Peninsular Spanish and Colombian Spanish can similarly be explained in terms of input diversity and ambiguity. More specifically, as some studies have shown, the range of constructions potentially involving null objects might be wider overall in some Latin American Spanishes than in Peninsular Spanish (Campos 1986; Garcia

---

[4] Since then, a similar but different approach to ambiguous input and its compatibility with a parameter setting approach has been proposed by Gould (2015, 2016). The timing of our work made it impossible to attempt to apply this promising model to the L1 development of transitivity.

Mayo and Slabakova 2015) as the examples in (28) attest (from Schwenter 2006).

(28)   a. Null objects when the referent is nonspecific:
        Fui a la tienda a comprar café pero no tenían Ø.
        "I went to the store to buy coffee but they didn't have (any)."
      b. Null objects in ditransitive pronominal constructions :
        se lo(s)/la(s) > le Ø; ya te lo dije > ya te Ø dije
        "I already told you (it)."
      c. Null objects when [-animate] 3rd person in monotransitives:
        A: Queremos el postre.
        "We want the dessert."
        B: Ya Ø traigo.
        "I'll bring (it)."

In contrast, Peninsular Spanish seems to only accommodate (28a) and, marginally, (28b). The input diversity hypothesis predicts longer resolution timing in the acquisition of direct objects in Latin American Spanish than in Peninsular Spanish and therefore higher object omission rates; this prediction is upheld, as we have seen in Table 3.2.

If this approach is on the right track, we must then ask how children eventually achieve convergence with the target grammar. The variational learning framework offers two concurrent mechanisms. In one scenario, reduction in the use of null objects by children may be achieved by successive (positive) experience with pronouns. Overall lower levels of exposure would reduce the opportunity for the algorithm to reward the nonnull object grammar. In the other scenario, the source of vulnerability is not rewarding the right grammar, but demoting the incorrect grammar. Such contexts could be negative contexts (e.g., *She is not eating*). This was explored in Pérez-Leroux et al. (2008b) and will be taken up in detail in Chapter 4.

To conclude, we have seen that object omission in child language acquisition is a cross-linguistic phenomenon and we emphasized two main characteristics: children go through an object omission stage across languages and resolution times for object omission vary across languages. We have proposed that these timing differences are due to differences in the quality of the input (diversity and ambiguity) within monolingual development. This makes us suspect that we should also find an effect of input quantity given that under reduced input conditions the relevant triggering experiences, which are a crucial component in the explanation of timing in the variational model, might become sparser.

Under normal conditions, we cannot set up an experiment with children that reduces their natural language input. Fortunately, we do not have to. This setup occurs in nature for approximately half of the world's population, namely children growing up in multilingual settings. As a rule, and on average, such a setting entails that children spend less time hearing or using a given language than their monolingual counterpart for the same language. In bilingual children, constructions involving a lexical learning component were found to be more vulnerable to quantitative input effects (Unsworth 2014 and references therein). In our modular approach, lexical learning is part of the explanation for how children arrive at the target complementation properties in each language (more on this in Chapter 5). Bilingual development is therefore the logical place to look for additional input effects in the acquisition of direct objects.

3.6   *Going Beyond One Language: Bilingual Acquisition*

Exposure to and use of two or more languages such as in bilingual (or multilingual) development often results in patterns of development not encountered in monolingual acquisition, although the learning tools employed are presumably the same (Zurer-Pearson 2008). Even though the addition of one or more languages does not inherently threaten native attainment in at least one of the languages, by its nature bilingual acquisition for even a balanced bilingual child already presents one characteristic which sets it apart from monolingual development: less input than for monolinguals (Paradis and Genesee 1996). Could this inherently reduced input have effects in some domains, independent of the specific language combinations? We will see below that a range of studies show that reduced input – in both balanced and unbalanced acquisition – does indeed affect certain domains.

Under normal conditions, monolingual acquisition offers a relatively stable exposure to input in childhood. There are environmental effects in monolingual language development but these only become apparent in large-scale studies and with global measures of language (Dale, Dionne, Eley and Plomin 2000), such that it is not likely we can rely on such variations as a tool for investigating specific syntactic development. In contrast, bilingual acquisition offers an excellent laboratory for how different amounts of language exposure can interact with the developmental timetable in normally developing children. The key point is that reduction in input quantity can have different effects in different domains of grammar. We now have a term for this, domain vulnerability (Hulk and Müller 2000). In some core domains of clausal structure, such as case, word order, verb finiteness or negation, input reduction does not seem to lead to delays (Paradis and Genesee 1996; Tsimpli 2014). In some other domains, diminished input leads to temporary or permanent delays. For example, delay in the weaker language has been documented in both lexical and grammatical domains. In the lexical domain, Cobo-Lewis, Pearson, Eilers and Umbel (2002a, 2002b) observed that English-Spanish children who receive more language input perform better on a variety of vocabulary measures, and this holds for both the minority and majority language. Similar results have been obtained for Moroccan-Dutch bilinguals by Scheele, Leseman and Mayo (2010) and for Welsh-English bilinguals by Gathercole and Thomas (2009). None of this is surprising; indeed, the relative stability of many properties in successful bilingualism was the surprise. The question is can we use this as a tool to test theories of grammatical development? Unsworth et al. (2014) propose more fine-grained measures of input quantity disentangling the overall length of exposure from current exposure in the measuring of input quantity. They found that the latter is the best predictor for the acquisition of grammatical gender in Dutch and Greek, along with intrinsic features of the construction in each language (opaque vs. transparent marking). While this structure is acquired later in the weaker language (Dutch), language exposure impacts acquisition in both languages. Some see these effects as temporary, i.e., a consequence of input quantity fluctuations in development, but some very recent studies seem to show that these effects can be long-lasting or recurring in reduced input conditions such as minority context or loss of contact (Flores and Barbosa 2014; Flores 2015).

Changes in the language context of children can have observable impact on the pace of development itself. Castilla-Earls et al. (2015) studied the production of target clitics and articles in children growing up bilingual in Arizona. Two facts stand out in their data. One observation is that the rates of target production in bilinguals is quite low relative to what one would expect from monolinguals at the same age, because they produce errors of omission and comission at ages where monolinguals are above of 90 percent target. The second observation is that the initial pace of development is robust but then slows down visibly as children approach the age of six. The authors attribute this to fluctuations in the input associated with the onset of schooling in the majority language, English.

Research on balanced bilingual acquisition has also uncovered some effects of the inherent reduced input in the domain of both the lexicon and grammar. For the lexical domain, the effects of reduced input in balanced bilingual acquisition have been well documented (see for example Bialystok et al. 2010 and references therein). Balanced bilinguals have a reduced lexicon size in each of their languages, something we have known since the work of Zurer Pearson, Fernández and Oller (1993). A variety of grammatical domains can also be affected in balanced bilingual acquisition (morphosyn-tactic areas such as gender marking in Dutch cf., Unsworth et al. 2011; phenomena at the syntax-semantics interface such as regulation of pronominal dependencies and object omission cf., Sorace et al. 2009; Pirvulescu et al. 2014; see also Meisel 2007; Paradis, Nicoladis and Crago 2007 for other examples). These effects appear in language combinations featuring typologically different languages as well as typologically related ones.

3.6.1   *Cross-Linguistic Influence vs. Bilingual Delay in Object Omission*

Bilingual effects in the domain of object omission have initially been interpreted only as cross-linguistic influence in language pairs where one of the languages is a null object language while the other one is not, and where both languages overlap to some extent with respect to null object representations. The work of Müller and Hulk (2001) and that of Yip and Matthews (2000, 2005) both look at the effect of a null object language (German and Cantonese) on a nonnull language (French and English). In the case of the German-French pair, bilinguals have a higher rate of omissions in French than French monolinguals but they seem to go through the same developmental phases as monolingual children and use the same type of structures containing omissions. In the case of the Cantonese-English pair, both quantitative and qualitative differences were found in English between monolingual and bilingual children. Bilinguals omitted more in English than monolingual English children while omissions in Cantonese were similar in bilinguals and monolinguals. Qualitative effects were also found; for example, the use of the verb *put* without a referential object but followed directly by a locative is argued to follow the Cantonese structure. Another example is the use of null objects in topicalized object structures as in (29), again arguably following a Cantonese pattern.

(29)   Schoolbag put _ here, put _ at the door. (Timmy 2;07,12; Yip and Matthews
         2005: 2427)

In both studies the effect is unidirectional (however, a comparison between German in monolingual and bilingual children is not offered in Müller and Hulk 2001) and the authors propose either indirect cross-linguistic influence under language overlap (Müller and Hulk 2001) or cross-linguistic influence plus language transfer (Yip and Matthews 2000, 2005). Under the specific analysis of Müller and Hulk (2001), the case of object omission meets both conditions they stipulated for cross-linguistic influence: the phenomenon is at the syntax-pragmatics interface and there is partial overlap between French and English. Moreover, they propose that object omission (or object drop) in initial grammars can be characterized universally as an instance of empty topics licensed via a default discourse licensing strategy. This developmental phase, termed the "Minimal Default Grammar" by the authors, has the properties found in a language such as Cantonese. The combination of languages, such as German and French, presents the necessary structural overlap for cross-linguistic influence: the default discourse-based strategy (discourse licensing of empty objects) is present in both languages in the early grammar.

The problem with investigating bilingual acquisition of two typologically different languages with respect to object omission (such as German and French) is to tease apart the effects due to language influence (cross-linguistic influence) from the effects due to input quantity. It is necessary to investigate two relevantly similar languages, i.e., where null referential objects are not allowed or are highly restricted in both. The bilingual acquisition of French and English is such a case. For both French and English, it has been proposed that instances of referential null objects are highly restricted, contextually or lexically, but that they do exist. We know that the issue of input ambiguity and diversity is relevant for monolingual acquisition of the null object construction; as such, these effects should also be observed in bilingual acquisition. In addition, we have seen above that reduction in the input can affect some grammatical domains. Is this true of objects?

Studies of bilingual acquisition of French and English pronominal direct objects show that there is indeed a bilingual delay in this domain for this language combination. In Pérez-Leroux, Pirvulescu and Roberge (2009a), we tested monolingual children acquiring French in a French-English bilingual context, i.e., francophone children growing up in an English-speaking environment. These children had only an environmental exposure to English and, according to their parents, only spoke French. They attended schools with French-only policies, had two French-speaking parents, etc. However, they were growing up in the city of Toronto, where the Canadian census reports that less than 3 percent of households speak French. In that sense, it is not obvious to what extent they can be monolingual and our results were very suggestive in this respect. Indeed, the Toronto francophone kids had almost twice as many object omissions as francophone monolingual children from Montreal. Although, according to the parents, their bilingualism was limited to mere ambient exposure, it seemed to nonetheless have played a role in the domain of object omission. These were intriguing results. The explanation for the delay could not originate in the properties of English, the majority language. So, we sought to pursue this further, in a bidirectional study, where we could test omission patterns in one language and then the other, and calculate the relative effect of variation in dominance. Testing this proved quite difficult. We had to overcome the natural resistance (based on policy) of the Toronto French schools to allow the use of English in the schools. Teachers and principals in the schools feel that to support the retention of the language in a minority setting the maximum amount of input is to be provided. Ignoring the language restrictions to allow us to conduct an experiment in English went against the schools' mission to create a francophone oasis. We managed to eventually persuade a few French schools in Toronto to grant us permission to run a bidirectional study. The data, reported in Pirvulescu et al. (2012, 2014), replicate our initial observations. Bilingual francophone children omit more object clitics than monolingual francophone children, even absent an explanation based on cross-language influence (the other language being English). Since the null object stage ends earlier in English than in French monolinguals (Pérez-Leroux et al. 2008a), it is not a case of English (a faster language) influencing the timing of French (a slower language).

In Pirvulescu et al. (2014) language balance was explicitly included as a variable. We first analyzed balanced bilingual children, separated into three age groups, and compared them to monolinguals both in English and French. This followed previous elicitation studies on monolingual French and English children, where three-year-olds are shown to be in an omission stage (see Pérez-Leroux et al. 2008a) but resolution of the omission stage is different across languages. In studying this population, the aim was to examine whether a bilingual population would show alterations in the timetable of development in both French and English and, at the same time, to see whether the asymmetrical development observed in French and English monolinguals was reproduced in bilinguals. A bilingual effect was confirmed: there were more omissions in both French and English by bilingual children than in the production of their monolingual age-matched mates. Moreover, the rates of omission, even if higher in magnitude in bilinguals than in monolinguals, followed the behavior observed in French and English monolinguals in the literature (i.e., more omissions in French than in English for three-year-olds).

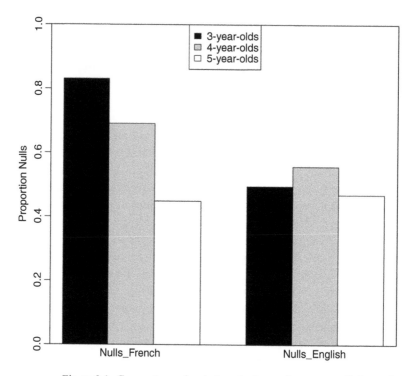

Figure 3.1 *Comparison of omissions in the two languages of bilingual children (mean proportions; from Pirvulescu et al. 2014: 504).*

We then compared groups of balanced and unbalanced bilinguals to the monolingual controls in each language. This analysis showed that balanced bilinguals omitted more than dominant children, in each language. In order to control for possible effects of English dominance over French, i.e., cross-linguistic influence resulting in the acceleration of pronominal convergence in French, the rate of omissions in the French of English-dominants was compared with the French of balanced and French-dominant bilinguals. It is interesting to note that asymmetrically bilingual children did not omit more in their weak French than balanced bilinguals did. The effect of bilingualism in the retention of null objects is evident, from cases of dominance in one language to cases of balanced bilingualism; however, further reduction in the input does not seem to have additional effects on the extent of omissions. There were no signs of English influence on the timing of French: having English as the other language does not lead to faster resolution of omissions in the French of these bilingual children.

What could the source of this bidirectional bilingual delay be? For Nicoladis (2012), bidirectional effects in French-English bilinguals are considered speech errors when there is structural overlap at the surface level. The fact that the languages of a bilingual are somewhat activated at all times, regardless of the language spoken, results in competition at a lemma level. That is, when one chooses the specific words and syntactic frame to convey the message, lexical competition should arise between similar words/syntactic constructions in the two languages. As such, bilinguals' activation of the typical word order of the possessive constructions in French and English at the lemma level would lead to mis-ordering constructions in both their languages.

Sorace et al. (2009) (English-Italian and Spanish-Italian bilinguals), following an approach dubbed the "interface hypothesis," consider bilingual effects to be due to the higher processing load present for bilinguals. Such effects are expected to be confined to (or concentrated at) the discourse level while the narrow syntax itself is predicted not to be affected. These effects result in "shallow" computation of reference resolution processes; the strategy used by bilinguals is thought to be the choice of a default form/structure, similar to the strategy used by monolinguals in challenging processing conditions. While in English overt pronouns are used for both topic maintenance and topic shift, in Italian a null pronoun is preferred for topic maintenance and an overt one for topic shift. English-Italian bilinguals have a preference in Italian for overt pronouns, which could be attributed to an influence from English. However, the authors show that the same preference for overt pronouns is present in the Italian of Spanish-Italian bilinguals, where priming from Spanish is excluded.

An alternative view is advocated in Hervé et al. (2016) and Hsin et al. (2013) who propose that the simultaneous acquisition and processing of two languages (executive control – language inhibition and language activation) affects the mental representations of syntactic structures in both languages. This results, to a certain extent, in shared mental representations between the two languages in bilinguals.

We see that in processing accounts mental representations, processing factors (language encoding) or semantic/pragmatic interpretations can all be affected by the acquisition of two (and presumably several) languages. This in turn amounts to saying that indeed everything is (or can be) different between bilingual and monolingual acquisition. This is a strong statement, so strong that it loses explanatory power. It is too blunt an instrument to account for the basic fact of bilingual effects: that much of the grammar of bilinguals lies within the footprint of the monolingual variants, while bilingual effects appear in a restricted (albeit consistent) manner. If an epitaph were provided for the contrastive analysis model of the sixties and early seventies, it would read: "not everything that can transfer does." More generally, we see that not everything that can be affected in bilingual acquisition in fact is. That is the basis for the autonomous development position (De Houwer 1990; Genesee et al. 1995; Meisel 2001). Moreover, while it is conceivable that language-processing mechanisms might indeed be affected by the acquisition of multiple languages, previous studies do not include online measures of language processing that can clearly differentiate between bilingual and monolingual acquisition. In addition, while priming effects between the languages of bilinguals are clearly demonstrated in Hsin et al. (2013), we do not know how long-lasting these effects can be and therefore if they indeed affect mental representations in a significant manner.

In our work, we advocate for a grammatical explanation based on the same underlying mental representation in both bilinguals and monolinguals. The child has to resolve a syntactic problem, namely, to determine under what conditions each language allows object omission (i.e., restriction of the default representation). We propose that the extended null object stage in bilinguals is a consequence of overall reduction in input and of the greater degree of input ambiguity and diversity. The input to which bilingual children are exposed contains more variety (variation both within and across languages) and is at the same time less robust in each language than is the case for monolinguals by virtue of a reduction in language exposure. From the perspective of a variational learning model, such as the one discussed in Section 3.5, reduction in the input, even in the case of balanced bilinguals, leads to a weak "signature" and therefore to a longer acquisition timeline. In addition, learning of complementation possibilities involves an important lexical component (the verb), which, as is known, is sensitive to fluctuations in the input.

3.7   *Conclusion*

Our objective in this chapter was to show that among the diversity we hear in child production, within and across languages, there is a constant silence that, we contend, can be traced back to a null object representation, unfolding according to constraints of the environment. The null object stage in development is detectable across languages, with some languages as exemplars (French) and others less clear (Spanish, Romanian). This is what we would expect for a phenomenon that has many dimensions. In this sense, the initial null object, satisfying the minimal instantiation of transitivity (MIT), leads to the rich cross-linguistic inventory of developmental patterns and, ultimately, to the null object possibilities attested in the languages of the world.

Patterns in the input reflect in patterns of acquisition and result in language-specific timelines. The matching of the input patterns by the children is not perfect, though: children prove one more time to be both conservative learners and innovators. In the same way children indirectly interpret what is missing from adult utterances, in the next chapter we will try to interpret the missing object in children's utterances with the help of contiguous theoretical proposals and carefully designed experiments. The silent objects are indeed quiet, and it is our job to draw out their meaning by carefully observing and investigating the available data.

4 *Interpreting the Missing Object*

> The disparities between what the grammar generates and usage both BY the speaker and usefulness TO the speaker are striking. We see this in the centrality of full argument structure to grammar, even if that full argument structure is rarely expressed.
>
> (Newmeyer 2003: 701)

4.1 Refining the Problem: Silent Objects Are Quiet

The previous chapters have brought us to a crossroad: we have an attested and fascinating phenomenon, namely object omission in L1 acquisition across languages, but the data available, although rich and complex, may not be sufficient to allow us to decide between several alternative approaches that have been developed to explain them. Indeed, we could take a variety of different routes depending on whether we conceive of this phenomenon as attributable to a pragmatic deficit, a performance deficit or a computational deficit in child production.

Our work so far, however, has taken us on a different route; we propose that object omission can be analyzed, without invoking any sort of deficit, by appealing to basic grammatical tools and the notion that parametric learning must be represented in terms of lexical learning.

Data, as the saying goes, do not speak for itself. Science is the art of asking probing questions and of learning how to observe (or listen) carefully. This is important because sometimes there is too much noise in the room, or too many data points speaking to us all at once, or because, we are warned, their voices might be too soft or even sly. To make the data talk the best approach is triangulation, i.e., the strategy of examining phenomena from different angles in search of converging evidence. Thus, in this chapter, we look at omission beyond the basic literature on elicited production surveyed in the previous chapter. We concentrate on the discourse-based recoverability of

106

empty objects. We examine our predictions, which have been developed in the context of elicited *production* data from preschool-aged children, against three different sets of evidence:

- Evidence from discourse-sensitivity in children at the telegraphic speech stage;
- Experimental evidence on how children *interpret* sentences with missing objects in controlled settings;
- Recent observations on intervention effects in the association between the null object site and the left periphery.

Our goal is to refine the learnability perspective introduced in Chapter 1 by incorporating our views with some core assumptions from linguistic theory and the field of L1 acquisition, namely Chomsky's Uniformity Hypothesis and two corollaries of the continuity hypothesis: Tom Roeper's approach to early meaning (Roeper 2007), and Luigi Rizzi's grammar-based and performance-driven approach (Rizzi 2002).

This cannot be done until we establish more specifically the inner workings of the grammatical machinery involved. So, we will start in Section 2 by becoming more explicit (and inevitably more technical) about the mechanics of object generation and object interpretation in adult grammars before we explore: discourse context and how grammar interacts with the input (Section 3); evidence from children's interpretation of null objects in comprehension studies (Section 4); and various pieces of grammatical evidence in L1 studies that show linking between certain null objects and the left periphery of the clause (Section 5).

4.2   Null Objects and the Uniformity Hypothesis

Up to this point we have been working with a set of assumptions on the form and function of verbal complementation, presented in Chapter 2; the results of our L1 acquisition studies point to an initial null object stage attributable in part to the Transitivity Requirement paving the way to the full adult grammar. The aim of this section is to present hypotheses as to how theory and experimental results can be linked. In order to do so, a preliminary discussion on cross-linguistic variation and L1 acquisition is in order.

4.2.1   Parameters and the Uniformity Hypothesis

Pinker (1984) proposes a relevant extension of the UG hypothesis in acquisition, the continuity hypothesis, which states that children's linguistic substantives (categories and computational processes) are fundamentally the same as those of the adult grammar, and therefore do not change in their essence. The strong version of the continuity hypothesis (Pinker 1984, 1989; Crain and Thornton 1998) holds that stages in acquisition may reflect parameter settings that are not valid in a particular adult grammar but are part of the UG inventory. In other words, when systematic patterns emerge in the data we should assume that they point to alternative parameter settings.

Our view of grammar has changed radically since the days of classic Principles and Parameters (P&P) approaches (Chomsky 1981). Naturally however, contemporary L1 acquisition research does not always automatically incorporate insights from the minimalist framework into the descriptions made of the acquisition process (Lorenzo and Longa 2008, 2009). A good example, of special interest here, is the Uniformity Hypothesis (UH), formulated by Noam Chomsky in "Derivation by Phase":

> Uniformity Hypothesis: In the absence of compelling evidence to the contrary, assume language to be uniform, with variety restricted to easily detectable properties of utterances.   (Chomsky 2001: 2)

The UH implies that while the computational system is assumed to be invariant, basic feature inventories can vary across languages (Chomsky 2001: 10). This assumption fundamentally revises the notion of grammatical categories and is crucial for work on language typology and acquisition. On the theoretical side, it has promoted comparative work and provided methodological constraints on the interpretation of cross-linguistic differences.[1]

From the acquisition perspective, the UH circumscribes the task of the learner to acquiring the features of the various categories of the grammar; this idea is not new in acquisition (Borer 1984), but the current UH makes lexical-functional learning the only form of learning. For instance, given the fine grained nature of typological variation in the semantic representation of categories, the acquisition of a functional category must include refining aspects of interpretation of specific categories (Pérez-Leroux 2005; Valian 2009; Pérez-Leroux and Kahnemuyipour 2014). While language learning in a parametric system amounts to selecting among UG-generated options (Rizzi 2002; Snyder 2007), Minimalism deconstructs the options and reduces them to minimal elements that are learned lexically. Although the debate on the validity

---

[1] As pointed out by Matthewson (2013: 338) linguistic diversity plays an important part in generative grammar and "a null hypothesis of universality is not the same thing as expecting all languages to look the same."

of the parametric approach to cross-linguistic variation and L1 acquisition continues (Boeckx 2011; Newmeyer 2005; Holmberg and Roberts 2014), it is at times difficult to tease apart terminological differences from more substantive disagreements. It seems clear however that the "deep" parameters (e.g., the prodrop parameter) that the P&P quest sought to discover appear to have been abandoned in much of the current acquisition research.

Be that as it may, our results point in the direction of the view articulated in Holmberg and Roberts (2014: 4), namely:

> that the simplest, arguably the most "minimalist," view of syntactic variation is that small parts of UG are underspecified and that the inherent computational conservatism of the learner interacts with the Primary Linguistic Data (PLD) in such a way as to impose a structure on the space of variation that this underspecification creates. The structural units in this variation can be called "parameters" (although, if we were starting from scratch, we would probably call them something else).

In order to avoid terminological issues, we refer to this approach as weak(ly)-parametric to convey the view that parameters correspond to areas of grammar that UG does not care about and thus where variation is expected. Applied to our particular studies, and as we have seen in the previous chapters, everything seems to function as though children in the early stages have access to an all-purpose empty category, used in object position and whose content is more flexible than observed in the adult grammars.[2] In addition, grammatical development in this domain appears to consist of a refinement of what the child knows about the recoverability of the null objects (in the referential cases) or the representation of the information necessary for the interpretation of the null object (in the nonindividuated, activity interpretation cases).

With this in mind, let us ask what a traditional parametric approach to the development of direct objects in L1 acquisition would look like. Recall that, under this view, early grammars may differ from adult grammars in the setting of a parameter. To draw an analogy to early work on the null subject parameter, let's assume the existence of a null object parameter [± referential null object]. If such a parameter existed, Portuguese would most likely be [+ referential null

---

[2] In Holmberg and Roberts' terms the empty category would be underspecified for the relevant features. This description is also compatible with earlier (general) notions of acquisition defaults (Lebeaux 1988; Roeper 1992).

object] while English would represent a [– referential null object] setting. Such a parameter would come from UG with a default setting (and the trigger needed to reset it), determined by a combination of logic and observed behavior in children (Hyams 1983; Berwick 1985; Manzini and Wexler 1987). In the case of null subjects, for instance, the initial setting for the parameter is [– null subjects], which can then be reset to [+ null subjects] based on exposure to sentences with null subjects. Now, because of the noncompulsory nature of null objects in many adult grammars, our parameter should similarly (and logically) be set to [– referential null object] and children would need to be exposed to referential null objects in their input to reset it to its positive value. Of course, this predicts the opposite of what we observe cross-linguistically as established in Chapter 3; if there exists a null object stage in L1 acquisition, the positive setting must precede the negative setting. Yet, an initial positive setting would lead to a logical dead end inasmuch as it would be impossible to retreat to a negative setting based on the input, which would have to provide (negative) evidence for the absence of null objects.

But the parametric approach as presented above is an oversimplification; if there is a parameter responsible for referential null objects, its nature is probably more complex than can be expressed by our simple formulation. Crucially, and significantly from our perspective, a null object parameter has never taken hold in the field although the term itself is sometimes used without concrete elaboration in both the typological and acquisition literature.

A slightly more sensible null object parameter would naturally be linked either to the use (or nonuse) of a topic drop construction (as in Mandarin or Japanese), or to the availability (or nonavailability) of a null pronominal empty category such as *pro*. To our knowledge, the only well-articulated parameter setting account of object omission in L1 acquisition comes from the pioneering work of Aafke Hulk and Natascha Müller, to which we referred on numerous occasions in the preceding chapters. They argue that object omissions in early French correspond to a free topic drop construction of the Chinese type. The null object is a variable and a recoverability mechanism allows the recoverability of the null object from the discourse through a null topic adjoined to the sentential projection (Müller et al. 1996; Müller and Hulk 2001).[3] For their part, Schmitz et al. (2004) suggest that omissions are due to the recourse to a Japanese-style grammar, with *pro* occupying the null object position and bound by a discourse-identified zero topic.

---

[3] See Section 4.3.3 for a fuller discussion.

As Snyder (2007) points out, a parametric approach to child language is a broad research program dedicated to understanding how children learn the abstract properties of grammar. Despite the undeniable insights stemming from those parameter-based contributions, the range of variation and types of null object constructions observed cross-linguistically combined with L1 acquisition results shed doubt on the validity of a traditional parametric approach. In the case under study here, if target languages cannot easily be organized in types based on a null object parameter, it is doubtful that the acquisition engine in the domain of verbal complementation would be driven by such a parameter. In addition, a classic "deep" parametric account would refer to clusters of properties, as is the case for null subjects and this has never been argued for in the domain under study here.

Rather, the approach we are advocating is Minimalist and, as such, claims that nontarget early child production reflects the interplay between a small, underspecified part of UG (the recoverability/interpretation of a null category in object position) and the input (comprised of a variety of null objects with different interpretations using different recoverability mechanisms). Learning in this case does not consist in simply determining whether or not *pro* exists as part of the lexical inventory of the target grammar, or in rightly/wrongly assuming that the target grammar is topic-drop. We take learning instead to be weakly parametric and the rest of this section presents an elaboration of this approach.

4.2.2   Transitivity, Variety and L1 Acquisition

The minimal instantiation of transitivity (MIT) introduced in Chapter 2 represents the initial underspecified state provided by UG and can thus be seen as the default representation of transitivity, applicable to all Vs.[4] What does this mean in terms of L1 development? Let's first attempt to answer this nontechnically, at an intuitive level. Since MIT provides the basis for all possible verbal complementation representations then what a child actually needs to learn, from the input, are the components of target representations that are not provided by MIT. In other words, the issue boils down to determining the nature of the null element involved in MIT. For the sake of the presentation, let us assume for the moment (subject to modification in Section 4.2.3.1) that this element is essentially similar to a null cognate

---

[4] See also Roeper's (2006) Minimal Default Grammar (MDG): the Initial State projected from UG. MDG contains nodes that are universal in a hierarchical relation.

object à la Hale and Keyser (2002). For instance, for a language like English, MIT is pretty much it: unergative constructions with null or overt (potentially cognate, or transitivizing) objects, and transitive constructions with overt DP or null cognate object, as exemplified in (1).

(1)   a. John ran.
       b. John ran a race.
       c. John ate.
       d. John ate an apple.

What is not provided by MIT are the recoverability mechanisms distinct from hyponymic identification. For a target language like Russian, MIT is insufficient: a referential null object representation must be added to the English possibilities. For French, a language with accusative pronominal clitics, this construction, which involves a null object, must also be learned. And so on and so forth for any, and all languages.

How can this happen? MIT gives unergatives and transitives with a null implicit object (1a and c) – they are the same – for free. If children can produce DPs, then they can generate transitives with overt objects and unergatives with overt cognate objects (1b and d). The rest, beyond MIT, crucially depends on the input; so in a language with accusative clitics, the clitic construction exposes the child to a referential null object in canonical object position. Other languages have other types of constructions that also provide input containing a referential null object. Keep in mind though that while there are languages, like English, that do not provide input exposing children to referential null objects we nonetheless observe referential null objects in the L1 development of all languages, whether these correspond to the target or not (see Chapter 3). Our results show that nontarget-like referential null objects remain longer in languages that allow referential null object constructions. Following this reasoning, what remains to be determined is the nature of the nontarget-like null objects as well as how children grow out of them. Crucially, we cannot hypothesize that the nontarget-like referential null objects are attributable to the input; if they were, we would expect them to correspond to a confusion found only in languages with referential null objects and they would not show up in the acquisition of a language like English. As we saw in Chapter 3, the input critically influences development but, as our results show, only in the developmental timeline not in the basic representations that are observed in child production; these representations are the same cross-linguistically.

Therefore, our problem has something to do with the nature of the null object involved in MIT and its recoverability or, to put it differently, it is an issue with empty categories. Descriptively speaking, the empty category used for null object constructions in the initial stage of development appears to have multiple referential and nonreferential uses. Finally, since the empty categories we are concerned with are nominal in nature, then there must be interactions with DP development in L1 acquisition, a domain that has (thankfully) been studied extensively in the literature. Let us turn our attention to empty categories.

4.2.3   On Empty Categories

Whereas four "traditional" functionally determined empty categories (NP-trace, Wh-trace, PRO and *pro*) were central to the GB framework, the Minimalist approach is far from clear as to what it has in store for empty categories (Holmberg 2005). This deserves some attention on our part.

Certain approaches such as Krivochen and Kosta (2013)'s Radical Minimalism attempt to eliminate empty categories completely while others continue not only to assume their existence but also to actually expand the inventory; this can be seen in the numerous empty functional heads that are characteristic of minimalist derivations, especially carto-graphic accounts.

The main criticism linked to empty categories is that their motivation is mostly theory internal. For instance, subject *pro* in a null subject language is necessary because of the Extended Projection Principle (EPP). So, the argu-ment goes, unless one can adduce theory-independent evidence for the existence of empty categories then they should be eliminated. Why is this a necessary conclusion? Without wanting to be facetious, one could certainly build a descriptively adequate model that makes extensive use of empty categories. Should we automatically reject such a model? A direct answer is suggested by recourse to Occam's Razor: the simplest of two competing theories should be adopted. Two main reasons are typically given to argue that the no-empty-categories approach is simpler. First, empty categories have to be interpretively necessary. Krivochen and Kosta's model attempts to show that for all constructions/derivations in which empty categories have been postulated another derivation can be presented that respects Full Interpretation, without recourse to empty categories. Second, from a language acquisition perspective it would appear to make sense to assume that learning a system without having to worry about invisible elements represents a simpler task than learning one with missing constituents.

In this book however, we take the opposite view, i.e., that empty categories can be seen as (UG) built-in learning tools in that they help make sense out of silence. The relevant metric for simplicity shifts from the theory itself to the acquisition process: which theory offers the simplest account for the acquisition process? Although we argue that it is one that includes empty categories, our purpose here is not to present decisive evidence for or against the necessity of empty categories as a general statement on the nature of possible natural grammars or of mental linguistic representations. We do, however, want to motivate our recourse to empty categories in the representations of VPs; whether or not this view extends to other domains (PPs for instance) is reserved for future research.

4.2.3.1   TR and Empty Categories   How are we to treat the empty category that can be used to satisfy TR as instantiated in MIT? As we have seen in Chapter 2, in adult grammars (setting aside unaccusatives) the empty category can be null N (unergatives and transitives with a generic interpretation) or null DP (for referential null objects). Null DP corresponds to *pro* in GB whereas null N was not commonly used in that framework. For our purpose and in order to follow a more minimalist approach, we adopt a contextual determination of empty categories, according to which grammars do not have an inventory of different types of empty categories per se. Instead, a head or maximal projection can be empty and the different properties of those empty elements are simply those of the category they represent. This view of empty categories conforms to the weak-parametric view of L1 acquisition articulated above. Learning does not consist in acquiring different types of empty categories but in determining how empty categories are used in the target grammar, with no deep parameters involved.

We therefore adopt Krivochen and Kosta's (2013) definition of empty categories as a semantically interpretable syntactic node ($X°$ or XP) with no phonological features. The key in this definition is of course the term "semantically interpretable," which harkens back to the recoverability (of deletions) condition of early generative grammar (Katz and Postal 1964; Fiengo and Lasnik 1972's insightful contribution). The presence in a structure of an empty category that is not interpretable would make the whole phrase or clause uninterpretable.

For null DP, recoverability is anaphoric while, for null N, hyponymic identification is at play. As stated above, everything seems to function as though children in the early stages had access to an all-purpose empty category of a type that cannot easily be classified as *pro* or null N; this is in fact expected

in our approach to empty categories.[5] We also find that grammatical development consists in a refinement of what the child knows about the recoverability
of the null objects. This is evidenced by the nontarget referential use of the
empty category (the null object).

4.2.3.2   Analysis   Stated simply, what seems to be confusing for children
is to distinguish between null DP and null N in VP. Assuming that the
distinction between the two is not given directly by UG, it follows logically
either that one emerges out of the other or that both coexist but are not easily
distinguishable. We thus explore four options to account for the development
from MIT to target grammars with an intervening null object stage. They
can be characterized roughly as: neither-N-nor-DP, N-to-DP, N-and-DP or
DP-to-N.

The neither-N-nor-DP approach says that the initial empty category that is
used as a complement of V in child production corresponds to the rudimentary
version of the empty categories that will eventually exist in the evolving child's
grammar and its incomplete state gives rise to the different ways it can be used
initially. An analogy that comes to mind is that of an embryo: this initial empty
category eventually develops into different types, accounting for the observed
gradual development, but importantly does not exist as such in adult grammars.
This is where the weakness of this view becomes apparent; it is far from clear
what this constituent is and how development from a rudimentary to a full-
fledged version can occur. Additionally, as far as we know, this type of
approach finds no parallel in the development of overt nominals. For these
reasons, we set this option aside.

Under the N-to-DP view, the starting point for learning in the domain
of verbal complementation is Merge of a null cognate object (or the child
grammar equivalent) to all verbs. This single null N is initially used in all
contexts with all verbs and can be used referentially. Crucially, this approach
predicts that there should be evidence of similar development in the case of
overt DPs: children would start out producing bare nouns which would
gradually be replaced by DPs by structure building above N in the course
of development. Thus the N-to-DP view is the null analogue of traditional
structure building approaches such as Lebeaux (1988) and Roeper (1992).

---

[5] Ritter and Wiltschko (2016) categorize impersonal *pro* in Hebrew as a "small nominal" that is
caseless, has no specific reference, does not bear a person feature although it must have a human
referent. This impersonal *pro* is thus structurally deficient. The concept of "small nominal" may
represent a useful tool to describe the null element used by children in our work.

Pannemann (2007) portrays this bottom up approach as (2); accordingly, DPs get built from N as the various functional categories are acquired.

(2)   Pannemann (2007: 41)

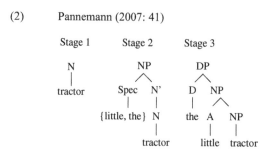

She subsequently offers a compelling alternative to the view that children start out with bare nouns on their way to using DPs. We will return to it shortly.

According to the N-and-DP approach, children initially have two empty categories: null N (nonreferential) and null DP (referential, equivalent to *pro*). The confusion responsible for the null object stage rests in an improper use of null DP, which functions in child grammar without a recovery mechanism to assign its reference. So in French, for instance, children would initially use *pro* without an accusative clitic. Something else must therefore provide the necessary interpretation and that could be an over-reliance on context.[6] The disappearance of null DP or the development of target-like recovery mechanisms would happen through an increased reliance on grammar instead of context. In that view, the null object stage does not have much to do with grammatical development per se, but follows "general" development: "[I]nference is cheap, articulation expensive, and thus the design requirements are for a system that maximizes inference" (Levinson 2000: 29). Although over reliance on context likely interferes with the grammar (see Section 4.3), this approach implies the loss of a possibility given by UG (i.e., *pro* as null DP) in acquiring languages without referential null objects. From a learnability approach this view is not particularly appealing since there is no mechanism for expunction.

The final option, DP-to-N, is the mirror image of the second but incorporates elements of the first option. Children's initial empty category is null DP (equivalent to *pro* in adult grammars) and as a result, their null objects

---

[6] This could help in accounting for the differences observed between spontaneous and elicited production as discussed in Chapter 3.

can always be referential. This approach to the development of null nominal elements follows the one suggested in Pannemann (2007) for overt nominals. Gradual development is accounted for by the "discovery" of null N as a possibility of a deconstructed or unraveled DP. The null object stage corresponds to the time period before the establishment of null N and the difference in timeline between languages can be attributed to the reinforcing role played by referential null object constructions in the input.[7]

Panneman proposes to invert the development of functional projections from bottom up to top down so that DP and not bare N is the initial category. Obviously, on the surface, children start with bare nouns. But according to Panneman, our analyses need to integrate the fact that early bare nouns truly have the referential properties of DPs. Panneman proposes that children initially map nouns to the maximal category (DP), and change this initial mapping with every step in learning the distribution of elements in the NP domain. In her view, children quickly detect the consistent presence of functional material to the left of nouns (i.e., determiners), but they might not be able to immediately interpret them. Mapping the determiner material reorganizes/unravels the structure of the nominal phrase:

> The presence of the determiner in the input leads to a retuning of the correspondence rule of the lexical item box_w such that this phonological string corresponds to a lower syntactic projection. (Panneman 2007: 72)[8]

Therefore, children can be structurally conservative, positing as little structure as possible, provided that it can accommodate the facts.

The evidence for Panneman's position is clear: studies with very young children (eleven to thirteen months) show that they are sensitive to determiners in the input; children produce a variety of DPs, including N, D-N, as well as others that are less relevant here (p. 31); and early determiners are not part of unanalyzed constituents (p. 34).

Panneman (2007: 46) argues that "in the absence of an overt determiner, bare nouns in child language have the same semantic properties as DPs in adult language (type-shifting, reference to particular instances, definite reference)," which cannot be accounted for by the structure building approach. For her, overt bare nouns in child production correspond to DP structures with null

---

[7] Note that this does not predict the use of pronouns in nonindividuated contexts; the null element used by children is nonreferential in this context.

[8] In Panneman the w subscript indicates that the expression has already been labelled as a word.

D. As a consequence, she argues that development is, to use our simplified terminology, from DP to N, instead of N to DP. In other words, "at the onset of acquisition, all nominal items correspond to DPs" (p. 95). The mapping between a nominal item to the functional maximal projection DP is provided in (3).

(3)   /X/object → DP

The similarities with our own observations on the behavior of null nominal direct objects are obvious and the clear advantage of DP-to-N over the other three is that it establishes a parallel between the development of overt and null nominals and sanctions the importance of the input in this development.

Additionally, this approach is fully compatible with the view expressed above that empty categories are not functionally determined but rather correspond to lexical items – in our case, empty Nouns or empty DPs; Panagiotidis (2002). For these reasons, we adopt it here and turn our attention to the recoverability of null objects in adult grammars as this is the source of the variation observed in the developmental timeline.

4.2.4   On the Recoverability of Null Objects

The development from the initial default correspondence in (3) is characterized by Pannemann as "structure unravelling," where the phonological material in the input corresponding to the noun phrase (determiner, adjective, noun) is successively reanalyzed within the syntactic DP shell until it reaches the target mapping. As we follow this approach and apply it to empty categories, an obvious difference arise; the overt nominals in (2) do not need to have their content recovered as they have inherent semantic/morphosyntactic content paired with phonological features which makes them visible and interpretable. In contrast, the content of empty categories needs to be recovered from the situational, discursive and/or grammatical context.

Sigurðsson (2011) presents a minimalist analysis of the recoverability of null referential arguments, which are presumed to be universally available in syntax. While all referential null arguments are subject to contextual recoverability, some languages require an additional clause-internal identification mechanism such as, for example, Pashto where dropped arguments must agree with the verb (Sigurðsson 2011: 268 example (5)). The rest of the syntactic structure becomes crucial for licensing purposes, in that all referential arguments must be licensed through a linking operation with the left periphery of the clause, a syntactic feature-matching operation Sigurðsson calls C/edge linking. C/edge linkers include features such as Topic features (aboutness-shift Topics, contrastive Topics and familiar Topics) and speech participant features (speaker and hearer).

While this approach does not suppose any null argument parameter, some cross-linguistic differences are made with respect to licensing (external licensing – through the discourse, and internal licensing – through antecedent logophoric and topic features on the C/edge) and identification of the arguments as phi-silent or phi-visible; these distinctions are operationalized at the level of syntactic derivations.

Putting all this together, we arrive at the following characterization of the development observed in our studies. Children start out with an empty or overt complement in object position in order to satisfy TR. Based on MIT, the empty category always has the potential to be used by the child with referential properties as argued above and, assuming Sigurðsson's approach, this is done through C/edge linking. Depending on the target language, other internal recoverability mechanisms (clitics, agreement) have to develop in parallel. This accounts for the coexistence of nontarget referential null objects and clitic constructions in French, for instance. The empty category used by children is essentially equivalent to a null DP and is used with unergatives and transitives. The null N manifestation of the empty category (for unergatives and transitives used generically) develops along lexical development. This is because null N can only be interpretively acceptable if it is in a proper semantic inclusion relation with the verb and this is only possible once the meaning of a given verb has been acquired.[9]

The developmental steps based on this approach proceed as follows:

- Learning of idiosyncratic verb meanings;
- Exposure to input that includes null object constructions;
- Contextual identification of null DP through C/edge linking (null object stage);
- Idiosyncratic verb meaning learned results in hyponymic identification of N.

---

[9] Under this view, it may be predicted that children can use a null referential object with unergatives. To our knowledge this has never been tested. Note however that given our approach to transitivity, the unergative-transitive dichotomy is a matter of continuum and, as such, it is not clear whether any given verb can be assumed to be clearly transitive or unergative in children's early production.

In the case of a language like English, the resulting adult system consists of null and overt N and overt DP and the null object stage is relatively short. In languages where exposure to the input provides more types of null object constructions, the null object stage is longer and the adult system might additionally include null DP.

4.3   *Pragmatics Meets Syntax*

Can syntax alone explain patterns of omission? For many, including us, the answer is no. Extensive research literature has focused on the properties of the utterance context contributing to omission patterns at the early stages of grammatical development, starting from the onset of word combinations and throughout the telegraphic speech stage. In this section, we review how these pragmatic perspectives contribute to our understanding of object omission in child language.

4.3.1   *Children's Sensitivity to Context*

The evidence on this point is quite clear, but it is often not integrated into accounts of object omissions. Children are highly sensitive to various discourse-pragmatic factors and adjust their speech accordingly. Sensitivity to context in the realization of arguments has been observed across languages, both in naturalistic (Allen 2000; Serratrice et al. 2004; Serratrice 2005) and in experimental settings (Salomo et al. 2010; Graf et al. 2014; De Cat 2009).

Context sensitivity in the situation that interests us here is linked to the availability of a referent in the extra-linguistic context or simply to sensitivity to the discourse context: when a referent is given, or identifiable in the context, children exhibit a tendency to omit the corresponding referential expression. It is simply a case of economy: why say it if it is obvious? There are two canonical cases of context sensitivity: reliance on null elements, or use of specific, contextually sensitive lexical expressions.

In the first case, the meaning of the utterance might involve a nominal expression whose referent is present in the context. Situational inference then trumps the use of an explicit lexical item, especially in child production (Roeper 1999: 171). In (4), for instance, the missing element (*the book*) is recovered through extra-grammatical inference directly from the context.

(4)   Here, take ___! (Instead of: Here, take the book!)

The second case is when the statement includes a variable referential expression, such as a pronoun, which is linked either to a referential antecedent in the discourse (5) or to a (nonexplicitly mentioned) referent in the extra-linguistic context (6):

(5)   Cotextual or discourse anaphora
        Student: "Do you know whether Mr. Smith is in his office?"
        Passing Lecturer: "No, he's not there." (adapted from Cornish 1999)

(6)   Contextual anaphora or exophora
        [In front of the locked door of the office of a member of academic staff [. . .].
        A student is hovering round the door, evidently interested in seeing the
        member of staff in question. Another lecturer, who knows the colleague in
        question, passes by and, observing the situation, remarks:] "He's not there!"
        (Cornish 1999: 119)

Pragmatic approaches in language acquisition assert that the information status of the argument is essential in the choice young children make between overt and null referential expressions. The evidence is fairly clear. Depending on the grammatical function (subject or object) and language type (whether the language requires obligatory vs. optionally realized arguments), both adults and children tend to omit or pronominalize referents that are easily recoverable in the discourse. These are considered highly accessible; the notion of conceptual accessibility of a referent is defined as "the ease with which the mental representation of some potential referent can be activated in or retrieved from memory" (Bock and Warren 1985: 50, from Hughes and Allen 2013). The forms used to identify various referents can be hierarchically ordered as shown in Table 4.1 (from Hughes and Allen 2013, based on Ariel's 2001 accessibility theory).

A range of comprehension experiments clearly confirms the observations from naturalistic studies that children are extremely sensitive to context. Matthews et al. (2006) reports that children can assess early on whether an object is accessible to the interlocutor based on the previous discourse

Table 4.1 *Four referential forms – A hierarchy of accessibility markers*

Low Accessibility Marker	Lexical NP	Boy go. (Brian, 2;07,01)
	Demonstrative	This go round here. (Fraser, 2;00,20)
	Pronoun	It goes there. (Annie, 2;00,25)
High Accessibility Marker	Null	Ø want chips. (Eleanor, 2;00,15)

information. Three- and four-year-olds switched from DP to a pronoun for the subject constituents in their responses if the utterance leading to the question contained a previous mention of that referent:

(7)   Prompt: That sounds like fun! What happened?
         Preferred response: The clown is jumping.
         Prompt: Was that the clown? Oh! What happened?
         Preferred response: He is jumping.

Two-year-olds also adjusted their utterances, but in a different way. When the subject was not mentioned in the preceding verbal context, their responses used a subject noun phrase: "clown!" When it was, they were more likely to offer the verb as a response: "jumping."

Other studies show that children are sensitive to both the verbal and the situational context. The best demonstration of this is given in a very simple experiment reported by Salomo et al. (2010). These investigators presented children with short video clips showing either a sequence where the same action affects different patients (frog washing *ladybug, hedgehog* and *duck*), or different actions that affect the same patient (frog *feeding* duck, *combing* duck and *washing* duck). So, by the time the experimenter asks target question *What is frog doing now*? the same thing is happening in both conditions: the frog is washing the duck. Children's responses patterned according to prior context. Whenever the patient was the same across the situations, children primarily gave null object responses (*washing*), and almost never gave an object-only response (*the duck*). When the action remained constant, and the objects varied, children mostly answered with the full predicate (*washing the duck*), although object-only responses were frequent as well. In a second version of the study, the audio script was modified to eliminate mention of the referents or the action, leaving only neutral comments "That's great!" As in the first experiment, children mostly realized the object when it was new and mostly did not when it remained constant across the scene. However, objects were realized more often when the script-modeled transitive sentences than when the verbal descriptions were removed.

In studies on child production or omission of arguments, various features have been identified as relevant. Some pertain to the accessibility of the referent; others, to the importance of the information contributed by the given argument. For example, Greenfield and Smith (1976) note that children tend to encode (i.e., realize) those aspects of the event that are most informative and not to encode those aspects of the event that are presupposed, such as the subject or the agent. Along similar lines, many authors consider newness of the information to be the most relevant feature of informativeness. Therefore, arguments representing given referents will be omitted (Bloom 1990; Valian 1991; Hirakawa 1993).

Clancy (1993, 1997) found that omission of arguments in children acquiring Korean is influenced by newness as well as by other features of discourse prominence, including absence, contrast and query. More specifically, an argument is more likely to be omitted in the case of a referent that is animate, present in the context and not contrasted. Allen (2000), Allen and Schröder (2003), Serratrice et al. (2004) and Hughes and Allen (2013) have demonstrated that several of the discourse variables investigated – informativeness or accessibility features – were significant predictors of argument realization in their sample, and that the effect of these features was cumulative. Allen (2000: 486–487) summarizes her findings on child Inuktitut as follows:

> Thus, [children] will tend to omit arguments when the referent of the argument is maximally clear from the discourse and situational context, and they will tend to refrain from omitting arguments when the referent of the argument is in doubt for any reason.

Now, Inuktitut and Korean are argument drop languages; subjects in classic prodrop languages also demonstrate pragmatic sensitivity but the set of features under discussion might differ. Serratrice's (2005) study of Italian found that the feature [person] was a key factor, showing evidence of development, in that third person referents were more likely to be lexicalized. Other main factors in her study were discourse activation and need to disambiguate. Similarly, Paradis and Navarro (2003) analyzed subjects in spontaneous speech in very young bilingual and monolingual Spanish-speaking children. Monolingual children realized overtly arguments that were most informative, in terms of newness, contrast, query, emphasis and absence; but bilingual children realized more overt arguments overall, possibly under influence by English.

Which features turn out to be central for children vary somewhat from study to study. This is not surprising, given that there is a great deal of overlap in these factors, and some variation in the methods of analyses. Kayama (2003) in a study on Japanese found that adults relied more on saliency (in terms of topic-marking) whereas children relied more on (temporal) distance (in discourse). In a recent study of children learning English, Hughes and Allen (2013) found that three accessibility features – physical presence, prior mention and joint attention – were apparent from the age of two. Joint attention is the shared visual focus of two individuals onto an object. It is a common interaction between a child and parent. For instance, a baby looks at a dog, then looks at the mother and the mother looks at the dog and then the baby. Both attend to the same object while at the same time they are showing awareness of the other's attentional focus. Skarabela et al. (2013) propose that joint attention may explain why children omit certain referents that are not yet mentioned in discourse. Their analysis of conversation between Inuktitut children and their mothers suggests that children frequently omitted arguments when joint attention was present, yet used mostly lexical forms when it was not. A common alternative response used demonstratives: children tended to use demonstrative clitics when joint attention was present but preferred the full form when it was absent.

While prior mention lies within the domain of discourse anaphora proper, physical presence and joint attention pertain to exaphora, the linking of referentially dependent forms to the situational context. Physical presence of the referent affects not only omission patterns (in children, and in discourse-oriented languages), but also the types of pronouns used. In adult speech, pronouns (with special reference to third person) are not strictly used anaphorically. Such use of pronouns without an antecedent ranges widely in French and other languages: between 16 percent and 50 percent of pronouns from different corpora lacked NP antecedents (Belzil et al. 2008, and references therein). In spontaneous production, children's use of object clitics in French tends to be exophoric rather than anaphoric (Belzil et al. 2008). In other words, an important number of clitic pronouns are used early on not with a linguistic antecedent but with a contextually available referent instead. This use does not seem confined to pronominal clitics but also extends to strong pronouns (Rozendaal 2006).

This raises a question for a subset of the data that preoccupy us here. Could the physical availability of the referent be responsible for the considerable number of omissions of pronominals in child experimental and naturalistic data (where overt pronouns would be preferred in adult speech)? In other words, are children omitting because they are so focused on the here and now of situations that syntactic forms do not really matter as much?

While clearly playing a role, exophoric uses of null elements could hardly represent the whole story of null arguments in general, nor of null objects specifically. First, if the only cause of omission phenomena were children's hypersensitivity to context, the degree of cross-linguistic variation in the omission of clitics in clitic-languages would not be expected. But, as we saw earlier in Chapter 3, variation is widespread. Focusing on the same age, in comparable studies across varieties of Romance, we saw that object clitics are omitted significantly less in European Spanish and Romanian but appear somewhat later in Colombian Spanish, and much later in French and Catalan, with Italian somewhat in between. The pragmatic strategy based on cognitive-based primacy of argument accessibility predicts universal patterns of omission. Second, as we will discuss in 4.5, pronominal omissions interact with syntactic structure. The conclusion is that there has to be more to the story than pragmatics alone. The key question is how to integrate pragmatic accounts to appropriate grammatical representations. As we look to previous attempts to integrate pragmatic recoverability strategies and syntactic development, two previous proposals stand out: Schaeffer's specificity hypothesis (1997, 2000) and Müller and Hulk's (2001) interface hypothesis.

4.3.2   Schaeffer's Specificity Hypothesis

The first work to simultaneously address the syntax, semantics and pragmatics of objects was that of Schaeffer (1997, 2000). Schaeffer proposed that certain aspects of the syntax of objects can be traced to the concept of nonshared knowledge. Because this pragmatic component is seen as missing in early child grammar, syntactic marking of specificity cannot be established and therefore object movement driven by specificity (object scrambling in Dutch and clitic placement in Italian) is problematic. One of the consequences of this gap in pragmatic knowledge is the inability to mark referentiality on *pro* and, therefore, to license a pronominal clitic. Schaeffer's proposal treats null objects as the result of a formal deficit at the interface between syntax and pragmatics.

This explanation is vulnerable to the criticisms leveled at pure pragmatic approaches, as noted above, namely, that it leads to some expectations of generality. In this case, the generalization is not about a form (null arguments) but about the relevant morphosemantic feature, specificity. If pragmatic-based difficulties with encoding specificity/referentiality was the only factor at stake in clitic omission, we should expect, across languages, all morphosyntactic forms dependent on the same feature to be vulnerable to early optionality. However, there is evidence that this is not the case. In a study of the acquisition of Swahili, Ud Deen (2004) shows that object agreement is acquired very early in Swahili, a language with obligatory agreement for specific direct objects. He finds that children reach 90 percent object agreement marking in obligatory contexts before the age of two, an early development much like that in Peninsular varieties of Spanish. Variation in timing of acquisition is also hard to integrate with accounts that posit such pragmatic deficits. The literature on early argument omission suggests the presence in children of an undeniably high level of general pragmatic sophistication, rather than a deficit in that domain. Importantly, Schaeffer's initial and subsequent work does not make a claim for general pragmatic immaturity. This particular proposal is carefully articulated on the basis of children's ability to distinguish systematically between their own beliefs and the belief state of their interlocutor (see Schaeffer and Matthewson 2005, for a detailed exposition).

Pragmatics is important, but not a cure for all our problems of grammatical development. This is evident in De Cat's (2009) argument that awareness of beliefs states of others (Theory of Mind) is neither necessary nor sufficient for mastery of the pragmatic determinants of subject syntax in French. In her study, children show early sensitivity to the discourse notion of topic, and almost exclusively link null subjects and subject clitics to discourse topics in experimental settings. However, they also continue to use clitics rather than full NPs to encode topics that are not salient enough in the context to avoid ambiguity. This is seen as suggesting that children over-rely on joint attention to minimize what they express with overt syntax. De Cat makes an important point about the nature of the syntax/pragmatics interface:

> The early mastery of the discourse notion of topic, at an age of well-documented processing limitations, implies that the integration of information from syntax and discourse is not per se too demanding for young children. Indeed, if such interface phenomena were by nature so costly to compute, then the architecture of the language faculty would be suboptimal from the start.   (De Cat 2009: 237)

4.3.3   Pragmatics and Syntax Meet Again: Müller and Hulk's Parametric Hypothesis

We have mentioned before Müller and Hulk's (2001) extremely influential proposal about early object omissions. To refresh our memory, these authors were concerned with object omissions in bilingual children simultaneously learning a Germanic and a Romance language. Theoretically, they sought to account for autonomous bilingual development – the fact that bilingual children manage by and large to develop two separate grammars – as well as the possibility of interdependence between the two languages (as evident from the presence of bilingual influence in this domain). While the details of that particular conversation are not of concern here, their formal analysis of illicit omissions involving an empty pronoun (PRO) connected to discourse and situated in the left periphery is of interest.

In their view, this configuration arises from a minimal default grammar, which they articulate under a parametric approach. As mentioned in Section 4.2.1, Müller et al. (1996) and Müller and Hulk (2001) treat omissions in early French as a free topic drop construction of the Chinese/Japanese type. The parameter concerning the direct object construction potentially involves either the availability of topic drop (as in Mandarin or Japanese) or the availability of different types of a null object pronominal *pro* (Müller et al. 1996; Müller and Hulk 2001; Schmitz et al. 2004). The null object in the configuration is a variable and a Chinese-like recoverability mechanism allows the content of the null object to be recovered from the discourse through a null topic that is adjoined at the sentence level (IP):

(8) $[_{IP}$ PRO$_i$ $[_{IP}$ Ivar répare pro$_i]$
        "Ivar fixes."

The change during the acquisition process from a Chinese-type grammar to a French-type grammar is triggered by representation of the clausal (CP) domain, which makes PRO illicit in the adjoined IP position. Refining this parametric approach further, Schmitz et al. (2004) suggest that omissions are due to a Japanese-style grammar where *pro* is present in argument position. This null argument is bound by a discourse identified zero topic.

According to this approach then children drop arguments because they can. Their initial representation allows a direct link to discourse, which, following the strong continuity hypothesis, is analyzed as involving the same mechanisms available in radical prodrop languages. The strength of this approach is that it provides a concrete formalism for how the syntax interfaces with pragmatics. However, their proposal, while laying out some of the groundwork for our own work, runs into some empirical problems. One problem is presented by their own monolingual data: since no correlation is demonstrated between the emergence of elements in the CP field and object clitics, this argues more generally against topic drop analyses of clitic optionality.

The two perspectives summarized so far represent diametrically opposed views as to how pragmatics and syntax are integrated in development. Under a pragmatic deficit model, children lack something in their pragmatic component, thus the syntax cannot be fully implemented. The second model attributes to the child representations that allow nontarget yet UG-compliant forms of recoverability while granting to children full pragmatic competence. This competence, manifested in the form of sensitivity to discourse and contextual features, is situated inside a specific construction, namely as topic drop.

If the first type of perspective pictures the pragmatic glass as half empty, the second deems it to be half full. So, although pragmatics and syntax likely both contribute to the null object stage in L1 acquisition, previous analyses have not succeeded in shedding light on the division of labour between them and the way they interact to produce this stage. The key to this interaction, we argue, is to be found in the input children are exposed to in the acquisition process. We proposed in Chapter 3 that cross-linguistic variation in the rates of omission is part of the signal. We showed that children are faced with substantial ambiguity in that omissions of the type in (9) are compatible with an object drop grammar:

(9)   I wish you'd stop hitting.

Intransitive instances of a verb as in the construction in (9) cannot be used to solve this particular parametric problem: whether the boy is hitting his brother, or just hitting is not particularly helpful in determining how a particular grammar functions since the latter includes the former: "hitting someone" is in a subset relationship with "hitting." It represents a semantic subset of the kind referred to by Crain and Thornton (1998). Learnability thus seems to be on the side of the null object approach because it predicts that the narrowest interpretation (anaphoric) should be available first such that "hitting" could mean "hitting someone" without overt expression of the object. Taken as a whole, context sensitivity supports this view but more fine-grained evidence is called for here. To obtain it, we must move out of the domain of production into that of comprehension.

4.4   *A Null Hypothesis for Null Objects: Experimental Approaches to Comprehension*

Many dimensions of grammatical learning go through extended stages of optionality. This leads to conflicting criteria for when a morpheme can be considered as acquired, which range between first productive uses vs. 90 percent insertion in obligatory contexts (see Paradis and Genesee 1997, for a relevant discussion). Logically, grammatical omissions can be considered in PF terms, derivational terms or LF terms. In essence, the whole grammar!

It is important to bear in mind that these are not competing possibilities; different kinds of factors may independently play a role in early grammatical omissions. However, in principle, one should be able to isolate the specific contribution of each of these dimensions even if, in the real world, everything happens at once. Starting from the left side (the PF interface), there is a solid body of evidence suggesting that rates of omission of various grammatical forms depend on the morphophonological and prosodic characteristics of the forms (e.g., prosody has been implicated in patterns of omission of determiners, plural *–s,* and other constituents). This is known as the Prosodic Bootstrapping Hypothesis (Demuth 1996; Demuth and Tremblay 2008, among others). For example, evidence from Greek (Tzakosta 2003) suggests that enclitics are less vulnerable to omission than proclitics. Similarly, in Spanish, Mateu (2015) shows that children perform better when the sentence is simpler (i.e., when it has fewer constituents and uses a simple instead of periphrastic tense). The position of the clitic is also a significant factor; children perform best when the clitic is in utterance final position, which is considered a salient position in processing, and otherwise, with preverbal rather than postverbal clitics.

Omission may also depend on factors related to the formal structure (syntax), the semantic representation (semantics) or, as we have seen, the interaction between meaning and context (pragmatics). As Paradis and Genesee (1997) indicate, it is not clear how nonuse or erroneous use in the intermediate phases can be dealt with only in morphosyntactic terms. In Chapter 3 we showed that proposals that focus only on clitic structures are insufficient because the properties of object omission extend to languages with no clitics, whether they are pronominal languages like English or Topic drop languages like Chinese and Japanese. Our account thus focuses on the interpretative side. Our specific proposal is that both optionality itself and variation in the rates of development across languages are a consequence of the natural course of development for morphosemantic knowledge. There is nothing extraordinary about this assumption: we have no guarantee that a form in children's language will have the same mapping as the same form in the adult grammar. Similar proposals have surfaced for other grammatical contrasts. In their study of early determiner optionality, Gavarro, Pérez-Leroux and Roeper (2006) suggest that bare nouns are possible in both adult and child language but have different semantic extensions (see Section 4.2.3.2 above). We consider the development away from the null object stage to be driven (at least in part) by children learning to restrict and fine-tune the various possible interpretations. However, taking this approach commits us to going beyond production and to seek evidence in children's interpretation of sentences with missing objects.

Others as well have attempted to elucidate clitic optionality via the comprehension route, for different purposes. These works seek to evaluate the possibility that clitic omission is exclusively a production phenomenon, under the assumption that production difficulties will not be evident in comprehension. Grüter's (2006) Decayed Feature Hypothesis is the first explicit model to pursue this.

(10)   Decayed Features Hypothesis (DFH)

Under limited working memory capacity, a syntactic long-distance Agree relation between two elements h_1 and h_2 may be computed incompletely, due to the activation level of (some of) h_1's features having decayed below the required threshold level by the time h_2 is merged. This may result in the underspecification of h_1 and/or h_2, and thus affect the choice of the relevant vocabulary item(s) selected at MS (Morphological Structure). (Grüter 2006: 178)

The DFH states that clitics are omitted because features decay on the path from base position to a higher clitic position. In taking this step, Grüter continues a long line of argumentation linking clitic optionality to computational difficulties stemming from the clitic configuration. As discussed in Chapter 3, according to authors such as Jakubowicz and Rigaut (2000), Jakubowicz and Nash (to appear) and Prévost (2006), children have difficulties with clitics because of their preverbal, noncanonical argument position. Grüter's work departs from these earlier computational accounts in that it concretely formalizes the role of online performance in the production of utterances with missing clitics. Under the DFH, omission (or underspecification) happens at the point of vocabulary insertion. The selection process linked to vocabulary insertion depends on the morphosyntactic features associated with a head position. If phi-features are decayed, either underspecification or omission can be expected. Decay depends on syntactic distance in the derivation, whose effects may only become apparent when there are limitations in working memory, such as in children.

This type of feature decay approach has two consequences. First, it predicts an association between children's clitic problems and limitations in their working memory. Second, it predicts a comprehension/production asymmetry. Because omission is linked to lexical retrieval in production, children should omit in production but succeed in comprehension. Comprehension evidence, according to Grüter, is essential to compare performance-based and representation-based accounts. This intuition is maintained, albeit with a different formalization, in Grüter's later work (Grüter and Crago 2012). While we agree on the centrality of evidence from comprehension, our approach happens to make the exact opposite prediction: if object optionality results from the availability of additional meanings for null objects, we should be able to tap into those meanings by studying null objects in comprehension. Comprehension studies have been conducted using two different methodological approaches with divergent results. Because the findings are contradictory, and the stakes are high, we pay much more attention to methodology in this section than we did in discussing other studies. Doing so leads to an elaboration of the role of the verbal lexicon in performance, foreshadowing some of the discussion in Chapter 5.

Constructing an experiment for null objects in comprehension is tricky business. One must find a way to make an objectless sentence contrast with a sentence with an overt object. The experimental literature has managed to find not one but two solutions to this problem. One solution is built on the causative/inchoative alternation; the other is built on optional transitivity.

4.4.1 Causative/Inchoative Alternation

In this type of alternation, the subject of the intransitive variant (inchoative) corresponds to the theme argument of the transitive equivalent (causative), as illustrated in (11).

(11)   a. The ball rolled down the hill.
         b. John rolled the ball down the hill.

A comprehension experiment can be built in order to test whether a subject+verb sequence corresponds to the inchoative sentence or to a causative sentence with a null object. Crucially, the scenarios corresponding to the inchoative interpretation and the causative interpretation do not overlap. All that is needed is an animate argument that can function as either the theme or the agent. Take (12) for instance.

(12)   John rolled.

Although in English this sentence can only be inchoative, the verb *roll* can also be used in a transitive construction and therefore could potentially be causative (meaning "John rolled something"). So, let's imagine that it can be inchoative in English, in which case we get two possible interpretations.

(13)   John rolled. = inchoative or causative

Crucially, the target interpretations are nonoverlapping. That "John is rolling down the hill" does not entail that "John is rolling something down the hill." Conversely, he can roll something without he himself rolling. There is no overlap in the scenarios to which each interpretation applies.

John himself rolling	John rolling something (but not himself)

In a null object grammar this sentence should be ambiguous, as schematized in (14).

(14)   a.   John rolled.   b.   John rolled Ø.
              theme   agent   theme

Applied to the work presented here, it could be assumed that children in the null object stage might be able to judge the sentence to be true in causative contexts. This approach is conditional on speakers' willingness to access both argument frames for the intransitive entry of the verb.

Grüter (2006, 2007) took this causative/inchoative route in designing her comprehension experiment. Her stories featured Caillou (a well-known character from a popular Francophone TV cartoon series), Dora (from a different TV series) and some other relevant inanimate objects, which were made salient in discourse and present in the accompanying picture. Those objects were meant to serve as potential antecedents to the null object in the causative frame, if such a null object was available in the child grammar. An example is given in Figure 4.1

Based on this illustration, children were asked to verify the validity of simple statements such as those given in (15).

(15)   a.   Caillou is hiding.   (Adult response: NO)
         b.   Caillou is hiding the car.   (Adult response: YES)
         c.   Caillou is hiding it.   (Adult response: YES)

In a transitive scenario, such as depicted in Figure 4.1, an adult response to an intransitive sentence would be negative (since Caillou is not hiding himself), while pronouns and DPs would be acceptable. Grüter speculated that if children have access to a null object representation, they should treat the statement in (15a) as ambiguous, accepting it both in response to scenes where Caillou was hiding the car (as in Figure 4.1), as well as to scenes where Caillou himself had hidden, which corresponds to the only acceptable possibility in English.

Figure 4.1 *An illustration of a transitive (causative) scenario (From Grüter 2007: 105)*

Since the choice depends on lexical ambiguity, Grüter predicted that the interpretation for this condition (which she calls the "null object" condition) should be (at least) occasionally available for children with a null object grammar. Consequently, even a low number of acceptances would be sufficient to support a null object grammar. However, very few children (in either English or French) accepted sentences with a null object interpretation (Grüter 2006, 2007). At the same time, children had no problem accepting transitive sentences in the causative scenarios or accepting the intransitive sentences in the inchoative scenarios. Grüter interprets this as evidence against the existence of referential null objects.

Grüter and Crago (2012) investigated null objects in comprehension and production in older children learning French as a second language, from both a Chinese and a Spanish background. They predicted that frequency of object clitic omission should be negatively correlated with working memory. Spanish learners of French produced clitics and DPs and few omissions, but the Chinese learners had nulls as their primary response to the elicitation task. For these learners, object omissions were correlated to an independent measure of working memory capacity (e.g., nonword repetition span), a fact that they interpret to support the performance hypothesis. Neither group accepted the null object condition. Grüter and Crago conclude that null objects do not transfer from the Chinese L1 into the French L2.

One noticeable pattern in the Grüter and Crago data is the relatively high rates of errors in the two conditions involving utterances with object clitics.

> ([S]ome) learners in both groups failed to accept utterances with a clitic in a transitive context, and failed to reject the same utterance in an intransitive context. This pattern of performance would be explained if a learner simply ignored preverbal clitics, which would render the utterance intransitive, and thus "false" in a transitive context (as presented in the TRANSITIVE (CLITIC) condition), and "true" in an intransitive context (as presented in the SUPERFLUOUS CLITIC condition).   (Grüter and Crago 2012: 10)

In other words, children heard a clitic sentence such as *Dora le monte sur le rocher* "Dora lifts it up the rock" and rejected it when Dora was lifting the backpack (with error rates of 25 percent for both groups of L2 learners), or accepted it when Dora herself was climbing up the rock (with 50 percent errors for the Chinese L1 group, and 18 percent for the Spanish L1) group. Mateu (2015) found a similar effect in children learning Spanish in Los Angeles, using a picture choice task instead of a truth-value judgment task. Younger children only managed to match the clitic sentence to the causative-transitive scene in 55 percent–60 percent of the trials, while four-year-olds managed to do it successfully 77 percent of the time (just above three out of four trials). As in Grüter's studies, children did not choose transitive pictures when the sentences had no overt object. Performance in those conditions was above 90 percent correct. In sum, intransitives were intransitives, but clitics were vulnerable and sometimes ignored.

How can we interpret this? Grüter (2006, 2007) and Mateu (2015) observe no null object errors but some clitic errors. We can propose a simpler explanation, which becomes prominent as soon as the lexical factor is taken seriously. Both these observations can result from a simple lexical preference for the intransitive entry of the verb. Grüter's children may reject the null object condition because this option is not salient to them. As pointed out by Wexler (2004), the causative/inchoative alternation is not productive in some languages (French and Spanish included). At the same time, there is an extensive body of evidence that children initially find this alternation difficult, and are initially unable to apply it to novel verbs (Tomasello 2000). An alternative account becomes obvious: perhaps children reject *He is hiding* in a context where Caillou is hiding the car because they simply fail to activate the transitive entry. That same lexical bias for the intransitive entry could lead them to ignore the clitic when present. As evidence against a causative gap in children's lexicon, Grüter cites the high rates of acceptance in the transitive condition (86 percent and 80 percent in different versions of the experiment). But this argument is not ironclad since children accept ungrammatical causatives structures. Naigles and Lehrer (2002) show that children are happy to comply with a transitive frame even if it is incompatible with the standard meaning of the verb (e.g., *Le tigre va le lion/ *The tiger goes the lion*).

Seeking to establish whether the causative entries of the verbs in her study were available at all, a subgroup of the children in her study were given another elicitation task to test whether they could use the causative entry in causative contexts. This task was identical to the standard elicitation task in the studies in Chapter 3 with prompts such as the one in (16).

(16)   What is Caillou doing with the car?

Grüter (2006: 46) concludes:

> In sum, there is indeed no absolute guarantee that the results reported in this chapter, i.e., the consistent rejection of null objects by French-speaking children, are not due simply to a strong preference for one interpretation of the test sentences over the other. However, there are at least three arguments that suggest that such an explanation is unlikely. First, French-speaking children rejected null objects just as often as English-speaking children. Second, at least two of the verbs used in the experiment were found in their transitive use in children's own speech, in two cases even with a missing object. And third, as pointed out earlier (6.1), the typical underlying "yes"-bias among children (Crain and Thornton 1998: 213) stacked the cards in favor of acceptance of null objects.

We find the assumption that the two tasks are doing the same thing questionable. In the elicited production task, the question sets up the object to be considered in the answer: the question is begging for a transitive answer. The intransitive entry would not even be considered; it would represent, at best, an implicit denial that the target object is implied and, at worst, a non sequitur (17).

(17)   A: What are you doing with that cake?
        B: I am dancing/hiding, etc.

A neutral statement, as used in the original Grüter experiment, which simply describes some elements in a visual context does nothing to force the speaker to include the object (the car) in the interpretation of the sentence given to judge. Hearers are free to assume that the utterance is about the subject and go with whichever lexical entry suits them best. Data from Portuguese prove this is the case. In such neutral contexts, Costa and Lobo (2009) found they could not elicit null object interpretations in Portuguese even though Portuguese is a null object language:

> While piloting the test, we realized that the eliciting sentence was crucial for obtaining answers compatible with the adult grammar, namely for obtaining a transitive reading for null objects. Therefore, a neutral lead-in sentence, like "let's see what happened", even with previously mentioned referents, did not provide an adequate context for eliciting a null object.   (Costa and Lobo 2009: 155).

To succeed at elicitation of a null object interpretation, these authors combined a direct prompt of the same type used in elicitation of pronouns with a deictic command (*look!*).

Lead: *Vamos ver o que o Rui fez ao cão.* Puppet: *Olha! Mergulhou na piscina!*
"Let's see what Rui did to the dog"   look   dove   in. the pool.
                                                      "Look! He dove it in the pool"
                                             [Adult answer: True]

Figure 4.2 *Example of test item for the null object condition (Costa and Lobo 2009: 72)*

In sum, when the prompt was neutral, Portuguese children did not opt for the null object. The available causative and inchoative options became accessible only when the target was preceded by a lead context; this is an important point of differentiation between Costa and Lobo's and Grüter's studies. This closes the case: asking for a judgment based on neutral prompts does not elicit null object interpretations, even in a language long known for its null object constructions (Raposo 1986).

To investigate the presence of null object interpretations in children's grammar, we really need to look elsewhere. We propose to go through the second experimental route, based on the optional transitivity alternation, where the agent argument remains the subject in both the transitive and intransitive frame.

4.4.2 Optional Transitivity

In comprehension, the problem with optional transitivity is that the two alternants do not lead to disjunct interpretations because the interpretation of a sentence with the overt object alternant is a semantic subset of the null object counterpart.

(18)   Johnny is eating that sandwich. ⊃ Johnny is eating.

Constructing a contrast in truth-values is more complicated with optional transitivity. To put it concretely, every situation of generic "eating" (which we call an activity interpretation meaning "eating something") includes situations in which something specific gets eaten.

Eating something	Eating a sandwich

The solution to this problem was hinted at earlier. Negation provides a way to eliminate the obligatory overlap. In a language like English, the null object is equivalent to a variable bound by an existential operator, with negation taking scope over it: *not eating* means "not eating anything," at least in adult English (19a). However, if *not eating* contained an anaphoric null object, this anaphoric null object, just like its overt pronoun or definite counterpart, would take scope over the negative operator (19b).

(19)   a. $\neg\exists x, eat(j, x)$
         b. $\lambda x!, \neg eat(j, x)$

Crucially, these two senses can apply to nonoverlapping scenarios. A situation of "not eating the sandwich" can extend to the situation of "not eating anything," but not necessarily so. Simply put, if you say that you did not eat the sandwich, you are not saying that you did not eat anything.

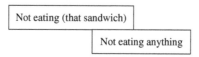

Embedding the verb under a negative operator thus de-couples the referential and the activity interpretations. We can then easily construct a scene where it is true for someone to not be eating a sandwich, but clearly false that the person is not eating anything. All it takes is something else that the person could plausibly be eating. To build an experiment on this approach requires that we demonstrate first that children can successfully judge negative sentences and that they can do so for the types of stories involved. We will return to this later; for now let's see how the solution based on negation has been implemented.

Two different experiments were independently developed on this basis. Tedeschi (2009) tested it in Italian, and Pérez-Leroux et al. (2008b) tested it in English. These two studies had slightly different implementations of the negation approach and arrived at similar results but reached distinct conclusions.

In one of the scenarios set up by Tedeschi (2009), a boy attempts to catch a smart fish but the fish escapes and the boy catches a frog instead. Italian-speaking children aged three and four participated in the exchange in (20).

(20)   Now, let's see if the puppet paid attention.
        Lumachina (a puppet), do you remember? There was a frog and a fish.
                        Cosa è successo al pesce?
                        "What happened to the fish?"
        Puppet's answer: Gino non ha pescato!
                        Gino NEG has fished (=caught)

Under the anaphoric reading ("he did not fish/catch it"), the puppet's answer is true. It is false, however, with the interpretation that Gino did not fish, because he did indeed fish something. Children often accepted these sentences (46 percent) but adults also accepted them at nonnegligible rates (30 percent). Tedeschi notes that there is a mismatch between the question under discussion (*what happened to the fish?*) and the statement (since the fish is not actually involved in the fishing event). She concludes that the null object interpretation exhibited by the participants has a pragmatic basis, with listeners forced to work with the most plausible interpretation. In her account, omissions happen because children over rely on the pragmatic principle of informativeness and, as a result, do not produce elements whose referents are easily accessible in the common ground. As such, this explanation is subject to the same criticism as pragmatics-only approaches.

In Pérez-Leroux et al. (2008b), we also implemented the negation approach using a truth-value judgment task. The stories were set up differently, in a way that there was no mismatch between the question under discussion and the target stimulus. The children's task was to evaluate the appropriateness of a statement provided by Froggy, a puppet portrayed as an unreliable storyteller. During a training phase, we established that the children were capable of judging simple negative sentences, without null objects. Children were presented sentences such as (21) and prompted to judge whether Froggy was right.

(21)   She is not wearing her red pyjamas.

    [True in a scenario where the pyjamas are pink]

Children were then presented with short stories as a preamble to the negative sentence in the intransitive form. The first picture, and the accompanying story, introduces an antecedent for the potential null object, namely, the fish (22).

(22)   David brought a fish to his mother, and says "Mommy can you cook this fish for dinner?" So, what do you think? Is the mother going to cook the fish or not? Froggy, what's happening in the next picture?

The second picture established that the potential antecedent was eventually not involved in the relevant event. In this case, the fish was not the object of the cooking. The illustration was designed to provide a rationale for why this is so, in this case, because the cat got the fish.

In the null object condition, the puppet describes the scene using the intransitive entry for the target verb (23).

(23)   Froggy: Oh look, the cat got the fish, so the mother is not cooking Ø.
        Experimenter: Is that right?
        Participant: No (Target)
        Experimenter: How come?
        Participant: Well, she is cooking eggs.

Figure 4.3 *Introduction of an Antecedent for the Potential Null Object: the Fish*

As the illustration shows that the mother is engaged in the target event with an alternative antecedent (i.e., eggs), the sentence *the mother is not cooking* can only be true if children allow a referential interpretation of the null object, i.e., the mother is not *cooking it,* meaning the fish. Under the activity interpretation, meaning the mother is *not cooking anything*, the sentence ought to be judged as false.

In a series of three studies, such null object sentences were counterbalanced with three different overt object conditions: pronouns, headless relatives and overt quantifiers. Consider Figure 4.4 as you read the following:

Study 1   Pronoun control: the mother is not cooking Ø vs. . . . is not cooking it.
Study 2   Headless relative control: the mother is not cooking Ø vs. . . . is not cooking what David brought.
Study 3   Quantifier control: the mother is not cooking Ø vs. . . . is not cooking anything.

Results indicated that for the intransitive form (*not cooking Ø*) English-speaking children generally preferred the anaphoric interpretation over the

Figure 4.4 *The Antecedent "Fish" Is Not Involved in the Relevant Event*

activity interpretation by a ratio of 3:1. Adults were more accurate but, as in Tedeschi's study, not perfect.

Children's performance with the overt object conditions was excellent. With overt object pronouns they gave close to 90 percent correct responses. With headless relatives in object position rates of rejections were similarly low. In each of these cases, there were substantively more rejections of the null objects than of the overt objects, indicating that a) children distinguished between the conditions, and b) that the activity interpretation remained available for the null object sentences.

Could these results simply reflect children's unwillingness to reject false targets? The training scenarios suggested this was not the case, but the true test was study three, which pitted null objects against quantified objects. Here, while acceptance was still the primary response for null objects, children correctly rejected quantifier sentences at levels that approximated those of adults. For adults, the activity reading is equivalent to the negative polarity quantifier sentence; adult performance with nulls and quantifiers was comparable in this version of the study. However, this was not the case for children.

This eliminates the possibility that over acceptance is due to pragmatic failure. The scenarios were explicitly designed to provide plausible reasons for dissent: *the mother is not cooking (the fish), because the cat got it* and she is in fact cooking something else. The story script openly encourages consideration of both alternatives: *So, what do you think, is the mother going to cook the fish or not?* Children were given sufficient warning and plenty of opportunities to reject the negative utterance. They did not take advantage of this opportunity for the null objects but had no problem doing so for overt quantifiers. This is as strong a piece of evidence as we could have hoped for.

4.4.3   Discussion

From the perspective of performance approaches the null assumption is that children's comprehension reflects their true grammar and their production reflects their capacity limitations. These approaches explicitly follow the logic of strong continuity, which a priori establishes that by the time we can study it grammatical learning has already taken place. For the null object approach, the null assumption is that both production and comprehension are reasonable exponents of the underlying grammar. The null hypothesis that children would treat nulls as they do other anaphoric elements is supported by our experiments.

For the null object approach, optionality in anaphoric contexts in production is taken to suggest that children allow such interpretations for their null objects, and that this interpretation needs to be expunged from the grammar. The evidence provided by children's interpretation of implicit objects under the scope of negation supports the existence of the null object stage. The strongest continuity approach would reject the likelihood of such a stage, possibly on learnability grounds. But note that elimination of the referential null object interpretation is not particularly mysterious as a learning step. It might take place by virtue of negative evidence (scenarios such as those developed here could provide the right triggering contexts), by positive evidence (as in Yang 2002, by simply rewarding the successful parses in activity contexts) or by bootstrapping (the association of implicit objects with adverbs and other contextual elements that favour the generic object/activity interpretation). Settling the development question would require a different kind of evidence from that examined here. However, we have clearly established that the performance account is not more parsimonious than the representational alternative and, under careful examination, not especially well supported by evidence from comprehension studies.

In our discussion, we left aside the argument of the association between verbal working memory and clitic omission. Recall that Grüter and Crago (2012) observed that Chinese-speaking learners' object omissions in production were negatively correlated with an independent measure of working memory (backward digit span); they concluded that object clitic omission is affected by processing limitations. Similarly, Mateu (2015) found that the only significant factor for object omission in elicited production was verbal working memory, which could account for most of the variance in their statistical model. This variable also turned out to be significant in the clitic comprehension errors in this study. While this piece of evidence is very important it does not warrant the inference that omission is a performance-only phenomenon. Firstly, by itself, it cannot explain why children learning Spanish stop omitting earlier than children learning French; memory is memory, age is age, and there is thus no reason for it to operate differently across languages. Secondly, verbal working memory for language correlates with many aspects of grammatical development (Gathercole and Baddeley 1993), therefore it is not surprising to find a correlation with clitic performance but it does not help characterize the null object phenomenon in a conclusive way.

Having shown that a null object is present in children's comprehension and production, it should be possible to reveal ways in which the interpretation of the syntactically present null object is sensitive to its syntactic environment.

4.5   Detecting the Presence of Null Objects

In this section, we show that object omission interacts with various syntactic phenomena, such as the manipulation of person features in subject position, left-dislocation and island constructions. All these suggest that, at least in these contexts, null objects in child grammar are present and behave as belonging to anaphoric dependencies. These data are also meant to strengthen the idea that reliance on pragmatics is mediated by the syntactic structure.

4.5.1   *Clitic Left-Dislocation*

Testing clitic left-dislocation can also reveal the anaphoric properties of the null object in child French. In French (and other Romance languages) topics are usually dislocated elements with both discourse and syntactic factors at play (Reinhart 1981; Lambrecht 1994; De Cat 2007). The Clitic Left-Dislocation (CLLD) construction involves a pronominal clitic that establishes the link between the topic and the complement position occupied by a null referential category *pro*. An example is provided in (24) (from Pérez-Leroux et al. 2011: 283).

(24)   a. Ton livre, tu devrais le   donner à Paul.
          your book you should it-CL-3SG-ACC give to Paul
       b. [$_{Top}$ Ton livre$_i$ [$_{IP}$ tu devrais le$_i$ donner pro$_i$ à Paul]]

De Cat (2004, 2009) shows that topics are encoded early in child production as dislocated elements (from age 2;06, in both naturalistic settings and experimental contexts). For example, in her experimental study eliciting subject topics (De Cat 2009), the youngest group (2;06 to 3;04) was able to use full dislocated NP 43 percent of the time, an older group (3;05 to 4;06) did so 46 percent of the time while for the oldest group (4;06 to 5;06) the proportion climbed to 84 percent. The rest of the answers still showed that children were highly sensitive to the topic status of the referent, using either clitics or null subjects without dislocation.

Research shows that object clitic production is drastically limited in the left-dislocation structures (Pérez-Leroux, Pirvulescu and Roberge 2011). Recall that in our original elicitation task (*What is she doing with the flower?*) a pronominal answer was expected (*she is drawing it*) but a nominal answer was also possible (*she is drawing the flower*), although not as felicitously. Left-dislocation in French on the other hand is a context where pronominal object clitics are normally considered obligatory (25).

(25)   a. J'ai   vu   Paul, mais Jean, je   ne l'   ai   pas vu.
          I have seen Paul but Jean I   not him-CL-3SG-ACC have NEG seen
       b. *?J' ai   vu   Paul,   mais Jean, je n'   ai   pas vu.
          I   have seen Paul   but Jean I   not   have NEG seen
       c. *J'   ai   vu   Paul,   mais Jean, je n'   ai   pas vu Jean.
          I   have seen Paul   but Jean I   not   have NEG seen Jean
          "I saw Paul but John, I did not see (him/John)."

This provides an ideal setting for further experimentation on null objects, which was done in Pérez-Leroux et al. (2011) using the set-up in (26), where children were asked to complete the sentence uttered by the experimenter.

(26)   Experimenter: Elle mange le sandwich, mais la pomme, elle ne ...
                         she eats the sandwich but the apple she neg
                         "She is eating the sandwich but the apple she (is) not ..."
       Expected answer: [i.e., starting point for completion]
                         la   mange pas.
                         It-CL-3SG-F-ACC eats   not
                         "(is) not eating it."

The results show a rate of omission that is even higher than in the experiment eliciting object clitics in simple clauses, where the clitic is only optimal and a full DP is possible, as stated above. An example of omission is provided here:

(27)   Prompt: Elle construit un château mais la voiture, elle ne ...
                 "She is building the castle but the car she is not ..."
                 Ø construit pas.
                   build not
                 "not building."

Omission of the clitic is uniformly high across the three age groups tested (three-, four- and five-year-olds), between 57 percent and 50 percent, with significant clitic responses only in the oldest group (37.8 percent). Importantly, as in De Cat's (2009) study, the clitic left-dislocation syntactic context is understood and complied with by the children, in the sense that they do not use DPs, which would be illicit (see (25c)). At the same time, this context forces them to use a syntactically referential null object if they do not use the expected pronominal clitic. Similarly, in De Cat's (2009) subject topic experiment children sometimes also prefer a null element to encode the target topic referent, in a reduced clause (no left-dislocated element):

(28)   Ø fait   dodo.
       Ø makes sleep
       "S/he is sleeping."

Interestingly, null subjects in subject position disappear in the older group (4;06 to 5;06), parallel to a significant drop in the use of the subject clitic in this reduced option. De Cat (2009) interprets this as indication that these are missing clitics, but does not elaborate on how this omission should be represented (morphophonological or syntactic). In Pérez-Leroux et al. (2011), we show that the results in CLLD structures suggest that the missing element is a referential null object.

4.5.2   *Person Manipulation Experiments*

Null objects in child language can also be shown to interact with their syntactic environment in what can appear at first to be puzzling ways. For instance, previous studies show that patterns of clitic optionality fluctuate based on the different syntactic and/or conversational contexts in which they are situated. One such study, Hill and Pirvulescu (2012), showed that the conversational setup – vs. context of indirect address – can have a significant impact on clitic omission. The rate of clitic omission is significantly higher in the context of indirect address such as when, for instance, a child talks about a character using a third person subject. Below we give examples of the contrast between the direct address condition (29) and the indirect address condition (30).

(29) Direct address elicitation procedure, with second person subject and third person object
Lead: Tu vois ici j'ai des sous. Maintenant regarde et écoute bien: je mets les sous dans la tirelire.
"You see, I have pennies. Now listen and look at what I'm doing: I am putting the pennies in the piggy bank."
Acting: The experimenter puts the pennies in the piggy bank.
Prompt: Dis-moi, qu'est-ce que je fais avec les sous?
"Tell me, what am I doing with the pennies?"
Acting: The action is still going on.
Expected answer: Tu les   mets dans la tirelire/dedans.
                          you them-PL-ACC put   in   the piggy bank/inside
                          "You are putting them in the piggy bank/inside."
Clitic omission answer: Tu mets Ø dans la tirelire/dedans.
                          you put   in   the piggy bank/inside

(30) Indirect address elicitation procedure, with third person subject/object
Lead: La mère a donné à sa fille un verre de lait. Et tu vois ici, la fille boit le lait.
"The mother gave her daughter a glass of milk. See here, the girl is drinking the milk."
Picture: A girl drinking milk
Prompt: Qu'est-ce qu'elle fait avec le lait?
"What is she doing with the milk?"
Expected answer: Elle le   boit.
                          she it-CL-3SG-ACC drinks
                          "She is drinking it."
Clitic omission answer: Elle boit.
                          she drinks
                          "She drinks."

Hill and Pirvulescu (2012) analyze the higher rate of object omission in direct address contexts (29) as a syntax-pragmatic interface effect. They suggest that the person features of the subject play a role in the left periphery of the clause and interfere with the syntactic computation of object clitics. Pirvulescu et al. (2012) replicated these results and refined the analysis using the model proposed by Sigurðsson (2011). The model provides different types of definite null objects and devises a mechanism through which these null arguments interact with overt manifestations of features of the syntactic and/or pragmatic context. This provides an interesting framework for the object clitic system in French, in particular for the child grammar where null objects are used alongside object clitics. Applying the distinction between phi-silent null arguments (Chinese argument-drop type) and phi-visible null arguments (Pashto null objects recovered by agreement) to null objects in French, Pirvulescu et al. (2012) link the null object, associated with a clitic, to a constituent in the edge of the clause (C-domain) that probes for a goal under Agree. They hypothesize that, contrary to the adult grammar, the child grammar contains a phi-silent null argument that is subject to intervention effects. According to Sigurðsson, "Radically phi-silent arguments differ from phi-overt arguments (including Romance Ø-Tphi) in that their C/edge linking is invisible, hence uninterpretable across a spelled-out intervener in the C-system" (Sigurðsson 2011: 270) Pirvulescu et al. (2012) propose that the following constructions are available in the child grammar for the direct object argument:

(31)   a. $[_{CP} \ldots CLn \ldots [_{TP} \ldots \emptyset \ldots]]$ = object omission > phi-silent; in situ null object
       b. $[_{CP} \ldots CLn \ldots [_{TP} \ldots Cl \ldots \emptyset \ldots]]$ = clitic construction > phi-overt; raising null object
       c. $[_{CP} \ldots CLn \ldots [_{TP} \ldots DP \ldots]]$ = overt DP object

In direct address contexts, with second person subjects, object clitic omission is disfavored and this can be interpreted as an intervention effect: the second person subject is an intervener between the C/edge linker and the null object. So for (31a), there would be impossibility of linking the null object, as shown in (32).

(32) $[_{CP} \ldots CLn \ldots\ldots [_{TP} \text{Subj 2pers} \ldots V \emptyset \ldots]]$

In contrast, (31b) is not problematic as the null object (assumed to be a *pro* in this case) links to the C/edge through the overt pronominal clitic which constitutes an overt trace of the linking, necessary according to Sigurðsson's model.

Effects of the syntactic context are also observed in object omissions in European Portuguese, where children overgenerate null objects both in contexts where clitics are not obligatory and in contexts where they are. However, in one of these latter contexts, a strong island construction, the rate of omission is lower than in the contexts where clitics are not obligatory indicating a level of sensitivity to the syntactic environment (Costa et al. 2012).[10]

4.6   Conclusion

As Roeper (2007: 127) puts it: "grammar carves out mental images in the mind that are so precise they give structure to silence itself." In this chapter, we explored some of the tools used by the grammar to 'carve' structure out of silence. We argued that the existence of a null object stage and the cross-linguistic differences observed in its duration, as established in Chapter 3, can be accounted for through an interaction between the Transitivity Requirement (presence of an object), pragmatics (the silent nature of the object) and the DP-to-N approach to the development of nominals in L1 acquisition (properties of the null object).

Grammar and pragmatics took center stage in this chapter as we attempted to demonstrate how their interaction is at the core of object omission phenomena in L1 acquisition. However, let's take a step back and recall the commonly shared – but incorrect – intuition discussed in Chapter 2 that learning transitivity and how to use verbs and their direct object is a matter of learning that there are verbs that take an object while some do not. Does claiming that this view is wrong commit us to denying any role to the lexicon and lexical learning? Not at all; in Chapter 5, the lexicon reclaims top billing.

---

[10] Another notable work on omission in island constructions is that of Brunetto (2010), who shows that clitic production is boosted in island constructions in Italian. Varlokosta et al. (2016) obtained high rates of clitic production across sixteen languages in an elicitation production task using a strong island context. Their results are less relevant for our discussion because they only tested five-year-old children. At this age, omissions are drastically limited in the standard root contexts as well.

5   *How Unusual Is Your Object?*

5.1   *Introduction*

Our null object approach is based on the fundamental assumption that missing components of sentences must be recovered. This is standard reasoning in generative grammar: null subjects, displaced elements, verbal and nominal ellipsis are generally treated in this way. However, there is no universal agreement as to how this standard view applies in the case of direct objects if at all, and if it does, whether it does for all verbs. We have argued that transitivity is a syntactic property and that it applies universally: across languages, across constructions and across lexical items. The lexical transitivity continuum simply reflects a selectional fact, but with underlying structural uniformity. The goal of this chapter is to spell out the consequence of this approach for the acquisition of lexical transitivity and to review the relevant acquisition evidence. But before we do that, we first review the basic facts of lexical transitivity.

5.2   *Lexical Transitivity*

As we know, verbs vary in their likelihood of being accompanied by a direct object. Intuitively, there seems to be an inverse relation between the range of types of direct objects a verb admits as a complement and the possibility of dropping that complement. The lighter the verb, the more obligatory its object appears. Light verbs impose little if any selectional requirements on their objects, thus accepting a wide range of objects:

(1)   a. Finish the dissertation/the boat/the race/dessert/painting the house/a magazine
        b. Get some money/coffee/sick/a job/a house/a husband/her husband.
        c. Take care/your passport/a magazine/the train/a pill/.

Their objects are essential to complete the meaning of the predicate; objects in essence define this meaning. Both *finish the dissertation* and *finish the boat* imply acts of creation, but the situations involved in each case are very different. A magazine and a dissertation both denote printed works, but upon hearing the minimal pair of sentences *John finished the dissertation* and *John finished the magazine*, we normally interpret them in complementary fashion, as "writing" vs. "reading," as such verbs actually select an event that remains implicit (i.e., "John finished reading the magazine"), resolving the discrepancy via the semantic operation of coercion (Pylkkänen 2008). But even verbs that straightforwardly select an NP are radically polysemous: *take a pill* is an ingestion event; *take the train* is not. Small differences in the complement give rise to radical meaning shifts: A single woman may set out *to get a husband*, but only a married woman can *get her husband*, say, to come meet the new neighbor.

Given these considerations it comes as no surprise that light verbs are the ultimate transitives. Too little meaning is left if the object does not appear; it is difficult to imagine a context that would license omitting an object for *get* or *take* (2a,b). However, even event selecting aspectual verbs such as *finish* or *begin* can have an implicit object that is recovered through context (2c).

(2)   a. *Can you get?
        b. *Can you take?
        c. Did you finish? (ok with contextual recoverability)

From this extreme of object obligatoriness, there is a transitivity continuum with various verb types being more or less likely to appear with a direct object. We illustrate a few facts about the transitivity continuum with the examples in (3).

(3)   Transitivity continuum

        a. She got *(it).
        b. She cut *(it).
        c. She broke *(it).
        d. She devoured *(it).
        e. She read (it).
        f. She ate (it).
        g. She painted (it).
        h. She danced (*it).
        i. She slept (*it).

At the top of the obligatoriness scale reside light verbs and change of state verbs. These are part of the subclass of result verbs that must realize their patient arguments, according to Rappaport Hovav and Levin (2005).

What is most salient, for us, is that the behavior of verbs along the continuum is not absolute. There are plenty of instances of transitivity transgressions. Many verbs traditionally described as obligatorily transitive (the classic *devour*) can be found with missing objects, as illustrated by the example from the British National Corpus quoted in Chapter 1 and repeated here in (4). However, these missing objects seem to emerge in special contexts, such as generic statements. In contrast, the direct objects of verbs such as *eat* seem truly optional – nothing special is expected of the context to support their missing objects.

(4)   Missing object with an obligatory transitive verb
        There are those who annihilate __ with violence, who devour __. (Cummins and Roberge 2004: 124)

Further down the transitivity continuum we have verbs like *read*, which are as likely to be used transitively as intransitively. The latter use focuses on the activity rather than on the theme affected by or resulting from that activity. At the intransitive extreme are unergatives such as *dance*, which tend not to have objects. However, as mentioned in Chapter 1, unergatives too can take objects but only of certain types: modified cognate objects, subtype objects and measure objects. The first two serve the purpose of hyponymic identification while the third provides delimitation for the event making them quantized or telic (de Swart 1998); key examples are reiterated in (5) and (6).

(5)   Direct objects of unergative *dance*

        a. Dance a slow dance. (Modified cognate)
        b. Dance a tango. (Activity subtype)
        c. Dance the night away. (Temporal measure)

(6)   Direct objects of unergative *run*

        a. Run a quick run. (Modified cognate)
        b. Run a marathon. (Activity subtype)
        c. Run 10 k. (Spatial measure)

In sum, the roots of omissibility have lexical, grammatical and contextual dimensions. It seems likely that internal components of verb meaning such as the incorporation of manner can predict omissibility patterns (as in the *eat* vs. *devour* contrast, where *devour* is "eat in a particular manner; greedily, ferociously"). Other dimensions of grammar that are pertinent to direct object omissibility include aspect, genericity and modality (Larjavaara 2000; Tsimpli and Papadopoulou 2006; Frolova 2013, among others). As we saw in

Chapter 2, there is a great deal of variation in the mechanisms that individual languages use to license, delimit and recover the null object and, as discussed in Chapter 4, the referential context is a key determinant of omissibility. The degree to which it is realized and the specific constraints and features involved vary across languages such that some languages appear to be very reluctant to allow referential null objects.

One could say that we are a bit like doctors who see signs of illness everywhere. For us, missing objects exist across types of verbs and constructions, and for all types of populations of speakers: child language, adult language, multilingual speakers. This is not quite true of every other type of missing material in early grammar, such as missing subjects, determiners or inflections. In those cases, the omission stage in acquisition is eventually superseded. For instance, when subject omission remains in use for adult speakers of a nonprodrop language, it normally occupies highly restricted registers (e.g., diaries) or constructions (e.g., imperatives). In contrast, variation in implicit objects does not depend on specific constructions, nor, as we argued above, can it be defined in terms of categorical lexical classes. Variation across null objects is best described in terms of the interaction between the various mechanisms available for recoverability: lexical knowledge, syntactic structure and context. The combined action of these independent factors leads to what may superficially look like a transitivity gradient.

Once this conceptual step is taken, we are committed to defining the acquisition task in terms of how children fine-tune the recoverability of the null objects, which must involve the integration of different sources of information. Thus, for us the growth of grammar is an interplay of modules (see Grinstead 2004, who advocates for a similar view on subjects).

It also commits us to defining the nature of the initial representation in child language as the simplest possible one. This chapter takes a further step in the exploration on what "simple" means in this context.

The previous chapters suggested the following developmental scenario: children start with what seems to be "early (hyper)sensitivity to the informational structure of events, and thus to pragmatic features of discourse," to repeat Shanley Allen's words (2000: 485). In this scenario, children eventually "retreat" to the target morphosyntactic mechanisms. Their overreliance on discourse linking to recover null arguments is replaced with grammar-internal mechanisms, including use of referentially dependent expressions, forms of agreement; these grammatical alternatives ultimately become entrenched. In this chapter, we see that additional forms of learning are involved in object acquisition. Up until now, our discussion has been mostly concerned with referential null objects,

Figure 5.1 *Accompanying picture for the elicitation of a nonindividuated object:* What is the dog doing? *(Pérez-Leroux, Pirvulescu and Roberge 2008a: 388)*

where the recoverability of the object depends on anchoring to discourse and where the distribution of null objects is pitted against that of pronouns. The reason for this focus on referential null objects is, of course, that they are illicit in some languages but present in children acquiring these languages. In this chapter, we turn to an entirely different type of null object, which is neither referential nor recoverable from discourse.

As before, it is best to illustrate with one of the experimental materials we have used, such as shown in Figure 5.1.

In informationally neutral contexts, such as the one provided by the broad focus question in (7a) or in predicate focus contexts as framed by the question in (7b), the speaker has the option of choosing to express the direct object either as a null or as a lexical DP. The quantity of information differs, but there are no differences in grammaticality or felicity.

(7)   a. What is happening?
      b. What is the dog doing now?
         Potential responses: Eating/eating something/eating his bone.

In our work we have called the null objects in these contexts "nonindividuated" to distinguish them from null anaphoric objects, which are "individuated" in discourse.

However, these null objects are not completely free. One interesting property, which we will delve into in some detail in Section 5.3.2, is that they seem to exhibit a prototypical interpretation, whereby the object associates with the most prototypical/generic theme compatible with the event denoted by the verb (intransitive *eat* refers to "eat foodstuff," intransitive *read* evokes the image of someone with a book or magazine in hand rather than the small print found on, say, an aspirin bottle). We argue that this special property of implicit objects shows that their interpretation reflects the verb's selectional properties.

Because null objects in this domain are generally not illicit, at least in European languages, nonindividuated null objects have not been generally considered problematic in acquisition and as such have received little attention. However, since TR predicts their existence, we believe these null objects are crucial for acquisition studies. In this chapter, we argue that there is in fact evidence of development in this domain, but given that no ungrammaticality is involved, the evidence is less prominent than in the case of referential null objects and has consequently been not properly examined in acquisition work. The primary goal of this chapter is to review this evidence and show how the null object approach can naturally encompass it.

The rest of this chapter is organized as follows. Section 5.3 establishes the structure of this interpretation of null objects. In Section 5.4 we revisit the question of lexical conservativity in children, across languages, and compare two approaches to development (from N to DP or from DP to N). In Section 5.5 we extend our approach to make new predictions concerning the typicality restrictions associated with implicit objects while in Section 5.6 we examine the empirical consequences of our approach, the form of the object as input to lexical learning and the general developmental associations between lexicon and syntax.

5.3   The Other Side of the Coin: Recoverability from Within

5.3.1   The Two Roles of an Object: Restriction and Saturation

The typological summary presented in Chapter 2 indicates that all (or nearly all)[1] languages have null objects, but their syntactic and semantic distribution varies across languages. We have proposed that variation depends on the

---

[1] Déchaine (2015)'s description of Yoruba indicates this language is an apparent counter-example to our "null objects everywhere" generalization. According to Déchaine, prosodic constraints dictate that all Yoruba verbs fit a CV template. Given this phonological restriction, the verbal inventory in this language is extremely limited; all verbs are, like light verbs, highly polysemic and as such occur exclusively in transitive frames.

mechanisms available for recoverability: fundamentally from context (syntactic or pragmatic) or from the lexicon itself.

While it is not impossible for these two mechanisms to coexist, there seems to be a tendency towards complementarity. We have seen in Chapter 2 (Section 2.2.1) that the literature suggests that Asian languages with anaphoric null objects tend to avoid cognate null objects. According to Thomas (1979), Japanese speakers tend to prefer null objects in referential contexts such as (8), and overt objects in activity contexts, such as in (9). Thomas calls these light objects "general" objects.

(8)   Q: Tofu wa   doko ni   aru ka
           Tofu-TOP where-LOC be-INT
           "Where is the tofu?"
        A: John ga   tabe-teiru.
           John-NOM Ø eat-PRES-PROG
           "John ate it."

(9)   Q: John wa   nani o   shi – teiruka
           John-TOP what-ACC do-PRES-PROG-INT
           "What's John doing?"
        A: Gohan-o tabe-teiru
           rice-ACC eat-PRES-PROG
           "Eating."

In a similar vein, Cheng and Sybesma (1998) indicate that Chinese speakers use overt generic dummy objects to represent activity readings (10), reserving null objects for contexts where they are identified by a topic, as in (11). These authors propose that the two observations are correlated: the presence of an anaphoric empty object in the grammar blocks the possibility of the null cognate reading (nonreferential *pro*, in their terms).

(10)   Lisi zai   chang ge
        Lisi-PROG sing   song
        "Lisi is singing."

(11)   (John$_i$), wo yijing   jian-guo le *pro$_i$*
        (John), I   already see-PAST-PERF
        John, I already saw him.

The semantic contribution of the object in these constructions can be described in terms of categories familiar in the noun incorporation literature, as either modificational (defining the event type) or classificatory (defining the range of objects to which the event applies), (Massam 2009).

Given these descriptions, the learning problem for children acquiring these topic-drop languages is to learn that null objects are blocked and dummy objects are preferred in nonindividuated, activity-focused contexts. This is the mirror image of what has to be learned by English, French and Spanish-speaking children: that null objects are blocked and pronominals must be used in anaphoric contexts. We can now formulate a new prediction: children learning Chinese and Japanese-style topic-drop grammars will also overgenerate null objects. In this case, it would not be a question of hypersensitivity to or over-intrusion of discourse, but because they have yet to block null objects from nonindividuated contexts in their language.

This claim is far from trivial; it essentially amounts to stating that, typologically speaking, learning to restrict the distribution of null objects in a given language is the consequence of the specialization of one of the two basic contributions of objects to sentence interpretation: as tools for predicate saturation or event restriction (Chung and Ladusaw 2003). These are two formally distinct ways in which arguments contribute to the description of the event denoted by a predicate. The former, saturation, is at the core of the standard Fregean approaches to the semantics of arguments. By analogy to the notion of valence in chemistry, predicates are treated as incomplete entities, whose argument structure is "saturated" by objects and other arguments. Saturation as a mode of composition provides the identity of participants in an event and function application renders the position unavailable for further composition.

The second role played by objects is that of predicate restriction, where the object argument is interpreted as a restrictive modifier of the predicate. In this mode of composition, the verbal predicate merges with a property, yielding another predicate but without altering the valence. The object contributes to the event composition by restricting the type of event denoted by the predicate. Using a lexical analogy, the activity of "cooking" might have different subtypes ("baking," "frying," etc.). In the same way, the addition of an object to the verb yields a subtype of activity (e.g., "cooking breakfast" is a subtype of cooking events). As a final step in the composition process is the rule of existential closure, which removes the remaining incompleteness of the predicate by binding an open variable. Although in languages like English restriction and saturation are conflated, we will rely on our quintessential optional transitive verb, *eat*, to provide a concrete illustration of how these two roles differ. Consider (12), where the definite direct object represents a previously introduced referent, the tofu.

(12)   John ate the tofu.

In addition to identifying the theme argument by linking it to a known referent, expressing the object simultaneously refines the event description. We are dealing with an instance of tofu-eating and hold this as distinct from events of noodle-eating, dessert-eating, etc.

Now, perhaps these two steps can be made distinct. The quantifier object in (13) illustrates how objects can saturate the predicate without providing any information that is useful in restricting the event.

(13)   John ate something.

Conversely, narrow-scope indefinite objects in characterizing sentences appear to contribute to identifying the type of activity rather than of the identity of the participants involved. Consider a sentence such as (14), in which the role of the object as event restrictor seems more prominent.

(14)   And what does this animal do? (pointing at a Panda Bear)
         Oh, that. It only eats bamboo.

No actual bamboo is under discussion in (14). The panda in question might be a stuffed toy, for all we know; but we are stating that the property of being a bamboo eater is a characteristic of its kind.

Null objects have something in common with narrow-scope indefinites. Upon hearing (15), we immediately conclude that something was eaten. No explicit mention of what was eaten is required.

(15)   Everybody ate Ø.

This type of indefinite interpretation results from the semantic operation of existential closure. Existential closure binds all open variables with the VP (Diesing 1992), saturating the relevant theta roles. It yields a narrow scope indefinite interpretation; it is the case that something was eaten by everybody, but various things, according to each individual. In previous work (Pérez-Leroux, Pirvulescu and Roberge 2013), we proposed that implicit objects behave like incorporated nouns, in that they are both scopally restricted and discourse-inert. As such, they cannot introduce a discourse antecedent into a discourse representation (Farkas and de Swart 2003). This latter property is shown by the paradigm in (16); implicit objects (16b) pattern with bare objects (16d) in that they fail to introduce a discourse referent.

(16)   a. John ate something. It was delicious.
         b. John ate. It was delicious.

    c. John ate some apples. They were delicious.
    d. John ate apples. They were delicious.

This much is uncontroversial. Yet, some interesting facts about the interpretation of null objects suggest that null objects contribute to event interpretation beyond representing the variable bound by existential closure. Specifically, despite their apparent lack of lexical content, null objects seem to be involved in event restriction. In the next section, we explore the relevant facts, expanding the initial characterization of the syntax and semantics of null objects laid out in Chapter 2.

5.3.2   *The Various Meanings of Implicit Objects*

Leaving discourse and scope properties aside, to simply equate implicit objects and indefinites is clearly insufficient. What is lost in this translation is the intuition that the interpretation of the null is narrower than that of "something" or "anything." The indefinite quantifier can refer to anything. Both (17a), which indicates that what was eaten was typical foodstuff and (17b), which refers to atypical, inedible stuff, are possible continuations.

(17)   The dog ate something . . .
      a.   There must have been something wrong with the food/his dinner/the meat, and it made him sick.
      b.   In fact, what he ate was paper/laundry soap/paper clips, and it made him sick.

For the null object counterpart in (18), only the first continuation is possible; the second would be anomalous.

(18)   The dog ate.
      a.   There must have been something wrong with the food/his dinner/the meat, and it made him sick.
      b.   In fact, what he ate was paper/laundry soap/paper clips, and it made him sick.

There seems to be a lexical dimension to the recovery of the implicit object. Psycholinguists have long observed (and exploited) the fact that lexical processing of a word leads to the activation of referents that are closely associated. For verbs, these tend to be prototypical direct objects. Recall the Runner and Baker experiment discussed in Chapter 2 (Section 2.3.4.1), where the experimenters were measuring the number of looks to the semantically related objects for verbs that differed in their transitivity properties. When participants hear either (19a) or (19b) their looks to *cake* increased not only when they heard the verb *bake*, but also again when they heard the auxiliary that supports the ellipsis construction (*did too*).

(19) a. Margaret baked a cake and Martin did too.
      b. Margaret baked and Martin did too.

A cursory inspection of the type of stimuli employed in their study gives a good range of examples of what we mean by prototypical objects *bake a cake, read a book, kick a ball*. These pairings are elicited from sentence completion tasks, or asking speakers for judgments. Nobody questions the idea that speakers have strong lexical associations between verbs and potential objects. What is novel about the transitivity approach is the proposal that speakers formally link that semantic association to a syntactically specified position.

The examples in (20), based on Gillon (2006) and already mentioned in Chapter 1, illustrate the variety of meanings we tend to ascribe to the null. What these interpretations have in common is that they reflect the most prototypical scenarios associated with each verb.

(20) a. Bill read this afternoon. (= "books/magazines/newspapers")
      b. Louisa ate late. (= "dinner/food")
      c. Hilary always leaves __ early. (= "places")
      d. John always washes/bathes __ before going to bed. (= "himself")
      e. Hilary and John met __ at noon for lunch. (= "each other")

Importantly, optionally transitive verbs behave like obligatory transitive verbs when the object falls outside the semantic selectional properties of the verb. In those cases, the object must be overtly realized. For instance, the implicit null object of *leave* has the interpretation of "some place," but cannot have an interpretation of "something" or "stuff." When what is left is a place, the speaker can opt for the implicit object, as in (21a). If what is left is not a place but a thing, say a wallet, the speaker cannot use (21b). In such context the object must be spelled out (21c).

(21) a. Hilary always leaves __ when she is in trouble. (= place)
      b. Hilary always leaves__ when she is in trouble. (≠ "things")
      c. Hilary always leaves her wallet.

English speakers realize anomalous objects overtly but have a choice of whether typical objects are realized or not. This is not just a mere statistical tendency; it really seems to act as a restriction. If you are in doubt, run the following experiment. Tell two different people about a TV show you watched last night. Then tell one of them that the show was about Suzy, a student with marginal cooking skills, as she prepares eggs for breakfast. The other person should hear that the scenario is about Mary, a daring young professional chef, who, aspiring to impress the jury in a cooking show, throws a flower arrangement into a wok. Then ask the first person what Suzy is doing and the second person what Mary is doing. They are likely to respond that Suzy is cooking or cooking eggs (22) but that Mary is cooking flowers (23). So, although the verb is the same, speakers will show you that the argument realization options are not.

(22)   Typical situation   Transitivity Patterns
        (Suzy is cooking some eggs)   Suzy is cooking ___.
                                        or   Suzy is cooking some eggs.

(23)   Atypical situation   Transitivity Patterns
        (Mary is cooking some flowers)   Mary is cooking some flowers.
                                              Mary is cooking ___.

The possibility of an implicit object is not equally distributed in the typical and the atypical scenarios. The implicit object is allowed to relate only to objects with the most representative attributes involved in prototypical scenarios associated with the verb. Or, to put it another way, the selectional properties of the verb *cook* are responsible for the "prototypical" interpretation of an unexpressed object such that the null object means "things you typically cook"; similarly, the null in *eat Ø* means "edible stuff," and in *kick Ø*, it means "a kick."

As stated in Chapter 2, in more formal terms, we propose that verbs enter into a relation with a null N complement where the core meaning of the verb identifies that of the object through "classificatory licensing" (Hale and Keyser 2002: 92), establishing a relation of hyponymy.

(24)   V   where N = prototypical, null object

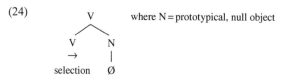

Hence verbs with implicit objects have a null cognate object as complement. There is nothing accidental or random about the typical interpretation of the null object: the semantic content of these nulls is recovered from the semantics of the selecting verb. Stated differently, the properties of the lexical root provide the basis for event restriction.

5.3.3   Aspect as a Relevant Factor

Aspectual distinctions are expressed by both lexical-semantic and grammatical means, these means presenting variation across languages. Within the larger IP projection, Aspect interacts with both the verbal argument structure and the temporal system. For example, in English we can find morphologically marked aspectual distinctions, as revealed in the difference between past and present participle in (25).

(25)   a. Anna wrote a book in 2014.
         b. Anna was writing a book in 2014.

In addition, verbs cluster around semantic classes of telic or atelic interpretation giving us distinctions such as those between atelic stative verbs (*to be, stay*) and telic punctual verbs (*to reject, miss*).

Object realization interacts with the aspectual system but there is no agreement as to how this observation should be interpreted. A range of views have been offered about the relationship between aspect and argument realization. That the object plays a key role in aspectual computation has long been recognized, from Dowty's inclusion of incremental themes as part of the range of proto-patient entailments to contemporary exoskeletal approaches such as Borer (2005). Incremental themes are objects whose quantity serves to delimit the bounded nature of an event (see also Verkuyl 1993). Tenny (1994) proposes a strong and explicit role for aspect in argument expression. Van Hout (1996) proposes that many argument expression alternations are instances of event type-shifting, i.e., aspectual reclassification, including conative, resultative formation and cognate object addition. Levin (2000) offers a more cautious view, arguing that the ontological types of events relevant to argument realization may not all be aspectual in nature. From her perspective, the links between aspect, lexical semantic representation and argument expression are neither simple nor transparent. Theoretical approaches and cross-linguistic empirical observations point to a natural association between nonindividuation in the event (habitual) and omission of the direct argument; it seems quite clear that individuated quantized aspect disfavors omissions.

With respect to the acquisition of transitivity, Ingham's observation about variation in the relationship between aspectual verb classes and argument realization is crucial. Specifically, Ingham (1993/1994) presents examples where verbs from the same aspectual semantic class may or may not allow direct object omissibility; an example is provided in (26) showing a change-of-state verb that must appear with a direct object and another that can be used without a direct object (Ingham 1993/1994: 102):

(26)   a. John mowed *(the lawn) in an hour.
         b. John tidied up (his room) in an hour.

This type of variation, as well as more regular instances of object realization in conjunction with aspectual manifestations, is inevitably part of the input the child is exposed to. What does this entail?

The aspect/object realization correlation has been tested experimentally in language development. Tsimpli and Papadopoulu (2006) show that in Greek the aspectual form of the verb affects the choice of overt vs. null objects for both adults and children (ten- to eleven-year-olds). However, the children prefer null objects significantly more than adults. The authors speculate that this preference might have a semantic/pragmatic base. Overall, their analysis suggests that null objects with imperfective verbs are a preferred option because of the lower number of operations involved (only Merge, no Move). This shows that, by age ten, children have in place the adult-like functional structure responsible for argument realization. This interaction between the clitic construction and the aspectual functional structure is not confined to older children; Avram et al. (2015) provide results for three-year-olds that seem to suggest that aspectual imperfectivity favours clitic omission in Romanian. Omissions with inherently atelic verbs *read* and *drink* are higher that with other verbs.

Frolova (2013) shows that Russian children are aware of the connection between the use of null objects and telicity in that they omit an object more often in optional contexts (atelic) than in obligatory contexts (telic). Overall, however, as in Greek, children omitted significantly more direct objects than adults and they did so even in contexts where for adults object omission is not possible, as in perfective nonreferential contexts. One interesting result from Frolova (2013) concerns the results across tasks involving direct object individuation and the interaction with the aspectual distinction. She used an experimental task closely approximating the individuated/nonindividuated conditions in Pérez-Leroux et al. (2008a). In that task Frolova shows that both the type of object (referential vs. nonreferential) and aspect play a role in object omission. Specifically, children omitted more referential objects and for a longer period of time. In both cases children still omit more objects than adults regardless of the distinction between the type of object (generic or referential). Aspectual distinctions do matter, in the sense that children omit more in the task where the verb is imperfective (optional omission) than in the task where the verb is perfective (omissions not allowed in the target grammar). Nontarget omissions in perfective contexts show that omission is not entirely regulated by aspectual distinctions nor by the type of object (referential vs. nonreferential) since in this context a nonreferential object is required in Russian.

The conclusion of this short presentation is that aspect is a factor in object omission but previous experimental results suggest that omissions trump aspectual distinctions as predicted by our null object approach. Before presenting further results, we turn our attention to an alternative, essentially lexical, approach to the acquisition of transitivity.

5.4   The View from the Lexicon

5.4.1   Lexical Transitivity and Faithfulness to Input Revisited

One alternative to our null object approach is a purely lexical approach according to which transitivity is fundamentally a lexical property (for us, transitivity is fundamentally syntactic). Under this view, all that a language learner needs to ascertain is the valence of each verb. However, as we have shown through our discussion of the transitivity gradient and transitivity transgressions, category-boundaries are ill-defined. On the surface there are no clear-cut categories, just gradience in the probability that a verb has to be followed by a direct object.

Usage-based models typically follow this lexical line and predict that children should match the probabilities of occurrence of a direct object as they exist in the input. How closely do they match it? Ingham's (1993/1994) analysis of Naomi's data (from the Sachs corpus) suggests that it is quite closely. This was also what Theakston, Lieven, Pine and Rowland (2001) found in their study of the speech of pairs of parents and very young children (between 1;10 and 2;00). They analyzed the correlation between the average proportion of use of the transitive frame with individual verbs in the input (with all parental data pooled) and in the children's speech (also as a whole). The resulting correlation was quite high and significant. Their conclusion is that children tend to realize direct objects with the verbs that most frequently appear as transitive in the input. Distributional regularities in the input are therefore guiding the learning task and, by extension, transitivity must be a lexical, gradable property.

However, it does not suffice to say that children learn about verbal transitivity from distributional regularities in the input. The most important question is: what components of verbal transitivity do they learn from the input? It seems obvious that input frequencies help children zero in on verbs at the extreme ends of the transitivity continuum, i.e., the contrast between verbs such as *eat* (less transitive) and *devour* (highly transitive) or between light verbs (highly transitive) and content verbs (less transitive). However, what distributional regularities cannot do is inform the child about the properties of direct objects of unergative verbs, the various meanings of implicit objects and the conditions under which these objects can be used. For these to be learned, a rich abstract system must be posited.

In our approach, we expect to detect visible effects of the underlying system that scaffolds the verb phrase. We believe that the development of language in this particular grammatical domain is buttressed by a system that: a) makes salient for children the relation between objects and verbs; b) projects a branching structure even in the absence of overt objects; and c) dictates how available structural and discourse information is used to recover the interpretation of objects.

Going beyond the field of linguistics we notice a parallel with developmental theories articulated for other domains of cognition. For instance, Gelman and Williams (1998) propose for cognitive development in general that skeletal, underspecified structures support development along a relevant learning path by encouraging attention to and fostering storage of data specifically relevant for that domain. They propose that there is a small set of domain-specific learning devices – each with a unique structure and information processing system – that support and facilitate learning in various cognitive domains. For us, the null object hypothesis can be seen as belonging to such a set and we expect to see its effects in cases where children diverge from their parents.

In Chapter 3 we touched on an artificial language learning experiment by Hudson Kam and Newport (2005) that suggests that children's language learning diverges from input in systematic ways. The "language learning" experiment makes up linguistic mini-systems in order to fully ensure that there has not been any prior experience with the target of learning. Experiments using invented language represent a classic tool for the study of language development, going back to Berko Gleason's clever Wug experiment (Berko Gleason 1958). In the case of Hudson Kam and Newport's study, this was not about small blue creatures and the words to name them. These authors invented a whole language so they could control for different percentages of realization of an artificial determiner. Hudson Kam and Newport found that children did not match the probabilities in the input but preferred instead categorical rules, unlike adults, who tended to match input probabilities. Children also systematically used fewer determiners, even in the condition where determiners were presented categorically (100 percent of the time). In other words, in artificial language settings, children acted as both regularizers and omitters. They followed the input less faithfully than adults and seemed more inclined to formulate new abstract rules. At the same time, in the face of the uncertainty of certain learning conditions, they choose to drop the constituent.

How should we interpret these observations? That children are regularizers and adults are not has enormous implications for many interesting and complex issues in language development. In addition, the fact that children are omitters is of course directly relevant to the null object approach. Children in Hudson Kam and Newport were relatively old in acquisition terms (mean age 6;04,10) and their sentences were, on average, adult-like in length. Therefore, it is unlikely that they favor omissions because their production is constrained. We believe that omission is a developmental strategy that consists in replacing target forms with minimal forms, until representations are fully acquired.

This interpretation in inspired by the literature concerned with a robust observation about children's morphological development. Children, until they have mastered a morphological paradigm, tend to overgeneralize the least informative form, which in many cases, such as that of determiners (and objects) happens to be the null form. Consequently, errors of omission are more frequent than errors of commission. In discussing this observation, Borer and Rohbacher (2002) propose that children's omissions originate from their (unconscious) awareness that their knowledge of a paradigm is incomplete (i.e., they are conservative, in the sense of Snyder 2007). These authors further propose that children interpret omitted structures through discourse-linking. This perspective is fully compatible with our null object approach to argument omission, where recoverability mechanisms also involve morphological means.

The evidence for systematic departure from input, of the sort uncovered in Hudson Kam and Newport, also shows up in the domain of verbal transitivity and again in the form of an omission bias. The evidence dates back as far as the initial study by Ingham (1993/1994), mentioned on several occasions throughout this book. Ingham wanted to test whether the lexical conservativity that he had observed in young Naomi's files was still a learning characteristic of older children. He presented two groups of four-year-olds with a set of six newly created verbs, such as *mivving* in (27). One group of children heard the verbs in transitive-only format while other heard them in mixed conditions, where the action was described half the time using a transitive (27a), and the other half of the time as an agent-intransitive (27b).

(27)   a. She is mivving the dough.
        b. She is mivving.

Ingham prompted the children with a standard predicate-focus question, such as we introduced in Figure 5.1. A child's response would provide indications as to whether the verb had been learned and, if so, whether it had been learned as a transitive or an intransitive. Children's responses clearly showed that the input condition determined their use of the novel verbs. They realized objects significantly more often in the consistent transitive condition than in the mixed condition. Of particular interest to us, children did not fully match the frequencies in the presentation. Instead, they produced omissions at higher rates that in the input. The children who heard the transitive-only presentation gave 19 percent omission responses, whereas the group in the optional transitivity condition produced 64 percent omissions, 14 percent more than the 50 percent baseline in their input. As in the Hudson Kam and Newport study, learning from the input did not translate into a faithful reproduction of the frequencies of realizations; a bias for null objects was revealed.

In sum, the problem with adopting the lexical transitivity view of acquisition is not that it is wrong, but that it is almost right. The observation that children are sensitive to lexical transitivity in the input is correct but insufficient. Input transgression examples are therefore crucial in showing that we need to consider the underlying system. In the next section we show that overgeneralization of implicit objects goes hand in hand with the overgeneralization of referential null objects.

5.4.2   Acquisition Experiments on Nonindividuated Objects

In Chapter 3 we examined (but did not exhaust) the treasure trove of studies focusing on pronominal contexts. Objects in nonindividuated contexts have been the topic of far fewer studies, and only for a few specific languages. However, those studies do provide additional evidence for the null bias phenomenon.

We first encountered this null bias in Pérez-Leroux, Pirvulescu and Roberge (2008a) when we compared object production in individuated/pronominal and nonindividuated, nonanaphoric contexts in French and English. We used existing, optionally transitive verbs, which ranged from very optionally transitive (*eat*) to much more transitive (*cut*). To elicit objects in nonindividuated contexts we used the simple predicate focus task we presented earlier in Figure 5.1. The results for the nonindividuated conditions, given in Figure 5.2, reveal a developmental decrease in the rates of omissions, in both languages. Three- and four-year-old French children had slightly more null objects in nonindividuated contexts than older children and adults. In English, the drop to adult baselines happened earlier, and was pronounced. However, these trends were not statistically significant.

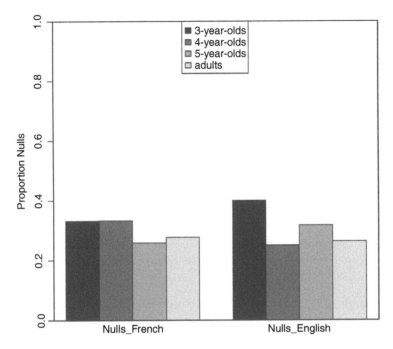

Figure 5.2 *Proportions of null object responses in nonindividuated contexts in the elicited production study of French- and English-speaking children and adults (Pérez-Leroux, Pirvulescu and Roberge 2008a: 391).*

The results show that in a discourse context that allows optionality, children have a slightly higher preference than adults for the null object option and they eventually grow out of it. Out of context, we could interpret the phasing out of developmental omissions as a relatively minor fact. We could interpret children's preference for leaving out the optional object as a consequence of the fact that their utterances tend to be shorter at younger ages. But what is more relevant here is not the reduction in the use of null objects, but rather, the timing of it. For one thing, the rates of null objects drop differentially in French and English and more interestingly, within each language, it happens at the same time in the individuated (pronominal omissions) and nonindividuated condition (DP omissions). In other words, the decrease in the grammatical null object in individuated contexts seems to coincide with the decrease in ungrammatical null objects in pronominal contexts. English children, who are quick to realize their object pronouns, were also quick to reduce developmental omissions in nonindividuated contexts. French children, who are slower in increasing their rates of object clitic realization, were also late in reducing their nonindividuated nulls. Many isolated accounts have been constructed to explain why French clitics are a late development, none of which can be brought to bear on this apparent developmental correlation.

In Pérez-Leroux, Pirvulescu and Roberge (2008a) we hinted at the possibility that the two phenomena were related: "[the] broad referential properties of the default initial N object are progressively replaced by lexical-semantic identification and by relevant mechanisms for linguistic recovery" (2008a: 395). We argued the following points:

- Children do not have a "pronoun drop" problem, but rather a case of null object overextensions;
- The two sides of the issue (individuated and nonindividuated null objects) may reflect a common development (restricting the various forms of recoverability)

In other words, the generalized null object stage predicts that children may tend to use more null objects not just when pronouns are expected but also in nonindividuated contexts, when nulls alternate with DPs. This is because their grammar offers this possibility. The nonindividuated context emphasizes an activity instead of the object that is affected by the activity. In such contexts, a pronoun should not be used.

(28)   a.   Nonindividuated
              What is she doing?   She is drawing.
                                        or   She is drawing the flower.
        b.   Individuated
              What is she doing with the flower?   She is drawing it.

Adults can use an implicit null object as a proper response in this context. However, here the null object patterns with full DPs, not pronouns. Interestingly, children appear to know this, and they did not respond to the prompt in (28a) with pronouns. In our view, the absence of pronominal overextensions demonstrates pragmatic sophistication. Another interesting observation was that in English there was a positive, significant correlation between omission in individuated and in nonindividuated contexts ($r = 0.551$, $p = 0.0001$). While we agree that this piece of evidence does not suffice to validate a null object stage, we found it suggestive and worth further investigation.

Experimental design affects results in subtle ways and rates of omission can be manipulated in different ways for individuated and for nonindividuated object uses. Moscati (2014) correctly points out that our results for nonindividuated context depend on the fact that we constructed our task around optional transitivity. Other verbs and other contextual conditions might have yielded different results. Comparing the methods in Tedeschi (2009)'s study on Italian to our 2008 study (Pérez-Leroux et al. 2008a), Moscati notes an important difference. In our design, the puppet provided an incorrect characterization of the picture and the child was invited to correct the statement. The consequence is that in the child's response there is corrective focus on the VP. Consider how the exchange went:

(29)　　STORY:　Franklin is sitting at the table with a crayon and a piece of paper.
　　　　　　　　He looks like he is having fun.
　　　　　　　　[Picture: Franklin at easel drawing a flower.]
　　　　CROCO:　Look! He is drinking juice.
　　　　CHILD:　＿＿＿＿＿[no]
　　　　CROCO:　No? Well, what is Franklin doing?
　　　　CHILD:　Franklin is drawing. / He is drawing a flower.

In other versions of this elicitation task, used by other researchers, the question is presented directly, without an incorrect statement triggering contrastive VP focus. In the absence of focus, Moscati argues, speakers will use the transitive version of the verb, with a concomitant reduction in the rates of null objects. His study tested this approach in French. Like in our study (Pérez-Leroux et al. 2008a), he concentrated on the contrast between anaphoric objects (which correspond to our individuated condition) and nonanaphoric objects (which correspond to our nonindividuated condition). He tested three- and four-year-old children as well as an adult control group. We leave aside the anaphoric results as they conform to expectations under most approaches to object omissions in L1 and because this is not our focus in this section. His data for the nonanaphoric context show the following patterns. Three-year-old children use more null objects than four-year-old children but the difference is quite small (~17 percent vs. ~15 percent). Importantly, this is in contrast with adults, who used null objects in less than 5 percent of their answers. Moscati focuses the discussion on the statistically significant contrast between children's more pronounced use of null objects in the anaphoric context in comparison to the nonanaphoric context (62 percent vs. 17 percent for three-year-olds) and suggests that this provides evidence against the generalized null object stage hypothesis, and favors instead accounts that focus on pronominal omissions. His interpretation of the null object approach is that the rates should have been comparable and therefore, according to him, these data represent a direct challenge to the null object approach.

Note, however, that his results still show more omissions in young children that in adults even in the nonindividuated condition. In Moscati's study, as in ours, children clearly behaved differently from adults, in both types of context. They visibly use more null objects than adults, which is what the null object hypothesis predicts. Additionally, comparing rates of nulls across individuated and nonindividuated contexts is not particularly useful; for us, it is in fact not even a valid comparison as the difference between the rates of null object responses in the two contexts receives a simple explanation. The key to understanding this contrast is found in the adult's obvious preference for overt DP answers in the nonanaphoric context; adults in his study accordingly produced a negligible amount of null responses. Clearly, this experimental approach makes a *He is drawing a flower* type of answer more felicitous than a *He is drawing* type. In this light, the 17 percent and 15 percent null objects produced by three-year-old and four-year-old children, respectively, can confidently be attributed to the null object stage and Moscati's results do not require us to reassess our null object hypothesis.

Finally, with respect to Moscati's claim that our discourse context (contrast) introduces corrective focus on the VP and therefore a preference for the null, this seems to be correct, as we see that removing this element from his elicitation task had the effect of reducing the proportion of null responses.

5.4.3   Unexplained Omissions: the Case of Topic Drop Languages

In the Previous Section we offered evidence for a null bias in nonanaphoric (i.e., nonindividuated) contexts. The purpose of this section is to make the same point again, this time alluding to data from the acquisition of radical null object languages. The facts presented are solid. However, our interpretation requires connecting the dots in a way that seems obvious under the null object approach but that may be irrelevant under other views and is downright inconceivable under approaches limited to lexical transitivity.

The notion first occurred to us while rereading a classic paper on argument drop by Wang, Lillo-Martin, Best and Levitt (1992). Wang and colleagues compared controlled narrative data from English and Chinese wishing to test a parametric prediction, namely, that early argument omissions in the acquisition of English are the result of a radical prodrop grammar, as found in Chinese for instance. Results showed that Chinese speakers dropped subjects and objects at higher rates than English speakers. This was true for both children and adults. As such, the evidence did not support the parametric hypothesis. What attracted our attention was their observation that Chinese-speaking children had null objects at twice the rate as Chinese adults (Wang et al. 1992: 240–241).[2]

Furthermore, the level of object omissions remained steady across age groups and did not appear affected by growth in MLU. This was not true of subject drop, which decreased with age and by four approached adult baselines.

This is not an isolated observation. Kim (2000) similarly notes that, in general, very young Korean children start with lower rates of object realization than adults; indeed, some children seem to go through an early zero-object phase. For Cantonese (Lee 2000), argument drop starts high and tends to decline at very late stages (MLU Stage IV). The implications of the latter two studies are less clear: the children in Kim (2000) are quite young so their data is open to other interpretations and in Lee (2000) we see a developmental decrease but there is no adult baseline to compare to. So the clearest piece of evidence for the existence of a null object bias in the acquisition of radical prodrop languages comes from the four-year-old children in the study by Wang et al. (1992).

Why would children overgenerate null objects if the language already licenses discourse-recoverability for null objects? What would they be omitting? In Section 5.3.1 we suggested that children learning this type of language might have to learn that null objects should be restricted to anaphoric contexts, and not used in the activity-focused, "what-is-he-doing" type of uses. This proposal, at this moment completely untested, simply states that as children acquire sensitivity to the blocking effects described by Cheng and Sybesma, their rates of object realization in nonindividuated objects should converge with those of adults. To the best of our knowledge, this experiment does not exist and this hypothesis awaits confirmation.

Data from these radical prodrop languages has supplied an additional piece of evidence that turns out to be crucial to our understanding of the acquisition of transitivity. As we have acknowledged above, children show that they are conservative in their transitivity patterns. Is this true for children learning any

---

[2] The authors did a follow-up study with adults, where omissions where much higher (40.1 percent in the followup compared to 10.30 percent in the original experiment). The authors attribute the low percentage of null objects in the original experiment to that fact that the adults were told to narrate as if they were telling stories to their children. In the follow-up study the adults (n = 5) were interviewed in an adult-to-adult conversation. In addition to the small number of participants in this study, we note that child-directed speech is exactly the type of input the children are exposed to mostly and they learn most from. Variation in register has to be accommodated by the learning procedure; therefore, we believe that the results in the initial study are significant.

type of language? In other words, does language typology with respect to null objects influence the learning patterns? In 2008, O'Grady and colleagues published a study examining object drop in the spontaneous data of children learning Korean and Japanese. They set out to find whether children learning these languages exhibited an item-learning effect comparable to that found in Theakston et al. (2001) (see Section 5.4.1). O'Grady and colleagues examined utterances with missing direct objects in reference to previous lexical production of the same verbs by parents and in reference to discourse recoverability conditions. Their results are striking. There was no evidence that early direct object use was sensitive to parental use of individual verbs – be it with respect to cumulative rates in the corpora or in the immediate context. Their conclusion is that Japanese children obey general discourse constraints on null object use, but pay no attention to the lexical properties of the input. These results have two important consequences:

- The item-learning strategy evident in English does not reflect a generalized strategy of lexical learning;
- Japanese and Korean children must have an early insight into the argument drop phenomenon in the language that leads them "to actually avoid item-by-item learning" (O'Grady et al. 2008: 66).

Clearly, children are making very early, higher-order generalizations about how implicit objects are construed. Discourse recoverability is robustly supported by experience and this recoverability option becomes entrenched right from the early stages.

5.5   *The Implicit Learning of Implicit Objects*

Gillette et al. (1999: 171) provides a wonderful formulation of the approach that has guided us so far:

> The findings bolster the considerable accumulating evidence that lexical and syntactic knowledge in the child, far from developing as separate components of an acquisition procedure, interact with each other and with the observed world in a complex, mutually supportive, series of bootstrapping operations whose outcome is a lexicalized grammar.

In light of this, let's go back to our initial assumptions, which are: a) the existence of a transitivity requirement as a universal requirement imposed on all verbal predicates; and b) the instantiation of the initial option in child grammar of a null DP. We can understand the unravelling of the null DP as a process of going away from the "outer" pragmatic and syntactic recoverability mechanisms towards the "inner" layer of the lexical relation between the verb and its complement: the core semantic identification between the verb and its object. We have seen that in this inner core the hyponymic relation between verb and the implicit object is essential. What do children need to learn in order to arrive at the target patterns of omission of the nonindividuated null objects?

The hypothesis of DP-to-N development predicts that children may initially differ from adults in the restrictions imposed by a given verb on the type of null object it accepts. Children's possibility will be wider than adults' in the sense that they will apply contextual recoverability (syntactic or pragmatic) and will have to learn the item-specific lexical recoverability mechanisms. In this approach, there is a crucial link between the lexical learning of the verb-object relation and the null object stage: while learning various aspects of the "outer" recoverability mechanisms accounts for the generalized null object stage and input complexity accounts for differences between rates of omissions across languages, it is ultimately learning the lexical transitivity that ends the omission stage. In this sense, therefore, learning about implicit objects matters not only for the realization/nonrealization conditions of lexical DPs but also for the overall language-specific null object recoverability mechanisms.

In Section 5.3.1 we proposed two ways in which the direct argument contributes to the interpretation of the sentences: predicate saturation and event restriction. We can now link these mechanisms to our assumptions about the null object grammar. Recall that in Chapter 4 we proposed that null objects are contextually determined and specific properties allow us to identify a null N (for unergatives and transitives with a generic interpretation) or null DP (for referential null objects). These categorial labels align with different recoverability mechanisms and the mechanism themselves define which semantic processes incorporate both overt and null nominal into the event description. If we consider saturation and restriction as independent from each other, we come up with a four-way classification of potential object nominals, according to their possible contribution to clausal meaning.

Silent objects appear into all but Type I, which both introduces a referent into discourse and provides the required lexical content for it. In Type II, we have all forms of overt DPs that do not individuate an object, nor establish reference. These include bare nouns (*She collects stamps*), but not exclusively so: here we can include certain uses of Romance definites, which following Vergnaud and Zubizarreta (1992), are described as having a "type" interpretation; *Les enfants on levé la main* "The children raised their hands", which also exhibit number neutralization in the sense of Farkas and de Swart (2003). This

Table 5.1 *Types of object NPs classified according to their semantic relation with the verb*

		Saturation of event valence?	
		Yes	No
Restriction of event type?	Yes	I. Referential lexical overt DPs	II. Bare nouns or Nonspecific DPs
	No	III. Pronouns or demonstratives	IV. Pure expletives

category possibly (but not uncontroversially) includes bare nominals in Chinese type languages. Type III consists of expressions whose sole contribution is to link the argument position to a preexisting referent; thus saturating the relevant argument variable. As we discussed in Chapter 2, languages differ as to whether this is a grammatically governed option. If we follow assumptions laid out in syntactic work such as Sigurðsson (2011), as well as in work in semantics (Heim 2008) we would hold that the featural content of pronouns introduces presuppositions about the entity that saturates the event. These restrict the search space of potential antecedents (for instance, to only animate entities), but that contribution is not part of the characterization. *To eat sausages/eat the sausage* directly defines the act; *To eat it quickly* less so. Moving on to Type IV, we see this category includes classic expletives, which presumably fulfill a syntactic condition without contributing to sentence interpretation.

The three semantically deficient types (Types II, III, IV) have a null counterpart. The null counterpart of nonindividuated, restriction-only nominals (Type II) is our nonindividuated prototypical object. These have not always been acknowledged in the theoretical or the acquisition literature. As we have seen, implicit null objects corresponding to Type II are beginning to make an appearance in the psycholinguistics literature. It makes little sense, at this point, to ignore their psychological validity, as done in usage-based frameworks, or indeed, in all the analyses that relegate transitivity to a mere lexical fact. The null counterpart of overt pronominals (Type III), i.e. *pro*, has long been recognized as a parametric and a developmental option. Null pronominas also have featural content; an observation dating back to Rizzi (1986) and widely recognized in contemporary work. Finally, according to standard analyses, Type IV are the counterpart of expletives in null subject languages. The lesson from objects is that silent components of language are as systematically complex, and rigorously articulated as their overt counterparts.

To those who want to unravel the mystery of how children acquire language, we would say that ignoring this insight must be done at your own risk.

While learning event restriction from the verbal root (item-specific and language-specific), children will at the same time be using and refining their "outer" recoverability mechanisms. In the section below, we present studies designed to explore different predictions of our proposal. In Section 5.6.1 we show how children gradually restrict the interpretation of a null implicit object to the prototypical interpretation; we propose a mutual bootstrapping process in which overt objects support the learning of verb meaning, and in turn apply to restrict the denotation of the implicit object. We continue in Section 5.6.2 by discussing the importance of overt direct objects in the input to children while in Section 5.6.3 we provide evidence for the link between lexical development and the resolution of the null object stage.

5.6   *Empirical Consequences of the Proposal*

5.6.1   *Unusual Objects*

One of the direct predictions of our account of the null bias in nonindividuated contexts is that children should produce null objects independently of the typicality of their referent. In Pérez-Leroux et al. (2013) we set out to test this prediction. As we have mentioned, adults treat typical objects as optional arguments but tend to realize atypical arguments directly (see Section 5.3.2). Our initial claim was that this contrast follows from the hyponymic status of the implicit null object. We argued that even though children are sensitive to patterns of object lexicalization in the input, this sensitivity might not suffice to zero in on the relevant semantic restrictions. Learning that implicit objects are restricted to hyponymic readings requires substantive experience from the input. We argue that there are two components of knowledge involved in this process. The first is the general, conceptual learning about events and their typical participants. The second learning step is actually learning language-specific lexical constraints on the construal of null objects.

This required us to assume that sensitivity to conceptual anomalies emerges at an early age. This is a highly plausible assumption. Research on conceptual development (Gelman 2003) suggests that children are excellent at making inferences about generic properties of categories. One study in particular reveals early sensitivity to the typicality of the object-verb relationship. Valian et al. (2006) gave two-and-a-half-year-old children short sentences to repeat. These sentences contained typical and atypical verb phrases, such as *eat the food*, as opposed to *eat the sock*. Children clearly discriminated between predictable and unpredictable verb+object combinations. With unpredictable combinations the children more often failed to reproduce the verb. These results suggest that children first master typical uses and clearly react to the difference between typical and atypical uses. The ability to extend certain verb meanings to novel, unfamiliar uses continues to develop well past the preschool years, according to a study of children's comprehension of specified instrument verbs (Seston, Golinkoff, Ma and Hirsh-Pasek 2009). In addition, the interaction between typicality and the realization of objects involves learning subtle semantic restrictions, i.e., the interaction between verbal lexical semantics and the recoverability requirement of the null object. The identification of the verb root with the most prototypical associated events is neither a given nor a conceptual necessity but rather a fact about a specific language that children must acquire on the basis of experience. It develops during the preschool years, and presumably continues to do so later on. We therefore expect that young children will still have difficulties with typicality distinctions when null objects are involved.

We conducted a study to test this prediction with English-speaking children and adults (Pérez-Leroux, Pirvulescu, Roberge and Castilla 2013). To this end, we elaborated a version of the elicited production task for nonindividuated objects. The goal of the task was to allow us to control for direct object typicality to determine if it had an effect on the optionality of direct object realization. The verb+object combinations were similar to those in the Valian study. We read the children short stories about characters doing different things (some typical, some atypical). The actions themselves were not named, just illustrated by a picture. The stories involved one of the characters requesting help or attention and the other characters were described as "too busy" to provide it. The experimenter asked the children to explain what each person was doing. One of the stories is given in (30) to illustrate.

(30)   Image: A room with a large window; breakfast is ready. Various characters are involved in different activities that are either typical (paint a wall) or atypical (paint a pet dog).

Script: Look, here's another busy family . . . it's early in the morning and it's already such a beautiful day. Look here . . . breakfast is ready. Do you see the piece of toast and the nice cup of cocoa? But look . . . no one is sitting down because they're all too busy. Look outside . . . why is this little girl too busy to have breakfast? (distractor: *the girl is skipping*) Well, let's go inside . . . And why is she too busy for breakfast? (target: *the girl is painting the dog or the wall*) And why isn't this little girl sitting down to breakfast? (distractor: *the girl is speaking on the phone*) And what about her? (target: *the girl is cooking eggs or flowers*).

Two different groups of children heard the same story, but with different pictures. The pictures were counterbalanced for the typicality of the component of the scene described by one of the target verbs. Thus, while one group of children was prompted to describe a typical scene of cooking (as in "cooking eggs"), the other group of children saw a near identical picture that involved the atypical object (i.e., "cooking flowers").

Everyone gave more null objects for typical than atypical events, but age group clearly determined the magnitude of the difference. Compared to adults, children were less sensitive to typicality. They produced overall more null objects than adults and the difference in the proportion of these null objects between typical vs. atypical context was significantly smaller, particularly for the three-year-olds. With age and experience the contrast between typical and atypical increased but did not reach adult range even in five-year-olds.

From these results, we extracted the following inferences:

- Null objects in early grammars are less semantically restricted than in adult grammars;
- Children initially allow null objects to denote objects that are not part of the set normally captured by the verb's semantic selection.

In one sense, the learning step by which children restrict the meaning of the implicit objects occurs in the opposite direction of what is standardly described under the syntactic bootstrapping hypothesis (Gleitman 1990). Syntactic bootstrapping is the process of learning about the meaning of verbs from the types of structures in which they appear, i.e., their selectional contexts. First, children learn the meaning of the verb with support from the objects that accompany them; eventually such knowledge is applied to restrict the denotation of the implicit object. Verbs and their direct objects are learned by a series of bidirectional bootstrapping steps. As proposed by Seston and her colleagues (Seston et al. 2009), children's initial understanding of verbs is narrow; it takes time and experience for the interpretation of verbs to broaden. At the same time, we are finding that it takes time and experience for the interpretation of the null implicit object to become narrower and circumscribed to the typical. We thus propose a model of mutual bootstrapping between verb and objects as outlined in Figure 5.3.

The contribution of the overt object to the semantic interpretation of the verb is therefore a crucial step for the child to get to the relation between the verb and its implicit objects. In the next section we discuss data that show how children are sensitive to the different types of overt objects in their input.

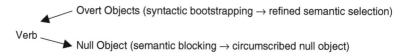

Figure 5.3   *A model of mutual bootstrapping between verbs and objects*

5.6.2   A Novel Verb Experiment

Children learn about verbs from their overt objects, and about (null) objects from their verbs. The form of bidirectional bootstrapping described above depends on: a) positing a null element in the representation, and b) attributing special status to (lexical) objects in making inferences about verbs, their meanings and their transitivity status. Object expression and object configuration varies quite a bit across languages and it is generally acknowledged that the cues to argument structure vary across languages (Naigles and Lehrer 2002; Lee and Naigles 2005; Oshima-Takane, Ariyama, Kobayashi, Katerelos and Poulin-Dubois 2011; Pye 1994; Göksun, Küntay and Naigles 2008; Matsuo, Kita, Shinya, Wood and Naigles 2012). The lexical object contributes both to the refinement of the selectional properties of the verb as well as to deeper semantic properties of event restriction and saturation. In contrast, morphosyntactic cues for verb argument structure should have various effects, depending on the larger syntactic structure of which they are part. If children are following patterns of object realization in the input, but at the same time overgeneralize based on the underlying abstract representation, variation in the realization of the object in the input should lead to innovations based on this basic abstract underlying structure.

Childers and Tomasello (2001) showed that two-year-old children were more likely to generalize the transitive construction to novel verbs when they heard both pronouns and nouns during the training phase. However, other forms of grammatical variation, such as the grammatical person of pronouns, do not particularly promote verb generalization (Smith 2011). A distributional learning framework for verb argument structure posits that consistently overt material in the input will provide the most reliable cues. As such, the authors found that pronouns schemas (*He's* [verb]-*ing it*) provided the most crucial role in the acquisition of the transitive structure.

In order to test whether different types of complement realizations lead to different types of responses, we designed an experiment for French in which children had to learn novel verbs in the context of various types of direct objects: lexical DPs, clitic pronouns and nulls. What interested us was the relation between the form of the object and how children use it as input. Specifically, we wanted to determine how input with pronominal clitic constructions in a language such as French shapes verb acquisition?

In French, direct objects are postverbal unless they are clitics, in which case they appear preverbally, in a noncanonical position. Thus, for a verb such as *manger*, "to eat," three possible types of direct objects (DOs) can appear: lexical (31a), clitic (31b) and implicit or null object (31c):

(31)   a.   La fille mange la pomme.   "The girl eats the apple."   (V + DO)
        b.   La fille la mange__.   "The girl eats it."   (pronoun + V)
        c.   La fille mange__.   "The girl eats."   (V + Ø)

Do children treat the input provided by a clitic sentence (31b) as similar to the input provided by the implicit object sentence in (31c)? Assuming that French has two positions for direct objects, one for regular NPs and another for clitic pronouns, and that children are sensitive to the distribution of these two types of direct object, we arrive at a null hypothesis: for French-speaking children, lexical NPs and clitics provide the same type of input for evaluating transitivity; after all the clitic is the object. However, if we assume that children represent clitic constructions with a null object, as proposed in the syntactic literature, we arrive at an alternative hypothesis. In this case, we predict that children will use more null objects when the input contains direct objects in the form of a clitic. If this is the case, our take on this would be the following: if children have an abstract representation of the null object, and if they use this abstract null object representation in the interpretation of a transitive sentence, then the clitic construction, involving a null category in the canonical object position, will elicit interpretations for which children rely on the null category, not the clitic, in order to interpret the verb as transitive.

The study we designed to test this prediction involved fifty-six monolingual French children recruited in preschools in Montreal (3;05 to 5;03). Groups were fairly matched for age: NPs-consistent (mean age 4;03,06, $SD = 5.5$ months, $n = 12$); NPs-mixed (mean age 4;03,02, $SD = 6.1$ months, $n = 12$); clitics-consistent (mean age 4;03,06, $SD = 6.0$ months, $n = 12$); and clitics-mixed (mean age $= 4;04$, $SD = 6.3$ months, $n = 12$).

We developed an elicitation task similar to the one employed in Ingham (1993/1994) and we also followed the minimal input design method (Bencini and Valian 2007). Children saw six short videos illustrating different activities.

Each video showed actors doing something with playdough. A recorded narrative described the situation using eight instances of a target verb. Three of the scenarios portrayed familiar activities described by existing verbs (*couper* "to cut," *mélanger* "to mix" and *presser* "to press"). The other three contained other activities described with novel verbs: *caniler*, "rolling and twisting the playdough," *pouquer*, "forming and pressing the dough in a particular manner" and *vimer* "putting the dough through a machine that transforms it into tiny balls."[3] At the end of the story, the video shows the two characters performing once again the various target actions. The experimenter then prompted the child with a verb-focused question, as exemplified in (32a), which gives the speaker the option of responding with either an overt (32b) or a null implicit object (32c).

(32) a. Dis-moi, qu'est-ce qu'ils font   "Tell me, what are they doing
          alors?   now?"
      b. Ils viment la pâte.   "They are viming the playdough."
      c. Ils viment.   "They are viming."

Input was treated as a between-subject factor, with individual children randomly assigned to one of the four input conditions.

(33)   Experimental conditions:
          a. Clitics/NPs with consistent transitive input: each verb token accompanied
             by an overt direct object (*la mélanger/mélanger la pâte* "to mix it/to mix
             the dough").
          b. Clitics/NPs with mixed transitivity input: half the tokens accompanying an
             overt direct object and half accompanying a null direct object (*mélanger Ø*
             "to mix Ø").

Results suggest sensitivity to the input that was provided during training. The number of NPs produced was higher in the two NP conditions than in the clitic conditions. Clitic pronouns were produced exclusively in the clitic conditions. Although the questions asked of the children do not target clitics (Pérez-Leroux et al. 2008a), speakers might produce them because the presentation reinforced the prominence of the object as an antecedent and provided a model. As for null objects, they were more prevalent for children in the mixed transitivity conditions than for children in the consistent transitivity conditions.

The rate of null objects show that they are more frequent in the responses given by children in the clitic input conditions than by those who were exposed to input with lexically realized NPs.

---

[3] The novel form *vimer* was chosen as a nod to Ingham's *miv*.

a language such as European Portuguese, which contains both discourse linked null objects and pronominal object clitics, this interaction is even more complex and a protracted object omission stage is predicted, which fits the available data. As we have seen in Chapter 3, the interaction between sources of recoverability can also account for the generalized bilingual effects; by necessity, children growing up bilingual face both a greater complexity in the input as well as a general reduction in the size of each single language lexicon, as shown in studies of the bilingual lexicon (Zurer Pearson, Fernández and Oller 1993; Marchman, Fernald and Hurtado 2010). In addition, solving parametric ambiguities has to be done independently in each language, so a generalized null object effect is predicted for bilingual development and, as we saw before, receives support from the evidence to date.

This takes us to a second prediction about the link between objects and lexical development. If it is true that learners rely on the mastery of lexical transitivity to solve the problem of the contextual distribution of direct object pronouns, children with more extensive vocabularies would be ahead in the null object game, and children with reduced vocabularies should have more omissions. This is an easy prediction to make, given our assumptions. What is difficult is to make it a clean prediction. The problem is that, in development, all the various dimensions of children's language development are growing. Children who are "good" at language, are "good" at vocabulary, are "good" at grammar, and so on and so forth. Developmental correlations between various components of grammar are so clear that authors such as Bates and Goodman 1999), for instance, go as far as claiming that vocabulary and morphosyntax represent a unitary system in development. From a formal perspective, this position is simply untenable. Lexical knowledge is representationally of a different type than grammatical knowledge: episodic, stored knowledge, as opposed to procedural, rule-based knowledge (Ullman 2001). Yang (2015), Lidz (2009), Naigles (2002) and others have argued quite convincingly against a stage without abstract grammar. A more plausible interpretation for these high correlations would be that they represent bidirectional bootstrapping effects between the two domains, where lexicon supports grammar and grammar supports lexicon. This is precisely how we described the relation between objects and verbs above and this is what Dixon and Marchman (2007) conclude from their modeling analysis of the developmental ordering relations in language acquisition. One of their key observations is that the growth relationship between vocabulary and grammar is synchronous rather than sequential.

However, if everything grows sort of at the same time, showing that the relationship between vocabulary and null objects is special becomes difficult.

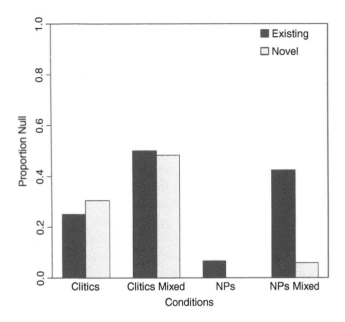

Figure 5.4 *Proportion of null object responses (from target verb responses) with novel and existing verbs across input conditions*

These results indicate that lexical NPs and clitics do not provide the same type of input for evaluating transitivity and provide support for our hypothesis. The presence of clitics affected the frequency of overt object realization in favor of missing objects. Clitic input led to more null object responses than input with lexically realized NPs, whether the children were learning novel verbs or producing existing verbs. On one hand, this confirms previous results showing that language-specific properties are relevant in the verb acquisition process. On the other hand, the results can be interpreted as showing that implicit objects, understood in our model as abstract null object representations, can prime and override overt morphosyntactic cues in the input.

Our results also suggest that sentences with direct object clitics in French may provide an additional layer of input complexity for the acquisition of verbal classes. This situation is similar to that of other languages examined in the literature, such as with the number of arguments in Turkish (Göksun et al. 2008). It adds one potential case to the list of observations showing that the age of acquisition of given phenomena may vary across languages (Slobin 1985).

Data from our French experiment also confirmed the fact that children are at the same time innovators and lexically conservative. The children in our experiment produced more null objects when verbs were presented as optional transitives (i.e., with both null and lexically realized direct objects) than when verbs were presented as obligatory transitives (i.e., with a direct object consistently realized) ($\beta = 1.99$, $Z = 3.30$, $p < .000$). In addition, they produced more NPs when NPs were present in the input and clitic pronouns were produced exclusively in the clitic conditions. With existing verbs, our results replicate in French the findings in Ingham (1993/1994). Children avoided object drop when verbs were consistently presented with a lexical NP, but alternated between overt and null objects when the input provided during the presentation phase was in a mixed transitivity frame.

This experiment again serves to confirm the null object bias in transitivity, while adding a further twist to the null object pronoun. Presenting children with French clitic input appears to increase the null bias in the standard nonindividuated task. According to the null object hypothesis, clitics and null objects have more structure in common than clitics and DPs, so this effect is not unexpected. It is difficult to see how the trend uncovered would fit a lexical transitivity approach, particularly given the earlier observation by Childers and Tomasello (2001), whose results show that pronoun use supported early verb learning in English.

5.6.3   *Lexical Development Matters (If You Are a Null Object)*

Last, we sought to explore one additional consequence of the null object hypothesis, namely that there is a special link between lexical development and resolution of the null object stage. We are not referring, as (incorrectly) assumed by Mateu (2015), to a direct item-by-item correlation between parental uses and children's level of realization; nothing as coarse as that can help us interpret the full cross-linguistic picture, which is the ultimate goal.

Our point of departure is in fact simpler: language varieties with a greater diversity of null object constructions would have a later resolution of the null object stage. In our view, this explains the French-English difference, rather than the structural contrast between the two types of pronouns, clitics and full pronominals. It also explains differences across varieties of the same language, as is the case of Iberian vs. American varieties of Spanish. Recall from Chapter 3 that children in Madrid had high rates of realization from the moment they could answer the task, whereas children in Cali, Mexico City, LA, and other places in the US had an early-disappearing but detectable null object stage. What can account for such differences? Based on our view, something as

small as the use of indefinite object drop in American variet[...] to introduce additional noise in the system and delay the r[...] object stage.

The second step in our reasoning is a bit more compl[...] input only displays categorical absence or presence of [...] transitivity, physical environment, discourse context, aspec[...] all can potentially contribute to the presence of a null o[...] Asian languages, it seems that children make a quick decisi[...] context and discount lexical transitivity. In other languag[...] forms of discourse or context recoverability coexist with[...] children have to rely on the latter to make fine-grained de[...] a certain form of context recoverability is to remain or b[...] grammar. The point is that children have to both learn the [...] and nulls across lexical items, i.e., the lexical component [...] must at least in part be responsible for the *eat*/*devour* con[...]

(34)   a. Spot is eating his food.
       b. Spot is eating.

(35)   a. Spot is devouring his food.
       b. *Spot is devouring.

They also have to learn, beyond the lexical contrast, the [...] discourse conditions, object realization is obligatory:

(36)   a. Q: What is the dog doing? A: He is eating. / He is [...]
       b. Q: What is the dog doing with the steak? A: He is [...]

From a learnability perspective the problem is the follo[...]

> The child is simultaneously faced with the prob[...]
> (lexical knowledge about optional *eat* vs. ob[...]
> language typology (grammatical knowledge [...]
> license referential null objects vs. those tha[...]
> about language typology based on optional v[...]
> referent can be recovered from the context, wo[...]
> they are properly mediated by the relevant lex[...]
> the child has mastered the crucial properties of [...]
> tions will occur. (Pérez-Leroux, Castilla and B[...]

The point is that learning the lexical fact is a prerequi[...] contextual distribution of null objects, which is a [...]

Pérez-Leroux, Castilla and Brunner (2012) make a specific proposal for a way out of this problem. Their proposal simply states that there are two distinct types of effects of vocabulary in grammar. The first type of effect, which they call the "general effect," should be true of all grammatical categories. It stands to reason that there must be a strong correlation between vocabulary and grammar: no words, then no phrases or sentences. Functional and relational terms, which form the basis of syntax, are types of words whose function is to link other words. And as everybody knows, to learn relational terms lots of other words and utterances are required as well (Gleitman et al. 2005). The second type of effect is called, perhaps rather too opaquely, the "specific effect."

> Specific effects can be examined in terms of children's ability to reliably insert certain functional elements in obligatory contexts and are best described in modular terms. We propose they arise in areas of grammar that require substantial knowledge of lexical-semantics before a learner can determine where certain grammatical markers fit in the typology of languages.
>
> (Pérez-Leroux, Castilla and Brunner 2012: 314)

In other words, certain fine-grained parametric decisions require children to have advanced vocabularies. Because of the intricate links between lexical transitivity and contextual recoverability, omission of anaphorically linked objects is one such domain. Indeed, the only one we can think of.

But the statistical problem remains. How can the two types of effects be distinguished? Correlations, no matter how strong, do not suffice. First, we need to demonstrate that the relation is directional (something that Dixon and Marchman argue is not true of general developmental associations between vocabulary-syntax, which they show to be bidirectional). Second, we need to show that they are distinct. For this, one needs a robust comparison case and those are hard to find.

Pérez-Leroux, Castilla and Brunner (2012) address the first problem by means of a statistical method known as Structural Equation Modeling (SEM), which is designed to test a conceptual or theoretical model. A SEM is a combination of two elements. One is a "measurement model" that defines latent variables (the underlying constructs in a model) using one or more observed variables (the actual measurements of things in the real world). The other is a "structural regression model," which serves to link the latent variables according to a theory. SEM models do not merely test associations between observations; they test theories as a whole, including the predicted directionality of effect.

The goal was to put to the test the two theories of language development: the unidimensional theory, which lumps syntax and lexicon together as a single component of development, and the specific effects theory, which is in essence a modular, two-dimensional theory. The specific theory predicts that vocabulary would have a general effect on utterance complexity (defined simplistically in terms of length of utterance and subordination index), which then could have general effects over various types of functional omissions, under the rather sensible claim that children who produce longer sentences are less likely to leave functional words out.

Solving the comparison problem was the most challenging task. For any set of two distinct functional elements there can be so many differences in development that we are likely to find ourselves comparing apples and oranges. We need a category that is very much like that of object pronouns, except that it is not. Pérez-Leroux, Castilla and Brunner (2012) argued that (definite) determiners could be such case, at least in a language like Spanish. Spanish represents the perfect storm of comparability between clitics and definite articles so it is not surprising that the generative analysis viewing clitics as D-heads was initially proposed in a classic paper on Western Romance by Uriagereka (1995). In Spanish, definite determiners and direct object clitics share form and features, which is unsurprising given their shared historical origins. Both categories descend from the same set of Latin pronouns. Accordingly, articles and direct object clitics share phonological and prosodic characteristics (homophonous sets of unstressed forms prosodically attached to the verbal or nominal head they associate with). The parallels are not just formal but also semantic and discursive. The accusative clitics and the definite articles are both semantically definite, in the sense that they link to a referent previously identified in the discourse model.

In Spanish, the rates of early omissions in elicitation tasks are comparable for definite articles and object clitics and, even better, the ages of resolution of early omissions seem to be comparable. Despite the extensive commonalities, this is not a guaranteed outcome. In French, another Romance language, definite articles and object clitics are alike but behave differently in development. French, like Spanish, is a language where developmental article omissions are resolved early in the preschool years (Guasti et al. 2008), but object clitic omissions are not. So, this comparison is reasonable in Spanish but would not work in French because the timetables of development are so dramatically different.

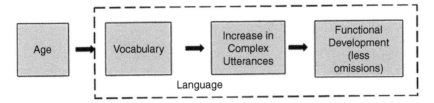

Figure 5.5 *Common sense model of language development (the general, unidimensional model)*

To conduct the experiment the authors reanalyzed the data in Castilla's dissertation (Castilla 2008), a developmental study of children growing up in Cali (Colombia), which includes multiple measures of vocabulary and grammar development including a full set of tasks eliciting object clitics and definite articles, among other things. The two theories were turned into testable statistical models, using a variety of structural equation modeling known as path analyses. This statistical approach is used to describe the directed dependencies among a set of variables and to test the fit of such models to data. The general model of development, according to the theory, has very little structure. It only contains Age (which is a known variable) as a causal link (indicated by an arrow) to (general) Language Development, which collapses the growth of vocabulary and grammar. This unitary latent variable was built from all the observed variables selected from Castilla's dissertation. Figure 5.5 represents this general model.

Pérez-Leroux, Castilla and Brunner proposed to compare this "General" unidimensional model to a second two-dimensional model, which they called the "Specific" model, for reasons that will become apparent shortly. The "Specific" model contained the same observed variables as in the "General" model, but organized them differently in two regards. First, it separates lexical development from syntactic development. For your average linguist, this is a fairly obvious step and it is hard to fathom why anyone would conduct a study to show that lexicon and grammar are two different things. Bear with us; what is obvious within the language sciences may still need proof within the developmental sciences.

The second feature of the proposed model is that it treats omissions separately. The specific model tells the story of development in the following way. The first portion of the model (from the bottom) represents the fact that age (a reasonable stand-in for experience, at least in monolingual children) leads to lexical development. Development of the lexicon leads to utterance

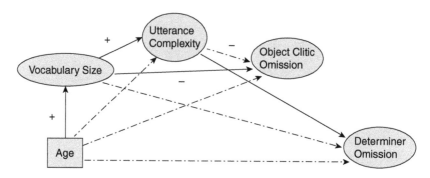

Figure 5.6 *Two-dimensional model of language development (the specific model)*

complexity, which stands for general grammatical development. The variable for utterance complexity links to two additional latent variables: one for object omissions and one for article omissions. These two constructs were put as a test of the assumption that transitivity puts specific demands on vocabulary development. One feature of path analyses is that the theory puts the variables (represented as boxes) and the causal links (represented as arrows) in place. The role of the statistical test is to verify the significance and the polarity of the overall model. Figure 5.6 portrays the results of the analysis, following the convention that solid arrows represent significant effects. The model confirmed a positive link from age to vocabulary and from vocabulary to utterance complexity. The results show that the links between complexity of utterance and omissions were not significant. What this means is that measures of omissions and utterance complexity may have surface correlations (they do!) but these do not constitute an underlying relationship. This analysis reveals that the fact that the longer the children's utterances are the less omissions we find in them is nothing but an epiphenomenon. The second finding of this study important to the goal of this book was that the specific link from vocabulary to clitic omissions was negative and significant, meaning that children with higher vocabularies are less likely to omit, above and beyond the general contribution of vocabulary to growth of sentence complexity.

The results also suggested that the two-dimensional model provided an acceptable fit for the data. This finding stood in contrast to the performance of the unidimensional model, which had a very poor fit to the data.

Pérez-Leroux, Castilla and Brunner (2012) reached the conclusion that lexicon and syntax constitute separate developmental components. Well, this is not going to impress the linguists. However, in the context of the more general discussion in the developmental field, this is quite an essential demonstration. Genetic studies on the heritability of language learning skill in children fail to detect dissociations between lexicon and grammar (Dale et al. 2000; Dionne, Dale, Boivin and Plomin, 2003; Hayiou-Thomas et al. 2006). Results such as those in Pérez-Leroux et al. (2012) serve as a warning to rampant antimodularists that conflating grammar and vocabulary runs the risk of masking the complex dynamics of interactions between dimensions of language abilities.

Beyond the general contribution to the study of language development, we find that with recourse to sufficiently powerful models we can test the types of fine-grained theories of development that can be drawn from formal linguistics. In pursuing this goal, this study produced exciting new evidence for the null object hypothesis. We now have verification that the lexicon has a special place in the resolution of clitic omissions. Just what the transitivity hypothesis would predict.

5.7   *Conclusion*

The modular perspective we endorse in this book entails that many dimensions of syntax, semantics and pragmatics intervene in the licensing and recoverability of null elements and while their combined effect leads to the appearance of a continuum, the contribution of each factor remains categorical. More specifically, in this chapter we showed that lexical transitivity is indeed at play in whether direct objects are realized as DPs or remain implicit. We argued that omissibility looks like a continuum but that it is only by considering the contributions of each component involved in its recoverability that we can hope to find out how speakers make the very categorical choice of realizing an object or leaving it implicit. This move gives us a way to incorporate into our analysis the fact that the probability of a verb to appear with an overt object is an affair of degree, as in the *eat/devour* contrast, but that transitivity itself is categorical.

6   *Conclusion*

6.1   Introduction

And so, we have reached the end of our journey and it is time to take stock of what we have seen and learned on this (grammatical) trip. In our introductory chapter, we stated that in order to reach a satisfactory level of understanding of missing objects in early children's speech, it was necessary to dig quite deeply into the essential nature of many aspects of the language faculty and that to do so required a technical apparatus (or theory) that provides the tools needed to tackle our research questions, as well as appropriate experimental methods. As a result, Chapters 2 to 5 presented detailed and at times intricate reasoning and conclusions that readers with less interest in all the steps of our argumentation might find too abstract. And so our first order of business, as promised at the end of Chapter 1, is to present a summary of the material found in those chapters before we enumerate our main findings. We then take the final step in our journey, one that brings us back to fundamental questions concerning the nature of language learning and will likely lead to challenging new journeys.

6.2   What We Have Done

Following a general presentation in Chapter 1 of the problem of missing objects in child language and of the learnability approach, which constitutes the basis of our methodology, Chapter 2 developed the hypothesis that missing elements in young children's production do not necessarily correspond to an absence, but rather to a special syntactic representation. Under this view, missing objects are actually represented in the structure and it is their properties that make them "invisible." We presented matters related to the input that are relevant for the development of transitivity in child L1. More specifically, given the considerable cross-linguistic diversity present in null and overt object constructions, we argued that it cannot be the case that a child simply has to be exposed to the behavior of a particular verb to learn how to use it. The adult input thus plays a crucial role not merely in "telling" the child which verbs can or not appear with a direct object but rather in displaying for her the types of constructions or contexts in which an object can be left unexpressed. This also serves to reveal (to both linguists and children!) the complexity of verbal transitivity and the various modules that can contribute to it. In other words, as Roeper (2007: 3) puts it: "As children progress, adult expressions provide endless puzzles for them to solve. The puzzles lead to "mistakes," which often elicit smiles or laughs from adults. Looking at those mistakes closely will, I believe, turn casual amusement into profound respect." With this lay of the (adult) land in mind, we then turned to null objects in child production noting significant methodological issues in identifying licit and illicit null objects in children. In naturalistic production, how do we decide if a particular utterance is "target-like" in a given context? What if it is not target-like for the language at stake but perfectly fine if it was a different language that was being acquired? We argued that a properly configured grammatical perspective was necessary and, since the central concept at stake is verbal transitivity, we shifted our focus to how best to characterize this concept. The conclusion we reached is that transitivity is more than just lexical semantics and actually incorporates a significant syntactic or structural component. This lead to our adoption of the Transitivity Requirement (TR), a hypothesis targeting the structural object position in VPs. We discussed four possible implementations of TR and proposed to pursue the strongest (obligatory objects). A weaker version of TR according to which there is optional merging of an object to the verb (modulated by some other component such as satisfaction of selectional features) was not pursued. In essence, this weaker version corresponds to the traditional lexical account of transitivity and as such does not provide useful insights into missing objects in child production and its generalized nature. TR in its strong form leads to a further hypothesis, namely that there exists a minimal instantiation of transitivity corresponding essentially to Hale and Keyser's (2002) representation of unergative (intransitive) verbs. In this representation V s-selects a bare N, which is consequently, in the default instance, implicit (or generic, nonreferential) corresponding to something like *John is reading* in English. This initial reasoning on the nature of transitivity and the diversity of null object constructions in the languages of the world inevitably leads to the view that object omissions in early child production must be studied from a "null object" perspective, not as a "deficit" but rather as a step towards the adult system. The approach we take is thus in keeping with much of the work done in the generative tradition since its beginnings as expressed by Newmeyer (2003: 690): "[...] speakers mentally represent the full grammatical structure, even if they utter only fragments." Since, after all, children are speakers too, our research question boils down to determining the appropriate representation for their utterances with missing objects.

Crucially, the null object approach predicts the same starting point across languages but differences in children's developmental timelines depending on the specific grammatical options that need to be acquired. In other words, "Universal Grammar is very tight in its underlying principles, but very broad in their varied expressions. It is the surface ambiguities that can obstruct the child and make the process slower. Indeed, it seems that acquisition would be simpler if nature spared us some of these puzzles" (Roeper 2007: 15). It follows that a null object stage should be observed in the acquisition process across languages but in a way that is tuned to the particular language at stake. This is the theme explored in depth in Chapter 3. To do this we collate results from previous studies on various languages to show that a null object stage is indeed attested, albeit not uncontroversially so. Part of the controversy stems from different results from different researchers for the same language. However, such differences can be unpacked and accounted for on the basis of different methodological approaches, MLUs of children observed and dialectal differences (in keeping with the importance of the diversity in null object constructions). In addition, our work reveals important asymmetries between elicited and spontaneous production data and we conclude that a controlled setting yields more reliable data, especially under a necessarily comparative approach such as ours. Another aspect of the controversy originates from the fact that a null object stage in child grammar was initially proposed for languages with object clitics like French. Research on object omission was, for a certain period of time, based on the assumption that this phenomenon happens only in languages with pronominal objects clitics and not in languages with strong pronouns, such as English. However, we presented and discussed recent work on nonclitic languages applying a methodology similar to that used for the elicitation of object clitics; this work shows relatively high rates of object omission in pronominalization contexts in those languages. Omission is also reported in contexts in which a full noun phrase direct object is obligatory. Based on available results, it seems quite evident that there is no clear and categorical divide between two developmental patterns across languages, one with omissions and one without. Rather, object omission is observed to a certain degree in all the languages that have come to our attention and this is why analyses focusing on only one language (such as French) or only on a certain type of omission (the omission of clitics, for instance) cannot fully account for all of our observations so far.

One crucial piece of evidence as a starting point to build our analysis comes from languages such as European Portuguese and Polish, which show that when both null objects and pronouns are available the rate of omission is higher than when there is no such alternation. In other words, this observation demonstrates that the conditions for choosing the null object or the pronoun (or a lexical noun) partially intersect at the discursive and syntactic levels and that this may lead to an overextension of the null object option. Input diversity, understood as the variety of relevant constructions as well as their potential ambiguity, plays an important role in the timing of the acquisition of direct objects. Ambiguous transitive constructions exist in many languages with some languages having more diversity than others. This points to the need for a learning model where input is linked to timing of acquisition; to this end, we discussed some ideas put forth in models such as Yang's (Yang 2004, 2010).

Before moving on to the details of our own analysis in Chapter 4, we made the observation that if indeed the diversity of null object constructions in a particular language is partly responsible for timing differences across languages in a monolingual environment, then we might expect that alterations in the quantity of input may also lead to alterations in the developmental timeline observed for the resolution of the missing object stage. This led us to wonder about object omissions in bilingual development. We reported on studies that confirm the predicted effects of inherently reduced input before presenting the results of our own study that revealed an extended null object stage in French-English bilinguals. At this point in our journey, we had observed the phenomenon of object omission in L1 acquisition and we had some idea as to how to study it, but no satisfactory explanation yet. The very scientific question to be asked was thus: What on earth is going on?

We suggested an answer in Chapter 4 that does not appeal to any sort of deficit in children but that is instead based on essential grammatical concepts and the notion that much of the learning that occurs is lexical. To zero in on an analysis, we took two different routes and identified where they converged. Our first route was determined by our theoretical approach.

The interplay between linguistic variation within the Minimalist framework, the Uniformity Hypothesis, empty categories and the Transitivity Requirement led us to characterize the object omission stage as an early stage in which children appear not to distinguish between null DP and null N in VP. Another way to state this would be to say that children in this stage use an "all-purpose" empty category that is neither pro (referential) or null N (nonreferential). When this view is combined with independent observations on the development of nominal expressions in children by other researchers, notably Pannemann (2007), a very compelling picture starts to take shape. She states that "at the onset of acquisition, all nominal items correspond to DPs" (p. 95) even though they may be uttered as bare nouns and she argues that such bare nouns in children's speech "have the same semantic properties as DPs in adult language (type-shifting, reference to particular instances, definite reference)" (p. 46). We only needed one more step in reasoning: if empty categories are semantically interpretable syntactic elements with no phonological features then nominal expressions in children should behave the same, whether they are null or overt. The (independent) development of DPs in L1 acquisition thus plays a major role in our analysis of the object omission stage. Our second route took us beyond elicited production data to examine evidence from comprehension studies and how pragmatics can help us make sense of the object omission stage. This of course assumes that comprehension data correspond to an accurate reflection of children's grammar, an assumption with which we agree. However, we pointed out that comprehension studies in the domain of verbal transitivity impose special challenges on experimental designs due mainly to the existence of various types of transitivity alternations. We suggested that studies based on the causative alternation (*The boy rolled the ball/The ball rolled*) are problematic and that the basic optional transitivity alternation (*The mother is cooking something/The mother is cooking*) provided more reliable results, which support the null object approach even in comprehension.

Everything we had seen up until then pointed to the fact that syntax alone cannot account for object omissions. Indeed, a fairly large body of literature had focused on the role of the utterance context in patterns of omission. Our task then consisted of exploring our options based on those previous studies. What became apparent was that the real issue consists in delimiting the role of each component (syntax vs. pragmatics) and the way they interact in the object omission stage. The key question we then explored was how to integrate pragmatic accounts into our grammatical representations and we showed that reliance on pragmatics is mediated by the syntactic structure. This point was reinforced in the Last Section of this chapter, where we presented results indicating that null objects can interact with elements in the left periphery of the clause. So, in addition to a clearer picture of the syntactic representations involved in the object omission stage, Chapter 4 helped us take a step towards a better elaboration of the modular approach. We did so through the inclusion of both pragmatics and the L1 development of nominal expressions as key components.

However, the modular picture remained incomplete until we could provide an appropriate assessment of the role of lexical development in object omission, which became the focus of Chapter 5. As should be completely clear by now, we do not subscribe to an exclusively (or even mostly) lexical view of the development of transitivity. Recall that according to this approach verbs are classified based on whether they are transitive or not, and children learn how to use verbs based on the usage of these verbs found in their environment (their input). Even setting aside the added complexity that the inclusion of further verb classes (such as unaccusatives and unergatives) and transitivity alternations would bring about, a lexical approach simply does not add up. As we said, the problem with this approach is not that it is wrong but that it is almost right! Since TR says that all verbs are in essence transitive, the L1 acquisition endgame cannot be to learn which verbs can or not have an object. Yet, transitivity undeniably relates to something lexical, given the obvious fact that not all verbs behave the same way in this respect; compare *take* to *sleep* for instance. One seems to "need" an object whereas the other "prefers" to have no object. TR states this differently: one "hates" null objects whereas the other "loves" them. And this, we believed, was where the key to a lexical approach was hidden: in the use of verbs in broad focus contexts such as the one found in answer to questions like *What is John doing?* or *What is happening? John/he is reading Ø*. This context differs from the one we had worked with up to this point, namely one that centered on the object (*What is John doing with the book?*) because we were interested in null objects that are anaphoric (i.e., that behave like pronouns: *He is reading it/Ø*).

The emphasis on the crucial role of nonreferential null objects (we used the term "implicit objects") in the acquisition of verbal transitivity constitutes another distinctive feature of our approach. The broad focus context allowed us to steer away from context and discourse linking considerations and to shift our attention to the relationship between the verb and its objects. The first step in our argumentation was to show that TR leads to the conclusion, based on influential work by K. Hale and S.J. Keyser, that there must exist a minimal instantiation of transitivity – a concept that was used in previous chapters – according to which a verb minimally appears with a null object that is specifically suited to its semantics, i.e., a prototypical null N. In a language like English, a good example would be something like *John plays Ø all the time*. Why should children's utterances involving this context be relevant at all? After all, where children seem to depart from their target language is in an overuse or even an inappropriate use of referential null objects; they have something like a null object bias. We could then phrase the question differently: is there a null bias in children even in the nonreferential context? The way to test this was to observe that while referential null objects in children correspond to pronouns, implicit null objects alternate with full DPs in adults (the children's input). So, returning to the example above, when one says *John plays Ø all the time*, one can also say that he plays computer games or the piano or something else. It just depends on how informative or specific one wants to be. We therefore compared children's and adult's uses of implicit null objects in an elicited production setting and found a slightly higher preference in children. Taken at face value, this might not be considered important or even interesting and the difference could be attributed to other factors than a null bias. However, we also found that the rates of implicit null objects decreased differentially in French and English and that the decrease happened at the same time as in the referential context, which is not only compatible with but also predicted by the null object approach.

   Could it be then that the null object used by children in referential contexts can also be used in the nonreferential context? And could it be that this happens as they learn the semantic restrictions imposed by a verb on its object? If that were the case, we would expect to be able to detect incompleteness in the semantic relationship between the verb and its complement. One way of testing this possibility would be to see if children can use an implicit null object for a given verb in alternation with a lexical object that is not prototypical for that verb. The type of alternation we used is exemplified as follows. Imagine a situation in which your friend is applying paint to something. If that something was a wall and someone asked you what your friend was doing you might reply with *He/she is painting Ø* or *He/she is painting a wall*. The null object answer is possible because the object is of a type that can normally be painted. Such an answer would not be expected if that were not the case, if a sofa was involved for instance. Your answer to the person's question would more likely be *He/she is painting a sofa* than *He/she is painting Ø*. It turned out that children produced overall more null objects, which we interpreted as an indication that objects are less semantically restricted than in adults. We proposed to apply a syntactic bootstrapping approach to explain this: through hearing verbs used with certain objects, children can eventually construct a meaning. What we see here shows that syntactic bootstrapping must also apply in the other direction in a process whereby the content of the implicit objects increasingly matches the lexical content of the verb.

With this summary in mind, let us now gather together the main findings of our investigation or, to continue with our journey analogy, the highlights of our trip!

6.3   *What We Have Found*

The following represents a list of the main findings, conclusions and contributions established in the previous chapters.

1. Our various investigations of the acquisition of direct objects and verbal transitivity provided us with a clear overarching finding: there is a cross-linguistically attested **object omission stage** during which children prefer omission of direct objects to their production and this in all the contexts we have looked at.

2. It follows that **omissions happen in parallel for pronominal and nonpronominal contexts** whereas in pronominal contexts, a pronominal object is strongly preferred in adult speech and in broad focus contexts (nonpronominal) both DPs and omissions are acceptable in adults. The decision to compare these two contexts has both empirical and theoretical motivations.

3. Empirically, research done on the typology of null objects shows that there are instances in adult speech where **the referentiality of the omitted object is not easy to pinpoint**; speech context can help but essentially these contexts are ambiguous.

4. Theoretically, object omission can be accounted for by a **null object approach**. Generally speaking, the recoverability of null objects obtains by combining semantic information from the verb and contextual (linguistic and extra-linguistic) information. Adults use this strategy to produce utterances with a nonreferential null object that is potentially discoursed linked; one can wonder how important such constructions are in the input to children. We looked for instances in child-directed speech in

both French and English corpora and found that the input to children contained substantial ambiguity. This formed the basis of our representational approach.

5. More specifically then, object omission in children corresponds to an indeterminacy stage in their use of null objects, where the null object appears to be of a multipurpose type. We refer to the construction used by children as a **default null object**. Therefore, the phenomenon defies language typology with respect to the existence of a null object stage and one remarkable fact unveiled by our work in combination with previous research is that object omissions exist across pronominal and nonpronominal languages, across clitic languages and nonclitic languages, across null object languages and nonnull object languages.

6. In addition, we found that the omission stage is resolved following **different timelines for different languages**. This is accounted for if learning (in this domain) consists of adjusting the default null object representation according to language-specific lexical typologies and modes of syntactic recoverability mechanisms. Consequently, the object omission stage will remain longer in children acquiring languages presenting more diversity of null object constructions than in those with less diversity.

7. A direct connection was established between the development of overt nominal expressions in children and the development of the default null object such that **overt DPs and null DPs develop in parallel** in clear support of a null object approach.

8. Extending this reasoning further, we showed that **bilingual children show retention of the null object default stage** that is independent from transfer. We attribute this result to the bilingual lexicon and thus interpret it as support for the developmental interaction of lexical transitivity and syntactic transitivity.

9. **When a pronominal is the only possibility children's predominant answer is omission**. This was shown via an experiment targeting Clitic Left-Dislocation in French, a construction where lexical DPs are not an option. This supports the "pronominal" flavor of the default null object. In previous elicitation contexts a pronominal (clitic) is optimal but not compulsory as alternation with a full DP is also possible and children distribute their responses across omissions, DPs and clitics.

10. **The default null object representation is active in comprehension** as shown by experimentation on the basic optional transitivity alternation and a study on verbs embedded under negation in a truth-value judgment task.

11. Proposed computational limitations or **"deficit" accounts cannot be the whole story of object omission** as they are insufficient to explain the extent of omissions and the resolution timing.

12. **Object omissions are not tied to past participle agreement** in Quebec French, contrary to what would be expected in a computational approach such as the UCC.

13. **The default null object interacts with the functional structure of the clause** as confirmed by experiments showing that object omissions interact with structures in the left periphery of the clause.

14. For instance, manipulation of the person features of the subject results in drastically different rates of object omission. Specifically, the context of direct address lowers the rates of clitic omission to almost target like, while high rates of omission were confined to the context of indirect address. We interpreted these results as stemming from intervention effects in the left periphery of the clause.

15. **Lexical development interacts with the development of direct objects.** A study on the acquisition of object clitics and determiners in Spanish, a language where those two functional categories share forms and features, showed that lexical development has a specific effect on the development of object pronouns, while only a general effect on the development of determiners.

16. In the course of learning the semantic hyponymic relation between the verb and its object, children **start by overextending null objects beyond the semantic selectional properties of the verb**. This was made evident in two experiments; one where implicit objects were targeted and a second testing the typicality of implicit objects. The first experiment confirmed that implicit null objects are overproduced by children, as is the case for referential null objects. The second experiment shows that children are less sensitive than adults to the typicality of the null object.

17. In addition, we found that the timing of conversion to the target for implicit objects correlated to the one for referential null objects.

18. Our studies have resulted in **new elicitation procedures**: a refinement of the analysis of spontaneous speech leading to solve asymmetries between experimental and spontaneous data, and an original comprehension methodology for null objects.

19. Some of our studies on spontaneous production **put to rest the assumption that elicitation procedures artificially inflate the rate of omissions**, showing that with proper methodology, the asymmetries disappear.

The points above portray our contributions in a very categorical manner for the sake of our presentation. To be realistic however, some might eventually be proven wrong or incomplete. That is what research is all about and we can only hope that our work will serve as the starting point for further testing, experimentation and reinterpretations. In the next section, we take a step back to reflect on what our contributions can tell us about the broader picture of language acquisition.

6.4   *Going Further*

By the time we were putting the last touches on the first five chapters of this book, we had spent several years working on the problem of null objects in acquisition. Our approach was used to build a consistent account across languages and across phenomena. It generated some unexpected predictions, like the pervasiveness of the bilingual null object effect, the developmental link between null objects and the lexicon, the indifference of discourse-oriented languages to lexical effects in omission. These predictions were proven correct by many subsequent results in the literature. But what are the implications of our findings for a conceptualization of "learning" and UG?

One nonnegotiable premise for us is that language development never starts from nothing, but rather starts with a variant of something. The question of course is to determine what this something corresponds to. Our transitivity requirement (TR) makes the strong hypothesis that many cases of object omission in L1 acquisition are an artifact of the acquisition of transitivity; direct objects are "special" as their acquisition starts with a UG-given "treelet" in which the verb merges with a multipurpose null object. Learning, as we said, thus consists in adjusting this default null object representation to meet language-specific lexical typologies (learning of the verb meaning) and modes of syntactic recoverability mechanisms (learning when the object has to be overtly represented and where it can remain null).

Our research brought direct empirical evidence mostly for the second component of the learning involved (the recoverability mechanisms). However, in Chapter 5, we tackled the issue of lexical development. Since TR gives us the minimal instantiation of transitivity, our assumption is that in learning the verb meaning children need to learn the semantic restrictions between the verb and its object. We proposed a mutual bootstrapping process in which overt objects assist in the learning of verb meanings, which consequently apply to restrict the denotation of implicit objects. The contribution of the overt object to the semantic interpretation of the verb is therefore a crucial step for the child to get to the relation between the verb and its implicit objects. The verb in turn restricts the interpretation of the null object to the prototypical one. For us, the relationship between the verb and its object is essential in the learning process. This is not, by any means, a universally shared assumption.

For example, Ninio (2015) provides a "pragmatic matching" approach to the learning of verb meaning, in fact as a fundamental process of learning, following Macnamara (1972):

> the alternative hypothesis to the theory of syntactic bootstrapping is that the interactive context of language use provides sufficient information for understanding parental utterances during acquisition, making it possible for the child to map meaning to a novel linguistic form. (Ninio 2015: 6)

Ninio sets out to specifically examine the association between single verb utterances (verbs in holophrastic contexts) and the interactional context in which they were uttered. One obvious way to test this is by looking at verbs when they are used without overt arguments and ask: Can single-word use of verbs by parents provide sufficient input to verb meaning? Her study uncovered two intriguing observations. First, that the frequency of single-word utterances in the input corpus predicts the acquisition of verbs by the children much better than the frequency of multi-word utterances, with the caveat that the data was pooled across all parents and all children. This is not predicted by syntactic bootstrapping, because under that approach relevant verb input must bring along a subcategorization frame. More important to our purpose was that she found that most single-verb uses were imperatives and for most of those definite objects at play were ostensive in the context. Parents used single-verb input to direct children's attentional focus (*Look! Take!*), to get them to act on an ostensive object (*eat, drink, push, open, turn*) or to negotiate an action (*try, stop, finish*). Thus, Ninio concludes, because the unexpressed semantic object of the verb is part of the shared attentional focus of the parent and child, children can exploit this both to retrieve the missing object, and to use the object to infer the meaning of the verb (2015: 25). In her view, this solves the thorny problem of how to get started with syntactic bootstrapping to begin with. Indeed, there is an inherent paradox in syntactic bootstrapping, namely, that children need to already have a mastery of the semantics of some verb and know how its arguments are expressed in a syntactically constructed sentence in order to learn that very verb (Ninio 2015: 26).

However, the paradox runs in both directions. By associating a single-word utterance consisting of a verb to a contextually salient, discourse-identified object, the child must already be assuming that the single word is a two-place predicate and that it should associate to the object in the shared attentional space. Returning to the premise stated above, this is the kind of "something" that the child starts with and which brings us back to our analysis of transitivity and especially TR. Moreover, as the author acknowledges, the study shows that children are capable of using verbs as single words in the correct context, as their parents do, but has nothing to say about whether the children have learned the correct verb semantics. As we have seen in Chapter 5, our experiment testing children's use of implicit objects shows that indeed children do not necessarily yet master the semantics of the verb-object association. In a recent paper, Hendrickson and Sundara (2017) examine how children understand utterances with unseen objects. They show that:

> infants' decontextualized absent object knowledge is in place at age 1;02, but fragile. Given highly familiar words, infants' absent object knowledge appears robust when given one prototypical exemplar, but too fragile to overcome the variation when that prototypical exemplar is presented alongside several atypical exemplars. This research contributes to the growing literature delineating how early word knowledge transitions to more adultlike knowledge states throughout the second year of life.   (Hendrickson and Sundara 2016: 14)

Lastly, let's not forget that in some varieties (Iberian Spanish, as we have shown), children by the age of 2 are capable of correctly using pronominalisation along with lexical DPs to express the direct object: this is direct proof that children do take into consideration the syntactic structure along with the visual context. So, although a verb may appear as a single word utterance, syntax is still at play providing a support for pragmatic matching. Thus, to paraphrase the title of a recent paper by Everaert et al. (2015), learning involves "structures, not just strings."

This of course leads us to a discussion of a model of UG and its relation to learning. A traditional approach to this in the generative framework is via parameter-setting: UG comes with parameters that can be set to one of different possibilities based on the evidence provided by the input. As we have argued, we find no obvious way to incorporate parameter setting into the learning of transitivity. Although languages seem to cluster around what appear to be "types," such as null object languages, nonnull object languages and mixed-languages, we have shown that this clustering is not categorical and when looked upon from the perspective of the recoverability involved (and not of the type of null object) we find ample instances of overlap. From the point of view of the child, the input is essentially ambiguous. For us, ambiguous input can only direct the child towards a null object grammar, a trace of which exists in every language. So, the different instantiations of the direct object in the input (null, DP, pronominal) are not signaling to the child nor do they commit the child to a "type" of grammar. The learning mechanism operates, unlike in the triggering model typical of parameter setting, in a domain-general way in the sense of Yang (2004): for parametric and nonparametric phenomena alike, the grammars compete for every input sentence encountered and the target grammar will win over the others as the most compatible one.

> There is evidence that statistical learning, possibly domain-general, is operative at both low-level (word segmentation) as well as high-level (parameter setting) processes of language acquisition. Yet, in both cases, it is constrained by what appears to be innate and domain-specific principles of linguistic structures, which ensure that learning operates on specific aspects of the input [...].   (Yang 2004: 455)

However, as we have seen, statistical learning is not the whole answer – but neither is UG alone or pragmatics alone. Together with UG principles, we acknowledge the contribution of pragmatics, subscribing to what Lorenzo and Longa (2009: 1308) deemed as an important shift to a "rigorous conceptualization of the acquisition of languages," namely that:

> the recognition that the contribution of the environment to the growth of a linguistic system in the mind of children should not to be restricted [*sic*] to those aspects in which languages differ. There is no a priori reason for the exclusion of stimuli (i.e., the positive

evidence within PLD) from the setting of conditions leading to linguistic uniformity. Thus, some neglected learning procedures, such as those of use-based treatments (Tomasello 2003), should be given new credit by generative acquisitionists.

(Lorenzo and Longa 2009: 1308)

It is in that sense that modularity, as we discussed in this book, provided a framework to help us uncover the architecture of null object constructions and we acknowledged that modularity should extend beyond the internal interfaces (semantic, lexical) to external interfaces (pragmatics, phonetics). But modularity should also extend to how we view learning in general by perhaps connecting two systems of learning: probabilistic (bootstrapping) and joint-attentional (pragmatics); this point is made clearly by Ninio (2015). Usage-based approaches, by emphasizing the role of the latter, also happen to tell a mostly true story, but being almost right is still being wrong. In reality, for usage-based accounts, the results presented throughout this book are bad news as they reveal the need for structural grammatical representations at very early stages. So, although UG does not dictate how learning happens, it provides directions as to what is learned. Because the model we envision incorporates discourse-based recoverability, we can take into account a wide range of results, originating from both sides of the theoretical divide, that show children's sensitivity to the conditions of the context.

This is an important and necessary move for us as it guides us in our attempt to discover how children recover the initial (multipurpose) null object. We have only begun to explore this question and many others remain. Along with recoverability from the pragmatic and discourse context, we have seen that various syntactic factors lead to increases or decreases in the use of null objects (manipulation of the functional structure or of features on the subject) but we believe we are still far from having uncovered all the factors, or their interplay, and new experiments need to be set to discover more of those factors. We have seen a qualitative resemblance between the development of null and overt DP but experiments have yet to be conducted to closely monitor such correlations, with the same pool of participants. Is the initial null object a feature of development, in the sense that it dissolves into the "stable" adult grammar, or might it recur under certain environmental conditions? We have observed that under input reduction the null object stage appears extended in bilingual children. Should we then expect null objects to reappear when fluctuations in the input are present, such as in bilingual and multilingual settings? This can only be looked at over a long window of time, whereas we, and most of the current research, commonly use narrow windows, for example children between three and five or six years old.

Finally, the transitivity requirement plays a crucial role in our analysis and although we have motivated its adoption from a grammatical perspective, its status in terms of UG remains unclear. To cite Lorenzo and Longa (2009: 1310):

> Hornstein et al. (2005) state that certain design features of human languages are so prominent that no serious theoretical approach can override them: the basic distinction between a lexical and a grammatical component, the existence of both meaningful and nonmeaningful or strictly formal items in any lexicon, the hierarchical arrangement of the phrasal structures that any grammar is capable of constructing, and so on.

Can TR credibly be counted as one of those design features? Probably not. As stated in Chapter 2, TR looks rather suspicious as a universal concept given current minimalist assumptions, which take Merge to be "the basic property of language" (Everaert et al. 2015: 730). If we attempt to describe TR in those terms, it consists in a mandatory application of Merge, specifically in the case of verbs. From this perspective, in evolutionary terms, we could hypothesize that V-Obj Merge operations have become so rooted in grammar as to become entrenched as a design feature of human language. In that sense, TR reduces to a statement about the defining nature of V, namely that contrary to other basic building blocks of grammar (except possibly P) that merely have combinatorial properties, V is intrinsically combinative. The plausibility of this view remains an open question.

In the end, it turns out our journey did not take us to a final destination but rather to a new crossroad where evidence from different languages meet, several grammatical modules intersect and structures superimpose on strings.

References

Aitchison, J. (1994). *Words in the Mind: An Introduction to the Mental Lexicon*. Oxford: Blackwell Publishers.

Akhtar, N., and M. Tomasello. (1997). Young Children's Productivity with Word Order and Verb Morphology. *Developmental Psychology 33*(6): 952–965.

Allen, S. (2000). A Discourse-Pragmatic Explanation for Argument Representation in Child Inuktitut. *Linguistics: An Interdisciplinary Journal of the Language Sciences* 38(3): 483–521.

Allen, S., and H. Schröder. (2003). Preferred Argument Structure in Early Spontaneous Inuktitut Speech Data. In J. DuBois, L. Kumpf and W. Ashby, eds., *Preferred Argument Structure: Grammar as Architecture for Function*. Amsterdam: John Benjamins Publishing, 301–338.

Amaral, L., and T. Roeper. (2014). Multiple Grammars and Second Language Representation. *Second Language Research* 30, 3–36.

Ariel, M. (2001). Accessibility Theory: An Overview. In T. J. M. Sanders, J. Schilperoord and W. Spooren, eds., *Text Representation*. Amsterdam: John Benjamins Publishing, 29–87.

Auger, J. (1994). *Pronominal Clitics in Québec French: A Morphological Analysis*. Doctoral dissertation, University of Pennsylvania.

Avram, L. (1999). Clitic Omission in Child Language and Multiple Spell-Out, poster presented at GALA 1999, University of Potsdam.

Avram, L. (2001). Remarks on the Optional Clitic Stage in Child Romanian. *University of Bucharest Working Papers in Linguistics* 3(1): 16–28.

Avram, L. and M. Coene. (2007). Object Clitics as Last Resort: Implications for Language Acquisition. In S. Baauw, M. Pinto and J. van Kampen, eds., *Proceedings of the Romance Turn II*. Utrecht: UiL LOT, 7–26.

Avram, L., M. Coene and A. Sevcenco. (2015). Theoretical Implications of Children's Early Production of Romanian Accusative Clitics. *Lingua* 161: 48–66.

Babyonyshev, M. and S. Marin. (2005). The Acquisition of Object Clitic Constructions in Romanian. In R. Gess, and E. Rubin, eds.,, *Theoretical and Experimental Approaches to Romance Linguistics*. Amsterdam: John Benjamins Publishing, 21–40.

Basilico, D. (1998). Object Position and Predication Forms. *Natural Language and Linguistic Theory* 16: 541–595.

Bates, E. and J. C. Goodman. (1999). On the Emergence of Grammar from the Lexicon. In B. MacWhinney, ed., *The Emergence of Language*. Mahwah, NJ: Erlbaum, 29–70.

Bedore, L. and L. Leonard. (2001). Grammatical Morphology Deficits in Spanish-Speaking Children with Specific Language Impairment. *Journal of Speech, Language and Hearing Research* 44: 905–924.

Belzil, I., M. Pirvulescu and Y. Roberge. 2008. Object Clitic Production and Omission in Early French and the Role of the Extralinguistic Context. In A. Gavarró, and M. J. Freitas, eds., *Language Acquisition and Development: Proceedings of GALA 2007*. Cambridge: Cambridge Scholars Press, 81–90.

Bello, S. (2014). Null Indirect Objects in Quebec French. Poster presented at the Canadian Linguistic Association (CLA). Brock University, St. Catharines, ON, May 25, 2014.

Bencini, G. M. L. and V. V. Valian. (2007). Abstract Sentence Representations in 3-Year-Olds: Evidence from Language Production and Comprehension. *Journal of Memory and Language* 59, 97–113.

Bender, E. (1999). Constituting Context: Null Objects in English Recipes Revisited. In J. Alexander, N. -R. Han and M. Fox, eds., *University of Pennsylvania Working Papers in Linguistics – Proceedings of the Annual Penn Linguistics Colloquium*, vol. VI (1). Retrieved from http://repository.upenn.edu/pwpl/vol6/iss1/.

Berko Gleason, J. (1958). The Child's Learning of English Morphology. *Word* 14: 150–177.

Bernard, G. (1991). Une conception linguistique méconnue de la transitivité. In Annie Montaut, ed., *Sur la transitivité dans les langues. Linx n° 17 (revue de linguistique de l'Université Paris* 10, 13–35.

Berwick, R. (1985). *The Acquisition of Syntactic Knowledge*. Cambridge, Mass.: MIT Press.

Bialystok, E., G. Luk, K. Peets and S. Yang. (2010). Receptive Vocabulary Differences in Monolingual and Bilingual Children. *Bilingualism: Language and Cognition* 13: 525–531.

Biberauer, T., A. Holmberg, I. Roberts and M. Sheehan. (2010). *Parametric Variation: Null Subjects in Minimalist Theory*. Cambridge: Cambridge University Press.

Blinkenberg, A. (1960). *Le problème de la transitivité en français moderne: essai syntacto-sémantique*. Copenhagen: Munksgaard.

Bloom, L., P. Miller and L. Hood. (1975). Variation and Reduction as Aspects of Competence in Language Development. In A. Pick, ed., *The 1974 Minnesota Symposium on Child Psychology*. Minneapolis: University of Minnesota Press, 3–56.

Bloom, P. (1990). Subjectless Sentences in Child Language. *Linguistic Inquiry* 21: 491–504.

Bock, K. and R. Warren. (1985). Conceptual Accessibility and Syntactic Structure in Sentence Formulation. *Cognition* 21: 47–67.

Boeckx, C. (2011). Approaching Parameters from Below. In A. M. Di Sciullo and C. Boeckx, eds., *The Biolinguistic Enterprise*. Oxford: Oxford University Press, 205–221.

Borer, H. (1984). *Parametric Syntax: Case Studies in Semitic and Romance Languages*. Dordrecht: Foris.

Borer, H. (2004). The Grammar Machine. In A. Alexiadou, E. Anagnostopoulou and M. Everaert, eds., *The Unaccusativity Puzzle*. Oxford: Oxford University Press, 288–331.

Borer, H. 2005. *Structuring Sense*. Oxford: Oxford University Press.

Borer, H. and B. Rohrbacher. (2002). Minding the Absent: Arguments for the Full Competence Hypothesis. *Language Acquisition* 10: 123–175.

Bowers, J. (2002). Transitivity. *Linguistic Inquiry* 33: 283–224.

Bowerman, M. (1982). Evaluating Competing Linguistic Models with Language Acquisition Data: Implication of Developmental Errors with Causative Verbs. *Quaderrni di Semantica* 3: 5–66.

Boeckx, C. (2011). Approaching Parameters from Below. In Di Sciullo, A. M. and Boeckx, C., eds., *The Biolinguistic Enterprise: New Perspectives on the Evolution and Nature of the Human Language Faculty*. Oxford University Press: Oxford, 205–221.

Bréal, M. (1897). *Essai de sémantique*. Paris: Hachette.

Brown, R. (1973). *A First Language: the Early Stages*. Cambridge, Mass: Harvard University Press.

Brunetto, V. (2010). Syntactic Diagnostics for Referentiality Marking in Early Null Objects: Evidence from Italian. In B. Heselwood and L. Plug, eds., *Leeds Working Papers in Linguistics and Phonetics* 15. Leeds: Department of Linguistics and Phonetics, University of Leeds, 1–13.

Cai, Z. G., M. J. Pickering, R. Wang and H. P. Branigan. (2015). It Is There Whether You Hear It or Not: Syntactic Representation of Missing Arguments. *Cognition* 136: 255–267.

Campos, H. (1986). Indefinite Object Drop. *Linguistic Inquiry* 17: 354–359.

Carroll, S. (2001). *Input and Evidence: The Raw Material of Second Language Acquisition*. Amsterdam: John Benjamins.

Carlson, G., and T. Roeper. (1981). Morphology and Subcategorization: Case and the Unmarked Complex Verb. In Hoekstra, T., H. van der Hulst, M. Moortgat, eds., *Lexical grammar*. Foris: Dordrecht, 123–164.

Castilla, A. (2008). Morphosyntactic Acquisition in Monolingual 3-, 4- and 5-Year-Old Spanish-Speaking Children, unpublished Ph.D. thesis, University of Toronto.

Castilla, A. P., A. T. Pérez-Leroux and A. Eriks-Brophy. (2008a). Omission and Substitutions in Early Spanish Clitics. In A. Gavarró and J. Freitas, eds., *Language Acquisition of French Pronouns in Normal Children of GALA 2007*. Newcastle, United Kingdom: Cambridge Scholars Press/CS, 112–122.

Castilla, A., Pérez-Leroux, A. T. and Eriks-Brophy, A. (2008b). Syntax and the Lexicon in Early Omission of Spanish Clitics. In H. Chan, H. Jacob and E. Kapia eds., *BUCLD 32: Proceedings of the 32nd Annual Boston University Conference on Language Development*. Somerville, Mass: Cascadilla Press, 72–83.

Castilla, A. and A. T. Pérez-Leroux. (2010). Omissions and Substitutions in Spanish Object Clitics: Developmental Optionality as a Property of the Representational System. *Language Acquisition* 17: 2–25.

Castilla-Earls A., M.A. Restrepo, A. T. Perez-Leroux, S. Gray, P. Holmes, D. Gail and Z. Chen. (2016). Interactions between Bilingual Effects and Language Impairment:

Exploring Grammatical Markers in Spanish-Speaking Bilingual Children. *Applied Psycholinguistics* 37(5):1147–1173.

Childers, J. B. and M. Tomasello. (2001). The Role of Pronouns in Young Children's Acquisition of the English Transitive Construction. *Developmental Psychology* 37 (6): 739–748.

Chillier, L., M. Arabatzi, L. Baranzini, S. Cronel-Ohayon, T. Deonna, S. Dubé, J. Franck, U. Frauenfelder, C. Hamann, L. Rizzi, M. Starke and P. Zesiger. (2001). The acquisition of French pronouns in normal children and in children with specific language impairment (SLI). In: *Proceedings of Early Lexicon Acquisition* [CD]. Lyon, France.

Chomsky, N. (1981). *Lectures on Government and Binding*. Dordrecht: Foris.

Chomsky, N. (1986) *Knowledge of Language: Its Nature, Origins and Use*. New York: Praeger.

Chomsky, N. (1995). *The Minimalist Program*. Cambridge, Mass: MIT Press.

Chomsky, N. (2001). Beyond Explanatory Adequacy. *MIT Occasional Papers in Linguistics*, 20. Cambridge: Mass.

Cheng, L. and R. Sybesma. (1998). On Dummy Objects and the Transitivity of Run. In R. van Bezooijen and R. Kager, eds., *Linguistics in the Netherlands*. Amsterdam: AVT/John Benjamins Publishing, 81–93.

Chung, S. and W. A. Ladusaw. (2003). *Restriction and Saturation*. Cambridge, Mass: MIT Press.

Clancy, P. (1993). Preferred Argument Structure in Korean Acquisition. In E. Clark, ed., *Proceedings of the 25th Annual Child Language Research Forum*. Stanford, Calif.: CSLI Publications, 307–314.

Clancy, P. (1997). Discourse Motivations for Referential Choice in Korean Acquisition. In H.–M. Sohn and J. Haig, eds., *Japanese/Korean linguistics* 6. Stanford, Calif.: CSLI Publications, 639–659.

Cobo-Lewis, A., B. Z. Pearson, R. E. Eilers and V. C. Umbel. (2002a). Effects of Bilingualism and Bilingual Education on Oral and Written English Skills: A Multifactor Study of Standardized Test Outcomes. In Oller D. K. and R. E. Eilers, eds., *Language and Literacy in Bilingual Children*. Clevedon, UK: Multilingual Matters, 64–97.

Cobo-Lewis, A., B. Z. Pearson, R. E. Eilers and V. C. Umbel. (2002b). Effects of Bilingualism and Bilingual Education on Oral and Written Spanish Skills: A Multifactor Study of Standardized Test Outcomes. In D. K. Oller and R. E. Eilers, eds., *Language and Literacy in Bilingual Children*. Clevedon, UK: Multilingual Matters, 98–117.

Coene, M. and L. Avram. (2011). An Asymmetry in the Acquisition of Accusative Clitics in Child Romanian. In A. Grimm, A. Muller, C. Hamann and E. Ruigendijk, eds., *Comprehension-Production Asymmetries in Child Language*. Berlin, New York: Mouton de Gruyter, SOLA Series, 39–67.

Cornish, F. (1999). *Anaphora, Discourse and Understanding: Evidence from English and French*. Gloucestershire: Clarendon Press.

Costa, J. and M. Lobo. (2007). Clitic Omission, Null Objects or Both in the Acquisition of European Portuguese? In S. Bauuw, F. Drijkoningen and M. Pinto, eds., *Romance languages and linguistic theory 2005: Selected Papers from "Going Romance".* Amsterdam: John Benjamins Publishing, 59–72.

Costa, J., M. Lobo, J. Carmona and C. Silva. (2008). Clitic Omission in European Portuguese: Correlation with Null Objects? In A. Gavarró, and M. J. Freitas, eds., *Language Acquisition and Development: Proceedings of GALA 2007.* Cambridge: Cambridge Scholars Press, 133–143.

Costa, J. and M. Lobo. (2010). Clitic Omission Is Null Object: Evidence from Comprehension. In J. Costa, A. Castro, M. Lobo and F. Pratas, eds., *Language Acquisition and Development.* Newcastle: Cambridge Scholars Press, 96–106

Costa, J. and M. Lobo and C. Silva. (2012). Which Category Replaces an Omitted Clitic? The Case of European Portuguese. In P. Guijarro-Fuentes, and M. Pilar Larrañaga, eds. *Pronouns and Clitics in Early Acquisition.* Berlin/New York: Mouton DeGruyter, 105–130.

Crain, S. and R. Thornton. (1998). *Investigations in Universal Grammar: A Guide to Experiments on the Acquisition of Syntax and Semantics,* Cambridge, Mass: MIT Press.

Croft, W. (1991). *Syntactic Categories and Grammatical Relations: The Cognitive Organization of Information,* Chicago: Chicago University Press.

Cuervo, M. C. (2014). Alternating Unaccusatives and the Distribution of Roots. *Lingua,* 141, 48–70.

Culbertson, J. (2010). Convergent Evidence for Categorial Change in French: From Subject Clitic to Agreement Marker. *Language,* 86(1), 85–132.

Culbertson, J. and G. Legendre. (2008). Qu'en est-il des clitiques sujet en français oral contemporain? *Proceedings of the 1er Congres mondial de Linguistique Francaise.* 1, 2663–2674.

Cummins, S. and Y. Roberge. (2004). Null Objects in French and English. In J. Auger, C. Clements and B. Vance, eds., *Contemporary Approaches to Romance Linguistics.* Amsterdam: John Benjamins Publishing, 121–138.

Cummins, S. and Y. Roberge. (2005). A Modular Account of Null Objects in French. *Syntax,* 8(1), 44–64.

Dale, P.S., G. Dionne, T.C. Eley and R. Plomin. (2000). Lexical and Grammatical Development: A Behavioral Genetic Perspective. *Journal of Child Language,* 27 (3), 619–642.

De Cat, C. (2004). A Fresh Look at How Young Children Encode New Referents. *IRAL,* 42, 111–127.

De Cat, C. (2007). French Dislocation without Movement. *Natural Language & Linguistic Theory,* 25, 485–534.

De Cat, C. (2009). Experimental Evidence for Preschoolers' Mastery of "Topic". *Language Acquisition,* 16, 224–239.

De Houwer, A. (1990). *The Acquisition of Two Languages from Birth: A Case Study,* Cambridge: Cambridge University Press.

De la Mora, J., J. Paradis, J. Grinstead, B. Flores and M. Sanchez. (2004). Object clitics in Spanish-speaking children with and without SLI. Poster presented at the 25th Annual Symposium on Research in Child Language Disorders, University of Wisconsin-Madison.

Déchaine, R.–M. (2015). What "Spell-Out" reveals: Niger-Congo prosodification constraints the syntax-semantics interface, ms. University of British Columbia. http://ling.auf.net/lingbuzz/002085

Demuth, K. (1996). The prosodic structure of early words. In J. Morgan, and K. Demuth, eds., *Signal to Syntax: Bootstrapping from Speech to Grammar in Early Acquisition*. Mahwah, NJ: Lawrence Erlbaum Associates, 171–184.

Demuth, K. and A. Tremblay. (2008). Prosodically-Conditioned Variability in Children's Production of French Determiners. *Journal of Child Language*, 35, 99–127.

Desclés, J.–P. (1998). Transitivité sémantique, transitivité syntaxique. In A. Rousseau, ed. *La transitivité*. Villeneuve-d'Ascq: Presses universitaires du Septentrion, 161–180.

De Swart, H. (1998). Aspect Shift and Coercion. *Natural Language and Linguistic Theory* 16, 347–385.

Diesing, M. (1992). *Indefinites*, Cambridge: MIT Press.

Dionne, G., Ph. S. Dale, M. Boivin and R. Plomin. (2003). Genetic Evidence for Bidirectional Effects of Early Lexical and Grammatical Development. *Child Development*, 74, 394–412.

Di Sciullo, A. M., and D. Isac. (2008). The Asymmetry of Merge. *Biolinguistics*, 2, 260–290.

Dixon, J. and V. Marchman. (2007). Grammar and the Lexicon: Developmental Ordering in Language Acquisition. *Child Development*, 78, 190–212.

Dobrovie-Sorin, C. (1998). Impersonal se constructions in Romance and the passivization of unergatives. *Linguistic Inquiry*, 29, 399–437.

Elliott, M. and M. Pirvulescu. (2015). Bilingual Delay in the Acquisition of Direct Object Clitics in the Spanish of Bilingual Spanish-French Children, paper presented at *Going Romance – 28th Symposium on Romance Linguistics*, Universidade Nova de Lisboa, Lisbon, Portugal.

Elliott, M. (in progress). Delay without Crosslinguisitc Influences: The Acquisition of Direct, Indirect Object Clitics and Clitic Sequences in the Spanish of 3–6-year-old Spanish-French Balanced Bilinguals, PhD Thesis, University of Toronto, Toronto, Canada.

Epstein, -S. D. and D. Seely. (2006). *Derivations in Minimalism*, Cambridge: Cambridge University Press.

Erteschik-Shir, N. and T. Rapoport. (2004). Bare Aspect: A Theory of Syntactic Projection. In J. Guéron, and A. Lecarme, eds., *The Syntax of Time*. Cambridge, Mass: MIT Press, 217–234.

Everaert, M. B. H., M. A. C. Huybregts, N. Chomsky, R. C. Berwick and J. J. Bolhuis. (2015). Structures, Not Strings: Linguistics as Part of the Cognitive Sciences. *Trends in Cognitive Sciences*, 19, 729–743.

Farkas, D. and H. de Swart. (2003). *The Semantics of Incorporation. From Argument Structure to Discourse Transparency*, Stanford, CA: CSLI Publications.

Fellbaum, C. and J. Kegl. (1989). Taxonomic Structures and Cross-Category Linking in the Lexicon. *Escol*, 93–104.

Fiengo, R. and H. Lasnik. (1972). On Nonrecoverable Deletion in Syntax. *Linguistic Inquiry*, 3, 528.

Fillmore, C. (1986). Pragmatically Controlled Zero Anaphora. In V. Nikiforidou, M. VanClay, M. Niepokuj and D. Feder, eds., *Proceedings of the Twelfth Annual Meeting of the Berkeley Linguistics Society.* Calif.: Berkeley Linguistics Society Publications, 95–107.

Flores, C. and P. Barbosa. (2014). When Reduced Input Leads to Delayed Acquisition: A Study on the Acquisition of Clitic Placement by Portuguese Heritage Speakers. *International Journal of Bilingualism* 18 (3), 304–325.

Flores, C. (2015). Losing a Language in Childhood: A Longitudinal Case Study on Language Attrition. *Journal of Child Language* 42 (3), 562–590.

Fodor, J. (1998). Unambiguous Triggers. *Linguistic Inquiry*, 29, 1–36.

Forsyth, J. (1970). *A Grammar of Aspect; Usage and Meaning in the Russian Verb*, Cambridge: Cambridge University Press.

Frazier, L. (1999). *On Sentence Interpretation*. Kluwer Academic Publishers: Dordrecht.

Frolova, A. (2013). Développement de la transitivité verbale chez les enfants russes, unpublished Ph.D. thesis, University of Toronto.

Fujino, H. and T. Sano. (2002). Aspects of the Null Object Phenomenon in Child Spanish. In A. T. Pérez-Leroux, and J. Muñoz-Liceras, eds., *The Acquisition of Spanish Morphosyntax*. Dordrecht: Kluwer Academic Publishers, 67–88.

Garcia Mayo M. del P. and R. Slabakova. (2015). Object Drop in L3 Acquisition. *International Journal of Bilingualism*, 19(5), 483–498.

García Velasco, D. and C. Portero Muñoz. (2002). Understood Objects in Functional Grammar. *University of Amsterdam Working Papers in Functional Grammar 76.* Amsterdam: Functional Grammar Foundation.

Gathercole, V., C., S. Mueller and E. M. Thomas. (2009). Bilingual First-Language Development: Dominant Language Takeover, Threatened Minority Language Take-Up. *Bilingualism: Language and Cognition*, 12(2), 213–237.

Gathercole, S. and A. Baddeley. (1993). *Working Memory and Language*, New York: Psychology Press.

Gavarró, A., V. Torrens and K. Wexler (2010). Object Clitic Omission: Two Language Types. *Language Acquisition*, 17, 192–219.

Gavarró, A., A. T. Pérez-Leroux and T. Roeper. (2006). Definite and Bare Noun Contrasts in Child Catalan. In V. Torrens, and L. Escobar, eds., *The Acquisition of Syntax in Romance Languages*. Amsterdam: John Benjamins Publishing Publishing, 51–68.

Gavruseva, E. and R. Thornton. (2001). Getting it Right: Acquisition of Whose Questions in Child English. *Language Acquisition* 9(3), 229–267.

Gelman, R. and Williams, E. M. (1998). Enabling Constraints for Cognitive Development and Learning: A Domain-Specific Epigenetic Theory. In D. Kuhn and R. Siegler, eds., *Cognition, Perception, and Language*, New York: John Wiley and Sons, 5th ed., Vol. 2, 575–630.

Gelman, S. (2003). The Essential Child: Origins of Essentialism in Everyday Thought, Oxford: Oxford University Press.

Genesee, F., E. Nicoladis and J. Paradis. (1995). Language Differentiation in Early Bilingual Development. *Journal of Child Language*, 22(3), 611–631.

Gillette, J., H. Gleitman, L. Gleitman and A. Lederer. (1999). Human Simulations of Vocabulary Learning. *Cognition* 73, 135–176.

Gillon, B. S. (2006). *English Relational Words, Context Sensitivity and Implicit Arguments*, Ms. McGill University.

Gleitman, L. (1990). Structural Sources of Verb Learning. *Language Acquisition*, 1, 1–63.

Gleitman, L., R. Cassidy, K. Nappa, R. A. Papafragou and J. C. Trueswell. (2005). Hard Words. *Language Learning and Development*, 1(1) 23–64.

Göksun, T., A. Küntay and L. Naigles. (2008). Turkish Children Use Morphosyntax in Extending Verb Meaning. *Journal of Child Language*, 35, 291–323.

Goldberg, A. (2001). Patient Arguments of Causative Verbs Can Be Omitted: The Role of Information Structure in Argument Distribution. *Language Science*, 23, 503–524.

Gordishevsky, G. and S. Avrutin. (2003). Subject and Object Omission in Child Russian. In Y. N. Falk, ed., *IATL* 19, University Ben-Gurion of Negev. Retrieved from http://linguistics.huji.ac.il/IATL/19/

Gordishevsky, G. and S. Avrutin. (2004). Optional Omissions in an Optionally Null Subject Language. In J. van Kampen and S. Baauw, eds., *Proceedings of GALA 2003*. LOT Occasional series 3, Utrecht University, 187–198.

Gould, I. (2015). *Syntactic Learning from Ambiguous Evidence: Errors and End-States*. PhD dissertation, Massachusetts Institute of Technology.

Gould, I. (2016). Learning Parameter Setting from Ambiguous Evidence: Parameter Interaction and the Case of Korean. In K. Kim, P. Umbal, T. Block, Q. Chan, T. Cheng, K. Finney, M. Katz, S. Nickel-Thompson and L. Shorten, eds., *Proceedings of the 33rd West Coast Conference on Formal Linguistics*. Somerville, MA: Cascadilla Proceedings Project, 157–166.

Graf, E., A. Theakston, E. Lieven and M. Tomasello. (2014). Subject and Object Omission in Children's Early Transitive Constructions: A Discourse-Pragmatic Approach. *Applied Psycholinguistics*, 36(3), 701–727.

Greenfield, P. and J. Smith. (1976). *The Structure of Communication in Early Language Development*. New York: Academic Press.

Grinstead, J. (2004). Subjects and Interface Delay in Child Spanish and Catalan. *Language*, 80 (1), 40–72.

Grüter, T. (2006). *Object Clitics and Null Objects in the Acquisition of French*, Ph. D. thesis, McGill University.

Grüter, T. (2007). Investigating Object Drop in Child French and English: A Truth Value Judgment Task. In A. Belikova, L. Meroni and M. Umeda, eds., *Proceedings of the 2nd Conference on Generative Approaches to Language Acquisition North America (GALANA)*. Somerville, MA: Cascadilla Proceedings Project, 102–113.

Grüter, T. and M. Crago. (2012). Object Clitics and Their Omission in Child L2 French: The Contributions of Processing Limitations and L1 Transfer. *Bilingualism: Language and Cognition*, 15(3), 531–549.

Guasti, M. T., A. Gavarró, J. de Lange and C. Caprin. (2008). Article Omission across Child Languages. *Language Acquisition*, 15(2), 89–119.

Haeckel, Ernst. (1866). *Generelle Morphologie der Organismen: allgemeine Grundzüge der organischen Formen-Wissenschaft, mechanisch begründet durch die von Charles Darwin reformirte Descendenz-Theorie*. Berlin: Verlag.

Hale, K. and S. J. Keyser. (1991). On the Syntax of Argument Structure. *Lexicon Project Working Papers* 34. Cambridge, MA: MIT Center for Cognitive Science.

Hale, K. and S. J. Keyser. (1993). On Argument Structure and the Lexical Expression of Syntactic Relations. In K. Hale and S. J. Keyser, eds., *The View from Building. 20*, Cambridge, MA: MIT Press, 53–109.

Hale, K. and S. Keyser. (2002). *Prolegomenon to a Theory of Argument Structure*, Cambridge, Mass: MIT Press.

Haegeman, L. (1987). Complement Ellipsis in English: Or, How to Cook without Objects. In A.–M. Simon-Vandenbergen, ed., *Studies in Honour of René Derolez*. University of Ghent, 248–261.

Hamann, C. (2003). Phenomena in French Normal and Impaired Language Acquisition and Their Implications for Hypotheses on Language Development. *Probus*, 15, 91–122.

Hamann, C., L. Tuller, C. Monjauze, H. Delage and C. Henry. (2007). (Un)successful Subordination in French-speaking Children and Adolescents with SLI. In H. Caunt-Nulton, S. Kulatilake and I. Woo, eds., *BUCLD 31: Proceedings of the* 31st *Annual Boston University Conference on Language Development*. Somerville, Mass.: Cascadilla Press, 286–297

Hayiou-Thomas, M., Y. Kovas, N. Harlaar, R. Plomin, D. Bishop and Ph. Dale. (2006). Common Etiology for Diverse Language Skills in 4 1/2 Year-Old Twins. *Journal of Child Language*, *33*, 339–368.

Heim, I. 2008. Features on Bound Pronouns. In D. Adger, S. Bejar and D. Harbour, eds., *Phi Theory: Phi Features across Interfaces and Modules*. Oxford: Oxford University Press, 35–56.

Hendrickson, K. and M. Sundara. (2017). Fourteen-Month-Olds' Decontextualized Understanding of Words for Absent Objects. *Journal of Child Language*, 44 (1), 239–254.

Hervé, C., L. Serratrice and M. Corley. (2016). Dislocations in French–English Bilingual Children: An Elicitation Study. *Bilingualism: Language and Cognition, FirstView Article, February* 2016, 1–14.

Hill, V. and Y. Roberge. (2006). A Locally Determined Verb Typology. *Revue Roumaine de Linguistique*, 5, 5–22.

Hill, V. and Pirvulescu, M. (2012). French Object Clitics, L1 and the Left Periphery. In S. Ferré, P. Prévost, L. Tuller and R. Zebib, eds., *Selected Proceedings of the Romance Turn IV Workshop on the Acquisition of Romance Languages*. Newcastle upon Tyne, UK: Cambridge Publishing Scholars, 169–189.

Hirakawa, M. (1993). Null Objects Versus Null Objects in an Early Grammar of Japanese. *McGill Working Papers in Linguistics*, 9, 30–45.

Holmberg, A. (2005). Is There a Little Pro? Evidence from Finnish. *Linguistic Inquiry*, 36, 533–564.

Holmberg, A. and I. Roberts. (2014). Parameters and the Three Factors of Language Design. In C. Picallo, ed., *Linguistic Variation in the Minimalist Framework*. Oxford: Oxford University Press, 61–81.

Hopper, P. and S. Thompson. (1980). Transitivity in Grammar and Discourse. *Language*, 56, 253–299.

Hornstein, N., J. Nunes and K. K. Grohmann. (2005). *Understanding Minimalism*. Cambridge: Cambridge University Press.

Hsin, L., G. Legendre and A. Omaki. (2013). Priming Cross-Linguistic Interference in Spanish-English Bilingual Children. In S. Baiz, N. Goldman and R. Hawkes, eds., *BUCLD 37: Proceedings of the 37th Annual Boston University Conference on Language Development*. Somerville, Mass.: Cascadilla Press, 165–177.

Huang, J. (1982). *Logical Relations in Chinese and the Theory of Grammar*. PhD dissertation, Massachusetts Institute of Technology.

Hudson Kam, C. and E. Newport. (2005). Regularizing Unpredictable Variation: the Roles of Adult and Child Learners in Language Formation and Change. *Language Learning and Development*, 1(2), 151–195.

Hughes, M. and S. Allen. (2013). The Effect of Individual Discourse-Pragmatic Features on Referential Choice in Child English. *Journal of Pragmatics*, 56, 15–30.

Hulk, A. (1997). The Acquisition of French Object Pronouns by a Dutch/French Bilingual Child. In A. Sorace, C. Heycock and R. Shillcock, eds., *Proceedings of GALA'97 Conference on Language Acquisition*. Edinburgh: University of Edinburgh Press, 521–527.

Hulk, A. and N. Müller. (2000). Bilingual First Language Acquisition at the Interface between Syntax and Pragmatics. *Bilingualism: Language and Cognition*, 3(3), 227–244.

Hyams, N. (1983). The Pro Drop Parameter in Child Grammars. In M. Barlow, D. Flickinger and M. Wescoat, eds., *Proceedings of the West Coast Conference on Formal Linguistics*, vol. II. Mass.: Stanford University, 126–139.

Hyams, N. (1986). *Language Acquisition and the Theory of Parameters*. Dortrecht: Reidel.

Ingham, R. (1993/1994). Input and Learnability: Direct Object Omissibility in English. *Language Acquisition*, 3, 95–120.

Ivanov, I. (2008). L1 Acquisition of Bulgarian Object Clitics: Unique Checking Constraint or Failure to Mark Referentiality. In H. Chan, H. Jacob, E. Kapia, eds., *Proceedings of the 32nd BUCLD*, Vol.1. Somerville: Cascadilla Press, 189–200.

Jakubowicz, C., N. Müller, O.–K. Kang, B. Riemer and C. Rigaut. (1996). On the Acquisition of the Pronominal System in French and German. In A. Stringfellow, D. Cahana-Amitay, E. Hughes and A. Zukowski, eds., Proceedings of the 20th BUCLD. Somerville, Mass.: Cascadilla Press, 374–385.

Jakubowicz, C., N. Müller, B. Riemer and C. Rigaut. (1997). The Case of Subject and Object Omissions in French and German. In E. Hugues, M. Hugues and A. Greenhill, eds., Proceedings of the 21st BUCLD. Somerville, Mass: Cascadilla Press, 331–342.

Jakubowicz, C., L. Nash, C. Rigaut and C.–L. Gérard. (1998). Determiners and Clitic Pronouns in French-Speaking Children with SLI. *Language Acquisition*, 7, 113–160.

Jakubowicz, C. and C. Rigaut. (2000). L'acquisition des clitiques nominatifs et des clitiques objets en Français. *Canadian Journal of Linguistics*, 45, 119–157.

Jakubowicz, C. and L. Nash. (forthcoming). Why accusative clitics are avoided in normal and impaired language development. In C. Jakubowicz, L. Nash and K. Wexler, eds., *Essays in Syntax, Morphology and Phonology in SLI*. Cambridge, Mass: MIT Press.

Jones, M. A. (1988). Cognate Objects and the Case Filter. *Journal of Linguistics* 24: 89–110.

Katz, J. and P. Postal. (1964). *An Integrated Theory of Linguistic Descriptions*, Cambridge, Mass: MIT Press.

Kayama, Y. (2003). L1 Acquisition of Japanese Zero Pronouns: The Effect of Discourse Factors. In S. Burelle, and S. Somesfalean, eds., *Proceedings of the 2003 Annual Conference of the Canadian Linguistic Association*. Retrieved from http://homes .chass.utoronto.ca/~claacl/2003/, 109–120.

Kim, Y.–J. (2000). Subject/Object Drop in the Acquisition of Korean: A Cross-Linguistics Study. *Journal of East Asian Linguistics*, 9 (4), 325–351.

Kowalski, A. and C. Yang. (2012). Verb Islands in Adult and Child Language. In A. K. Biller, E. Y. Chung and A. E. Kimball, eds., *BUCLD 36: Proceedings of the 36th Annual Boston University Conference on Language Development*. Somerville, Mass: Cascadilla Press, 281–289.

Krivochen, D. (2013). Towards a Geometrical Syntax: a Formalization of Radical Minimalism. Ms. Universidad Nacional de La Plata.

Krivochen, D. G. and P. Kosta. (2013). *Eliminating Empty Categories: A Radically Minimalist View on Their Ontology and Justification*, Frankfurt: Peter Lang.

Kuroda, S.–Y. (1972). The Categorical Judgement and the Thetic Judgement: Evidence from Japanese syntax. *Foundations of Language*, 9, 153–185.

Lambrecht, K. (1994). *Information Structure and Sentence Form: Topic, Focus, and the Mental Representation of Discourse Referents*. Cambridge: Cambridge University Press.

Lambrecht, K. and K. Lemoine (1996). Vers une grammaire des compléments zéro en français parlé. In J. Chuquet, and M. Frid, eds., *Absence de marques et représentation de l'absence*. Travaux Linguistiques du Cerlico 9, Rennes: Presses universitaires de Rennes, 279–309.

Larjavaara, M. (2000). *Présence ou absence de l'objet. Limites du possible en français contemporain*, Helsinki: Academia Scientiarum Fennica.

Larson, M. (2002). The Semantics of Object Drop in Baule. In M. Nissim, ed., *Proceedings of the seventh ESSLLI Student Session*. 1–10.

Lasnik, H. (2001). Subjects, Objects, and the EPP. In W. Davies and S. Dubinsky, eds., *Objects and Other Subjects: Grammatical Functions, Functional Categories, and Configurationality*. Dordrecht: Kluwer Academic Publishers, 103–121.

Lavidas, N. (2013). Null and Cognate Objects and Changes in (In)transitivity: Evidence from the History of English. *Acta Linguistica Hungarica*, 60, 69–106.

Lavidas, N. (2016). Development of Transitivity in a Language without/with Object Clitics: English vs. Greek (A Diachronic Contrastive Study). In M. Mattheoudakis and K. Nicolaidis, eds., *Selected Papers of the* 21st *International Symposium on Theoretical and Applied Linguistics (ISTAL 21)*, Prothiki: Aristotle University of Thessaloniki, 186–210.

Lazard, G. (1994). *L'actance*. Paris: Presses universitaires de France.

Lebeaux, D. (1988). Language Acquisition and the Form of the Grammar, Ph.D. thesis, University of Massachusetts.

Legate, J. and C. Yang. (2007). Morphosyntactic Learning and the Development of Tense. *Language Acquisition*, 14, 315–344.

Lee, T. H.–T. (2000). Finiteness and Null Arguments in Child Cantonese. *The Tsinghua Journal of Chinese Studies*, New Series 30, 365–393.

Lee, J.N. and L.R. Naigles. (2005). The Input to Verb Learning in Mandarin Chinese: A Role for Syntactic Bootstrapping. *Developmental Psychology*, 41(3), 529–540.

Levin, B. (1999). Objecthood: An Event Structure Perspective. In S. Billings, J. Boyle and A. Griffith, eds., *Proceedings of CLS 35, Vol. I: The Main Session*. ILL: Chicago Linguistic Society Billings, 223–247.

Levin, B. (2000). Aspect, lexical semantic representation, and argument expression. In A. Simpson, ed., *Proceedings of the 26th Annual Meeting of the Berkeley Linguistics Society*, 413–429.

Levin, B. (2013). *Verb Classes Thinking and across Languages*. Ms. Stanford University

Levinson, S. C. (2000). *Presumptive Meaning: The Theory of Generalized Conversational Implicature*, Cambridge, Mass: MIT Press.

Lizsckowski, D. (1999). On the Acquisition of Pronominal Object Clitics. Unpublished thesis. Harvard University.

Longa, V. and G. Lorenzo. (2008). What about a (Really) Minimalist Theory of Language Acquisition? *Linguistics*, 46, 541–570.

Lopez, L. (2003). Steps for a Well-Adjusted Dislocation. *Studia Linguistica*, 57(3), 193–231.

Lorenzo, G. and V. Longa. (2009). Beyond Generative Geneticism: Rethinking Language Acquisition from a Developmentalist Point of View. *Lingua*, 119, 1300–1315.

Luraghi, S. (2004). Null Objects in Latin and Greek and the Relevance of Linguistic Typology for Language Reconstruction. In *Proceedings of the* 15th *Annual UCLA Indo-European Conference*, JIES Monograph 49, 234–256.

Luraghi, S. (2010). Transitivity, Intransitivity and Diathesis in Hittite. In *ИНДОЕВРОПЕЙСКОЕ ЯЗЫКОЗНАНИЕ И КЛАССИЧЕСКАЯ ФИЛОЛОГИЯ* – XIV, vol. 2. St. Petersburg, Nauka, 133–154.

Macnamara, J. (1972). Cognitive Basis of Language Learning in Infants. *Psychological Review*, 79, 1–14.

MacWhinney, B. (2000). *The CHILDES Project: Tools for Analysing Talk*, Mahwah: Lawrence Erlbaum.

Manzini, R. and K. Wexler. (1987). Parameters, Binding Theory, and Learnability. *Linguistic Inquiry*, 18, 413–444.

Marchman, V. A., A. Fernald and N. Hurtado. (2010). How Vocabulary Size in Two Languages Relates to Efficiency in Spoken Word Recognition by Young Spanish–English Bilinguals. *Journal of Child Language*, 37(4), 817–840.

Marinis, T. (2000). The Acquisition of Clitic Objects in Modern Greek: Single Clitics, Clitic Doubling, Clitic Left Dislocation. *ZAS Papers in Linguistics*, 15, 259–281.

Massam, D. (1990). Cognate Objects as Thematic Objects. *Canadian Journal of Linguistics*, 35, 161–190.

Massam, D. (2009). Noun Incorporation: Essentials and Extensions, *Language and Linguistics Compass* 3/4: 1076–1096.

Massam, D. and Y. Roberge. (1989). Recipe Context Null Subjects. *Linguistic Inquiry*, 20, 134–139.

Mateu, V. E. (2015). Object Clitic Omission in Child Spanish: Evaluating Representational and Processing Accounts. *Language Acquisition*, 22, 240–284.

Matsuo A., S. Kita, Y. Shinya, G. C. Wood and L. Naigles (2012) Japanese Two-Year-Olds Use Morphosyntax to Learn Novel Verb Meanings. *Journal of Child Language*, 39(3), 637–663.

Matthews, D., E. Lieven, A. Theakston and M. Tomasello. (2006). The Effect of Perceptual Availability and Prior Discourse on Young Children's Use or Referring Expressions. *Applied Psycholinguistics*, 27, 403–422.

Matthewson, L. (2013). On How (Not) to Uncover Cross-Linguistic Variation. In S. Keine and S. Slogett, eds., *Proceedings of the North East Linguistic Society* 42, vol. II. Amherst, Mass.: GLSA, 323–342.

Meisel, J. M. (2001). The Simultaneous Acquisition of Two First Languages: Early Differentiation and Subsequent Development of Grammars. In J. Cenoz and F. Genesee, eds., *Trends in Bilingual Acquisition*, Amsterdam: John Benjamins Publishing, 11–41.

Meisel, J. M. (2007). On Autonomous Syntactic Development in Multiple First Language Acquisition. In H. Caunt-Nulton, S. Kulatilake and I. W. Kulatilake, eds., *Proceedings of the 31st Annual Boston University Conference on Language Development (Vol. 1)*. Somerville, MA: Cascadilla Press, 25–45.

Merlo, P. and S. Stevenson. (2001). Automatic Verb Classification Based on Statistical Distributions of Argument Structure. *Computational Linguistics*, 27, 373–408.

Moscati V. (2014). Discourse Adherence and the Pronominal Status of Null-Objects in French-Speaking Children. *Journal of Child Language Acquisition and Development* 2.4: 1–15.

Müller, N., B. Crysmann and G. Kaiser. (1996). Interactions Between the Acquisition of French Object Drop and the Development of the C-System. *Language Acquisition*, 5, 35–63.

Müller, N. and A. Hulk. (2001). Cross-Linguistic Influence in Bilingual Language Acquisition: Italian and French as Recipient Languages. *Bilingualism: Language and Cognition*, 4, 1–21.

Müller, N. (2004). Null-Arguments in Bilingual Children: French Topics. In J. Paradis, and Ph. Prévost, eds., *The Acquisition of French in Different Contexts*. Amsterdam: John Benjamins Publishing, 275–304.

Müller, N., K. Schmitz, K. Cantone and T. Kupisch. (2006). Null Arguments in Monolingual Children: A Comparison of Italian and French. In V. Torrens and L. Escobar, eds., *The Acquisition of Syntax in Romance Languages*. Amsterdam: John Benjamins Publishing, 69–93.

Mykhaylyk, R., Y. Rodina and M. Anderssen. (2013). Ditransitive Constructions in Russian and Ukrainian: Effect of Givenness on Word Order. *Lingua*, 137, 271–289.

Mykhaylyk R. and A. Sopata. (Forthcoming). Object Pronouns, Clitics, and Omissions in Child Polish and Ukrainian. *Applied psycholinguistics*.

Naigles, L. R. (2002). Form Is Easy, Meaning Is Hard: Resolving a Paradox in Early Child Language. *Cognition*, 86, 157–199.

Naigles L.R. and N. Lehrer. (2002). Language-General and Language-Specific Influences on Children's Acquisition of Argument Structure: A Comparison of French and English. *Journal of Child Language*, 29(3), 545–566.

Newmeyer, F. J. (2003). Grammar Is Grammar and Usage Is Usage. *Language*, 79, 682–707.

Newmeyer, F. J. (2005). *Possible and Probable Languages*. Oxford: Oxford University Press.

Nicoladis, E. (2012). Cross-Linguistic Influence in French–English Bilingual Children's Possessive Constructions. *Bilingualism: Language and Cognition*, 15:2, 320–328.

Ninio, A. (2015). Learning Transitive Verbs from Single-Word Verbs in the Input by Young Children Acquiring English. *Journal of Child Language*, available on CJO2015.

Noailly, M. (1997). Les mystères de la transitivité invisible. *Langages*, 127, 96–109.

O'Grady, W., Y. Yamashita and S. Cho. (2008). Object Drop in Japanese and Korean. *Language Acquisition*, 15, 58–68.

Olguin, R. and M. Tomasello. (1993). Twenty-Five-Month-Old Children Do Not Have a Grammatical Category of Verb. *Cognitive Development*, 8, 245–272.

Oshima-Takane Y., J. Ariyama, T. Kobayashi, M. Katerelos and D. Poulin-Dubois. (2011). Early Verb Learning in 20-Month-Old Japanese-Speaking Children. *Journal of Child Language*, 38(3), 455–484.

Panagiotidis, P. (2002). *Pronouns, Clitics and Empty Nouns: Pronominality and Licensing in Syntax*, Amsterdam: John Benjamins Publishing.

Pannemann, M. (2007). DP Acquisition as Structure Unravelling, unpublished Ph. D. thesis, Universiteit van Amsterdam.

Paradis, J. and F. Genesee. (1996). Syntactic Acquisition in Bilingual Children: Autonomous or Interdependent? *Studies in Second Language Acquisition*, 18, 1–25.

Paradis, J. and F. Genesee. (1997). On Continuity and the Emergence of Functional Categories in Bilingual First Language Acquisition. *Language Acquisition*, 6, 91–124.

Paradis, J. and S. Navarro. (2003). Subject Realization and Cross-Linguistic Interference in the Bilingual Acquisition of Spanish and English: What Is the Role of the Input? *Journal of Child Language*, 30, 371–393

Paradis, J., E. Nicoladis and M. Crago. (2007). French-English Bilingual Children's Acquisition of Past Tense. In H. Caunt-Nulton, S. Kulatilake and I.–H. Woo, eds., *BUCLD 31 Proceedings*. Somerville, MA: Cascadilla Press, 497–507.

Pearson, B. Z., S. C. Fernández and D. Kimbrough Oller. (1993). Lexical Development in Bilingual Infants and Toddlers: Comparison to Monolingual Norms. *Language Learning*, 43(1), 93–120.

Pearson, B. Z. (2008). *Raising a Bilingual Child: A Step-by-Step Guide for Parents*. NY: Random House.

Pérez-Leroux, A.T. (2005). Number Problems in Children. In C. Gurski, ed., Proceedings of the 2005 Canadian Linguistics Association Annual Conference, 1–12. http://ling.uwo.ca/publications/CLA-ACL/CLA-ACL2005.htm

Pérez-Leroux, A. T. and T. Roeper. (1999). Scope and the Structure of Bare Nominals: Evidence from Child Language. *Linguistics*, 37, 927–960

Pérez-Leroux, A. T., M. Pirvulescu and Y. Roberge. (2006a). Early Object Omission in Child French and English. In C. Nishida and J.–P. Y. Montreuil, eds., *New Perspectives in Romance Linguistics*, (vol. I). Amsterdam: John Benjamins Publishing, 213–228.

Pérez-Leroux, A. T., M. Pirvulescu, Y. Roberge, D. Thomas and L. Tieu. (2006b) *Variable Input and Object Drop in Child Language*. In C. Gurski and M. Radisic, eds., *Proceedings of the Canadian Linguistics Association Conference*, http://ling.uwo.ca/publications/CLA2006/Perez-Leroux_etal.pdf.

Pérez-Leroux, A. T., M. Pirvulescu and Y. Roberge. (2008a). Null Objects in Child Language: Syntax and the Lexicon, *Lingua*, 118(3), 370–398.

Pérez-Leroux, A. T., M. Pirvulescu and Y. Roberge. (2008b). Children's Interpretation of Null Objects under the Scope of Negation. In S. Jones, ed., *Proceedings of the 2008 meeting of the Canadian Linguistics Association*. Retrieved from www.chass .utoronto.ca/~cla-acl/actes2008/actes2008.html

Pérez-Leroux, A. T., M. Pirvulescu and Y. Roberge. (2009a). Bilingualism as a Window into the Language Faculty: The Acquisition of Objects in French-Speaking Children in Bilingual and Monolingual Contexts. *Bilingualism: Language and Cognition*, 12 (1), 1–16

Pérez-Leroux, A. T., M. Pirvulescu and Y. Roberge. (2009b). On the Semantic Properties of Implicit Objects in Young Children's Elicited Production. In J. Chandlee, J., Franchini, M. S. Lord and G.–M. Rheiner, eds., *Proceedings of the 33 Annual Boston University Conference on Language Development*. Somerville, Mass: Cascadilla Press, 398–409.

Pérez-Leroux, A. T., M. Pirvulescu and Y. Roberge. (2011). Topicalization and Object Drop in Child Language. *First Language* 31(2), 1–20.

Pérez-Leroux, A. T., A. P. Castilla-Earls and J. Brunner. (2012). General and Specific Effects of Lexicon in Grammar: Determiner and Object Pronoun Omissions in Child Spanish. *Journal of Speech, Language and Hearing Research*, 55, 313–327.

Pérez-Leroux, A. T., M. Pirvulescu and Y. Roberge, A. P. Castilla-Earls. (2013). On the Development of Null Implicit Objects in L1 English. *The Canadian Journal of Linguistics*, 58(3), 443–464.

Pérez-Leroux, A. T. and A. Kahnemuyipour. (2014). News, Somewhat Exaggerated: Commentary on Ambridge, Pine, and Lieven. *Language*, 90(3), 115–125.

Pesetsky, D. and E. Torrego. (2004). Tense, Case, and the Nature of Syntactic Categories. In J. Guéron and A. Lecarme, eds., *The Syntax of Time*. Cambridge, Mass: MIT Press, 495–537.

Pinker, S. (1984). *Language Learnability and Language Development*, Cambridge, Mass: Harvard University Press.

Pinker, S. (1989). *Learnability and Cognition: The Acquisition of Argument Structure*, Cambridge, Mass: MIT Press.

Pirvulescu, M. (2006a). Theoretical Implications of Clitic Omission in Early French: Spontaneous vs. Elicited Production. *Catalan Journal of Linguistics – Special Edition on Acquisition*, 5, 221–236.

Pirvulescu, M. (2006b). The Acquisition of Object Clitics in French L1: Spontaneous vs. Elicited Production. In A. Belletti, E. Bennati, C. Chesi, E. Di Domenico and I. Ferrari, eds., *Proceedings of GALA 2005*. Cambridge, UK: Cambridge Scholars Press, 450–462.

Pirvulescu, M. and Y. Roberge. (1999). Objects and the Structure of Imperatives. In J.–M. Authier, B. Bullock and L. Reed, eds., *Formal Perspectives on Romance Linguistics*. Amsterdam: John Benjamins Publishing, 211–226.

Pirvulescu, M. and Y. Roberge. (2005). Licit and Illicit Null Objects in L1 French. In R. Gess and E. Rubin, eds., *Theoretical and Experimental Approaches to Romance Linguistics*, Amsterdam: John Benjamins Publishing, 197–212.

Pirvulescu, M. and I. Belzil. (2008). The Acquisition of Past Participle Agreement in Québec French L1. *Language Acquisition*, 15:2, 75–88.

Pirvulescu, M., A. T. Pérez-Leroux, Y. Roberge and N. Strik. (2011) Pousse-le! Clitic Production across Tasks in Young French-Speaking Children, Presentation, LSRL 41, University of Ottawa, May 5–7 2011.

Pirvulescu, M., A. T. Pérez-Leroux and Y. Roberge. (2012). A Bidirectional Study of Object Omissions in French-English Bilinguals. In K. Braunmüller, C. Gabriel and B. Hänel-Faulhaber, eds., *Multilingual Individuals and Multilingual Societies*. Amsterdam: John Benjamins Publishing, 171–188.

Pirvulescu, M., A. T. Pérez-Leroux, Y. Roberge, N. Strik and D. Thomas. (2014). Bilingual Effects: Exploring Object Omission in Pronominal Languages. *Bilingualism: Language and Cognition*, 17(3), 495–510.

Pirvulescu, M. and N. Strik. (2014). The Acquisition of Object Clitic Features in French: A Comprehension Study. *Lingua*, 144, 58–71.

Postal, P. and G. Pullum. (1988). Expletive Noun Phrases in Subcategorized Positions. *Linguistic Inquiry*, 19, 635–670.

Prévost, P. (2006). The Phenomenon of Object Omission in Child L2 French. *Bilingualism: Language and Cognition*, 9 (3), 263–280.

Pye, C. (1994). A Cross-Linguistic Approach to the Causative Alternation. In Y. Levy, ed., *Other Children, Other Languages*. Hillsdale, NJ: Erlbaum, 243–264.

Pylkkänen, L. (2008). *Introducing Arguments*, Cambridge: MIT Press.

Radford, A. (1990). *Syntactic Theory and the Acquisition of English Syntax: The Nature of Early Child Grammar of English*, Oxford: Blackwell.

Raposo, E. (1986). On the Null Object in European Portuguese. In O. Jaeggli and C. Silva-Corvalán, eds., *Studies in Romance Linguistics*. Dordrecht: Foris, 373–390.

Rappaport Hovav, M. and Levin, B. (2005). Change of State Verbs: Implications for Theories of Argument Projection. In N. Erteschik-Shir and T. Rapoport, eds., *The Syntax of Aspect*. Oxford: Oxford University Press, 274–286.

Rappaport Hovav, M. (2014). Lexical Content and Context: The Causative Alternation in English Revisited. *Lingua*, 141, 8–29.

Reinhart, T. (1981) Pragmatics and Linguistics: An Analysis of Sentence Topics. *Philosophica*, 27, 53–94.

Reinhart, T. and Reuland, E. (1993). Reflexivity. *Linguistic Inquiry*, 24: 657–720.

Ritter, E. and Wiltschko, M. (2016). Humanness as an Alternative to Case-Licensing. Paper Delivered at the Annual Meeting of the Canadian Linguistic Association, University of Calgary.

Rizzi, L. (1986). Null Objects in Italian and the Theory of Pro. *Linguistic Inquiry*, 17, 501–557.

Rizzi, L. (2002). On the Grammatical Basis of Language Development: A Case Study, Manuscript Retrieved from www.ciscl.unisi.it/pubblicazioni.htm#2002.

Rizzi, L. (2009). On the Grammatical Basis of Language Development: A Case Study. In G. Cinque and R. Kayne, eds., *Handbook of Comparative Syntax*. Oxford-New York: Oxford University Press, 70–109.

Roberge, Y. (1990). *The Syntactic Recoverability of Null Arguments*: Montréal: McGill-Queen's University Press.

Roberge, Y. and M. Troberg. (2007). Les objets indirects non thématiques en français. In Radišić, M. ed., *Proceedings of the 2007 Annual Conference of the Canadian Linguistic Association*. www.chass.utoronto.ca/~cla-acl/actes2007/Roberge_Troberg.pdf.

Roberge, Y. (2002). Transitivity Requirement Effects and the EPP. Paper Delivered at the Western Conference on Linguistics (WECOL). Vancouver.

Roeper, T. (1992). From the Initial State to V2: Acquisition Principles in Action. In J. Meisel, ed., *The Acquisition of Verb Placement: Functional Categories and V2 Phenomena in Language Acquisition*, Dordrecht: Kluwer Academic Publishers, 333–370.

Roeper, T. (1999). Universal Bilingualism. *Bilingualism: Language and Cognition*, 2, 169–186.

Roeper, T. (2004). How Not to Undermine the Goal of an Acquisition Theory. *Journal of Child Language*, 31, 500–504.

Roeper, T. (2006). Watching Noun Phrases Emerge: Seeking Compositionality. In V. Van Geenhoven, ed., *Semantics in Acquisition*. Dordrecht: Springer, 37–64.

Roeper, T. (2007). *The Prism of Grammar*, Cambridge, MA: MIT Press.

Rosenbaum, P. S. (1967). *The Grammar of English Predicate Complement Constructions*. Cambridge: MIT Press.

Roussou, A. and I. M. Tsimpli. (2007). Clitics and Transitivity. In A. Alexiadou, ed., *Studies in the Morpho-Syntax of Greek*, Cambridge: Cambridge Scholars Publishing, 138–174.

Rozendaal, M. (2006). The Acquisition of the Syntax-Pragmatics Interface in French L1: Evidence from DP's and Pronouns. Paper Delivered at the Romance Turn 2, Utrecht.

Rizzi, L. (2016). The Concept of Explanatory Adequacy. In I. Roberts, ed., *The Oxford Handbook of Universal Grammar*. Oxford University Press: New York.

Roeper, T. (1999). Universal Bilingualism. *Bilingualism, Language and Cognition* 2, 169–186.

Roeper, T. (2014). Strict Interface Principles and the Acquisition Engine: From Unlabeled to Labeled and Minimal Modular Contact. *Language Sciences* 46, 115–132.

Roeper, T. (2016). Multiple Grammars and the Logic of Learnability in Second Language acquisition. *Frontiers in Psychology* 7, 1–15.

Ruda, M. (2014). Missing Objects in Special Registers: The Syntax of Null Objects in English, *Canadian Journal of Linguistics* 59, 339–372.

Runner, J. T. (2000). The External Object Hypothesis and the Case of Object Expletives. In K. Crosswhite and J. S. Magnuso, eds., *University of Rochester Working Papers in the Language Sciences*, 1 (2), 257–269.

Runner, J. T. and A. Baker. (2015). New Evidence for Sensitivity to Syntax in English Verb Phrase Ellipsis, poster presentation, The 28th Annual CUNY Conference on Human Sentence Processing, New York, March 19–21.

Sakas, W. and J. Fodor. (2012). Disambiguating Syntactic Triggers. *Language Acquisition*, 19(2), 83–143.

Salomo, D., E. Lieven and M. Tomasello. (2010). Young Children's Sensitivity to New and Given Information When Answering Predicate-Focus Questions. *Applied Psycholinguistics*, 31, 101–115.

Schaeffer, J. (1997). Direct Object Scrambling and Clitic Placement in Dutch and Italian Child Language, Ph.D. thesis, University of California Los Angeles.

Schaeffer, J. (2000). *The Acquisition of Direct Object Scrambling and Clitic Placement*, Amsterdam: John Benjamins Publishing.

Schaeffer, J. and L. Matthewson. (2005). Grammar and Pragmatics in the Acquisition of Article Systems. *Natural Language & Linguistic Theory*, 23, 53–101.

Scheele, A. F., P. P. M. Leseman and A. Y. Mayo. (2010). The Home Language Environment of Monolingual and Bilingual Children and Their Language Proficiency. *Applied Psycholinguistics*, 31. 117–140.

Schmitz, K., K. Cantone, N. Müller and T. Kupisch. (2004). Clitic Realizations and Omissions in Early Child Grammar: A Comparison of Italian and French, paper presented at the Romance Turn Workshop on the acquisition of Romance Languages, Madrid, Spain.

Schwenter, S. (2006). Null Objects across South America. In T. Face and C. Klee, eds., *Selected Proceedings of the 8th Hispanic Linguistics Symposium*. Somerville, Mass.: Cascadilla Press, 23–36.

Serratrice, L. (2005). The Role of Discourse Pragmatics in the Acquisition of Subjects in Italian. *Applied Psycholinguistics*, 26, 437–462.

Serratrice, L., A. Sorace, S. Paoli. (2004). Cross-Linguistic Influence at the Syntax–Pragmatics Interface: Subjects and Objects in English–Italian Bilingual and Monolingual Acquisition. *Bilingualism: Language and Cognition*, 7, 183–205.

Seston, R., R. Michnick Golinkoff, W. Ma and K. Hirsh-Pasek. (2009). Vacuuming with My Mouth?: Children's Ability to Comprehend Novel Extensions of Familiar Verbs. *Cognitive Development*, 24, 113–124.

Shetreet, E., N. Friedmann and U. Hadar. (2010). Cortical Representation of Verbs with Optional Complements: The Theoretical Contribution of fMRI. *Human Brain Mapping*, 31, 770–785.

Sigurðsson, H. Á. (2011). Conditions on Argument Drop. *Linguistic Inquiry*, 42, 267–304.

Skarabela, B., S. Allen and T. Scott-Phillips. (2013). Joint Attention Helps Explain Why Children Omit New Referents. *Journal of Pragmatics*, 56: 5–14.

Slobin, D. I. (1985). Introduction: Why Study Acquisition Crosslinguistically. In D. Slobin, ed., *The Crosslinguistic Study of Language Acquisition. Volume I: Data*. Hillsdale, NJ: Lawrence Erlbaum, 3–24.

Smith, M. A. (2011) Everyday Talk Informs Toddlers' Novel Verb Generalizations. *First Language*, 31(4), 404–424.

Snyder, W. (2007). *Child Language: The Parametric Approach*. Oxford, UK: Oxford University Press.

Snider, N. and J. Runner. (2010). Structural Parallelism Aids Ellipsis and Anaphora Resolution: Evidence from Eye Movements to Semantic and Phonological Neighbors. Talk Presented at *16th Annual Conference on Architectures and Mechanisms for Language Processing*. September 7–9, York, UK.

Sorace A., L. Serratrice, F. Filiaci and M. Baldo. (2009). Discourse Conditions on Subject Pronoun Realization: Testing the Linguistic Intuitions of Older Bilingual Children. *Lingua*, 119, 460–477.

Stampe, D. (1993). Object Agreement Summary, Linguist List 4.447. https://linguistlist .org/issues/4/4-447.html.

Tedeschi, R. (2008). The Syntax-Discourse Interface: Referential Expressions in Early Italian. In A. Gavarró and J. Freitas, eds., *Language Acquisition and Development: Proceedings of GALA 2007*. Newcastle upon Tyne: Cambridge Scholars Press, 457–466.

Tedeschi, R. (2009). *Acquisition at the Interfaces: A Case Study on Object Clitics in Early Italian*, Utrecht: LOT.

Tenny, C. (1994). *Aspectual Roles and the Syntax/Semantics Interface*, Dordrecht: Kluwer Academic Publishers.

Theakston, A. L., E. Lieven, J. M. Pine and C. F. Rowland. (2001). The Role of Performance Limitations in the Acquisition of Verb-Argument Structure: An Alternative Account. *Journal of Child Language*, 28, 127–152.

Thomas, A. L. (1979). Ellipsis: The Interplay of Sentence Structure and Context. *Lingua* 47, 43–68.

Tieu, L. S. (2007). Transitivity Requirements in Chinese: Putting the Generic Object in Context. In M. Radišić, ed., *Proceedings of the 2007 Annual Conference of the Canadian Linguistic Association*. http://homes.chass.utoronto.ca/~cla-acl /actes2007/Tieu.pdf.

Tomasello, M. (1992). *First verbs: A Case Study of Early Grammatical Development*, Cambridge, UK: Cambridge University Press.

Tomasello, M. (2000). Do Young Children Have Adult Syntactic Competence? *Cognition*, 74, 209–253.

Tomasello, M. (2001). The Item-Based Nature of Children's Early Syntactic Development. In M. Tomasello and E. Bates, eds., *Language Development: The Essential Readings*. Oxford: Blackwell Publishers, 169–186.

Tomasello, M. (2003). Constructing a Language. *A Usage-Based Theory of Language Acquisition*, Cambridge, MA: Harvard University Press.

Tomasello, M., N. Akhtar, K. Dodson and L. Rekau. (1997). Differential Productivity in Young Children's Use of Nouns and Verbs. *Journal of Child Language*, 24, 373–387.

Trzyna, M. M. (2015). Acquisition of Object Clitics in Child Polish: Evidence for Three Developmental Stages. *Lingua*, 161, 67–81.

Tsakali, V. and Wexler, K. (2004). Why Children Omit Clitics in Some Languages but Not in Others: New Evidence from Greek. In J. van Kampen and S. Baauw, eds., *Proceedings of GALA 2003*. Utrecht: LOT Occasional Series, 493–504.

Tsimpli, I.M. (2014). Early, Late or Very Late? Timing Acquisition and Bilingualism. *Linguistic Approaches to Bilingualism*, 4(3), 283–313.

Tsimpli, I.M., D. Papadopoulou. (2006). Aspect and Argument Realization: A Study on Antecedentless Null Objects in Greek. *Lingua* 116, 1595–1615.

Tuller, L., H. Délage, C. Monjauze, A.–G. Piller, and M.–A. Barthez. (2011). Clitic Production as a Measure of Atypical Language Development in French. *Lingua*, 121, 423–441.

Tzakosta, M. (2003). The Acquisition of Clitics in Greek: A Phonological Perspective. In B. Agbayani, P. Koskinen and V. Samijan, eds., Proceedings of the 31st Western Conference of Linguistics: WECOL 2002. Fresno: California State University, 306–321.

Ud Deen, K. (2004). Object Agreement and Specificity in Nairobi Swahili. In A. Brugos, L. Micciulla and C. Smith, eds., *Proceedings to the* 28th *Annual Boston University Conference on Language Development*. Somerville, Mass: Cascadilla Press, 129–140.

Ullman, M. T. (2001). The Declarative/Procedural Model of Lexicon and Grammar. *Journal of Psycholinguistic Research*, 30 (1), 37–69.

Unsworth S., F. Argyri, L. Cornips, A. Hulk, A. Sorace and I. Tsimpli. (2011). On the Role of Age of Onset and Input in Early Child Bilingualism in Greek and Dutch. In M. Pirvulescu, M. C. Cuervo, A. T. Pérez-Leroux, J. Steele and N. Strik, eds., *Selected Proceedings of the 4th Conference on Generative Approaches to Language Acquisition North America (GALANA 2010)*, Somerville, MA: Cascadilla Proceedings Project, 249–265.

Unsworth, S. (2014). Comparing the Role of Input in Bilingual Acquisition across Domains. In T. Grüter, and J. Paradis, eds., *Input and Experience in Bilingual Development*. Amsterdam: John Benjamins Publishing, 181–201.

Unsworth, S., F. Argyri, L. Cornips, A. Hulk, A. Sorace and I. Tsimpli. (2014). The Role of Age of Onset and Input in Early Child Bilingualism in Greek and Dutch. *Applied Psycholinguistics*, 35(4), 765–805.

Uriagereka, J. (1995). Aspects of the Syntax of Clitic Placement in Western Romance. *Linguistic Inquiry*, 26(1), 79–123.

Valian, V. (1991). Syntactic Subjects in the Early Speech of American and Italian Children, *Cognition*, 40, 21–81.

Valian, V. (2009). Innateness and Learnability. In E. Bavin, ed., *Handbook of Child Language*. Cambridge: Cambridge University Press, 15–34.

Valian, V., S. Prasada and J. Scarpa. (2006). Direct Object Predictability: Effects on Young Children's Imitation of Sentences. *Journal of Child Language*, 33, 247–269.

van Hout, A. (1996). *Event Semantics of Verb Frame Alternations: A Case Study of Dutch and Its Acquisition*. Doctoral dissertation, Tilburg University. Published in 1998. New York: Garland Publishing.

van Hout, A. (2008). Acquisition of Perfective and Imperfective Aspect in Dutch, Italian and Polish. *Lingua*, 118(11), 1740–1765.

van der Velde, M. (1998). L'acquisition des clitiques sujets et objets: Une étude sur deux enfants francophones, unpublished M.A thesis, Universiteit van Amsterdam and CRNS Paris.

van der Velde, M., C. Jakubowicz and C. Rigaut. (2002). The Acquisition of Determiners and Pronominal Clitics by Three French-Speaking Children. In I. Lasser, ed., *The Process of Language Acquisition, Proceedings of the 1999 GALA Conference*, Frankfurt am Main: Peter Lang, 115–132.

van der Velde, M. (2003). Déterminants et pronoms en néerlandais et en français: syntaxe et acquisition, Ph.D. Thesis, Université Paris 8.

Verdelle, A. J. (1995). *The Good Negress*, Chapel Hill: Algonquin Books of Chapel Hill.

Vergnaud, J.–R. and M. L. Zubizarreta. (1992). The Definite Determiner in French and English. *Linguistic Inquiry*, 23, 595–652.

Verkuyl, H. (1993). *A Theory of Aspectuality: The Interaction between Temporal and Attemporal Structure*. Cambridge: Cambridge University Press.

Varlokosta, S., A. Belletti, J. Costa, N. Friedmann, A. Gavarró and K. K. Grohmann, et al. (2016). A Cross-Linguistic Study of the Acquisition of Clitic and Pronoun Production. *Language Acquisition* 23, 1–26.

Wang, Q., D. Lillo-Martin, C. Best and A. Levitt. (1992). Null Subject versus Null Object: Some Evidence from the Acquisition of Chinese and English. *Language Acquisition*, 2(3), 221–254.

Wexler, K. (1998). Very Early Parameter Setting and the Unique Checking Constraint: A New Explanation of the Optional Infinitive Stage. *Lingua*, 106, 23–79.

Wexler, K. (2004). Lennenberg's Dream. In L. Jenkins, ed., *Variation and Universals in Biolinguistics*. Amsterdam: Elsevier, 239–284.

Wexler, K., A. Gavarró and V. Torrens. (2003/2004). Object Clitic Omission in Child Catalan and Child Spanish, *Reports de Recerca*, Grup de Gramatica Teorica, Universitat Autonoma de Barcelona.

Wexler, K., A. Gavarró and V. Torrens. (2004). Feature Checking and Object Clitic Omission in Child Catalan. In R. Bok-Bennema, B. Hollebrandse, B. Kampers-Manhe, and P. Sleeman, eds., *Romance Languages and Linguistic Theory 2002*. Amsterdam: John Benjamins Publishing, 253–268.

Yang, C. (2002). *Knowledge and Learning in Natural Language*, Oxford, UK: Oxford University Press.

Yang, C. (2002). *Knowledge and Learning in Natural Language*. Oxford University Press: Oxford.

Yang, C. (2004). Universal Grammar, Statistics, or Both. *Trends in Cognitive Sciences*, 8, 451–456.

Yang, C. (2010). Three Factors in Language Variation. *Lingua*, 120, 1160–1177.

Yang, C., and T. Roeper. (2011). Minimalism and Language Acquisition. In C. Boeckx, ed., *The Oxford Handbook of Linguistic Minimalism*. Oxford University Press: Oxford, 551–573.

Yang, C. (2013). Who's Afraid of George Kingsley Zipf?: Do Children and Chimps Have Language? *Significance*, 10(6): 29–34.

Yang, C. (2015). Negative Knowledge from Positive Evidence. *Language*, 91(4), 938–953.

Yip, V. and S. Matthews. (2000). Syntactic Transfer in a Cantonese–English Bilingual Child. *Bilingualism: Language and Cognition*, 3, 193–208.

Yip, V. and S. Matthews. (2005). Dual Input and Learnability: Null Objects in Cantonese–English Bilingual Children. In J. Cohen, K. T. McAlister, K. Rolstad and J. MacSwan, eds., *Proceedings of the 4th International Symposium on Bilingualism*. Somerville, MA: Cascadilla Press, 2421–2431.

Zesiger, P., L. Chillier-Zesiger, M. Arabatzi, L. Baranzini, S. Cronel-Ohayon, J. Frank, U.H. Frauenfelder, C. Hamann and L. Rizzi. (2010). The Acquisition of Pronouns by French Children: A Parallel Study of Production and Comprehension. *Applied Psycholinguistics*, 31(4), 571–603.

Index